SSrc

DHSS

Studies in Deprivation and Disadvantage 4

Disadvantage and Education

Studies in Deprivation and Disadvantage

Despite substantial economic advances and improved welfare services in Britain since the Second World War, there has been a conspicuous persistence of deprivation and maladjustment. In June 1972 Sir Keith Joseph, then Secretary of State for Social Services, drew attention to this. In particular it seemed to him that social problems tended to recur in successive generations of the same families – to form a 'cycle of deprivation'. Subsequently the Department of Health and Social Security, through the Social Science Research Council, made available a sum of money for a programme of research into the whole problem.

Academics and practitioners from a wide range of disciplines and professional backgrounds were invited to investigate many aspects of deprivation and the process of transmission. Their findings are now becoming available and many of the empirical studies, together with literature reviews and the final summary report on deprivation and social policy, are being published in this series of *Studies in Deprivation and Disadvantage*.

Studies in Deprivation and Disadvantage 4

Disadvantage and Education

Jo Mortimore and *Tessa Blackstone*

Heinemann Educational Books · London

Heinemann Educational Books Ltd
22 Bedford Square, London WC1B 3HH
LONDON EDINBURGH MELBOURNE AUCKLAND
HONG KONG SINGAPORE KUALA LUMPUR NEW DELHI
IBADAN NAIROBI JOHANNESBURG
EXETER (NH) KINGSTON PORT OF SPAIN

British Library Cataloguing in Publication Data

Mortimore, Jo
    Disadvantage and education. – (SSRC/DHSS studies
    in deprivation and disadvantage; 4)
    1. Educational equalization – Great Britain
    I. Title   II.Blackstone, Tessa   III. Series
    370′.941   LC213.3G7

    ISBN 0-435-82608-5
    ISBN 0-435-82609-3 Pbk

Typeset by Inforum Ltd, Portsmouth
Printed by Biddles Ltd, Guildford, Surrey

Contents

List of Tables

Acknowledgements

This review has been funded as part of the DHSS/SSRC Transmitted Deprivation Programme. The authors wish to thank Alan Crispin, Tony Green, Peter Mortimore and John Welton for their helpful comments. Thanks are also due to the project secretary, Julia Perry, and to Caroline Bridges, Jean Griffiths and Joan Ridgewell who all assisted with the typing of the manuscript.

Introduction

This literature review is concerned with the effect of certain social policies on educational disadvantage. The material reviewed covers the past thirty years but the emphasis is on the last decade or so.

Social research is of considerable importance for those in a position to formulate policy for it provides information, if not understanding, about social conditions and attempts to rectify them. However, as the review demonstrates, there are limitations to what research can tell policy-makers. There are inconsistencies and contradictions between some of the research findings of different studies and where this is the case we can only record them, until further research is undertaken which may help to iron them out. Furthermore, the review is not comprehensive. As with any work of this kind, there are omissions due to the limitations of time, the inaccessibility of material, the failure to locate relevant studies and the need, when faced with a mass of material, to be selective. Moreover, the reviewer is limited by the constraints of the original research which may not have been carried out with 'disadvantage' as its prime focus or which may be of a short-term or descriptive nature, which makes it harder to draw inferences about long-term effects or to evaluate change.

In addition to education the review presents some research findings in related areas on the assumption that educational disadvantage is in part a result of other forms of disadvantage and therefore needs to be considered in the wider social context. These areas will, however, be dealt with more fully in other concurrent reports commissioned by the SSRC.

Sex differences in education are not discussed specifically. Where research findings differ markedly between boys and girls, for example in access to day-release provision, this is noted. There is a growing body of literature on sex differences in child-rearing, aspirations, expectations and attainment which could well form the subject of a separate review. In the same way, ethnic differences have not been considered separately. This too is an area of great importance, particularly in the light of the evidence to the Select Committee of the House of Commons on Race Relations and the findings of the interim report of the Rampton Committee (DES, 1981).

We do not enter the continuing debate over the relative influence of genetic inheritance or environment on educational performance. The literature on genetic inheritance, IQ and educational performance is the subject of a separate review in this series by Brown and Madge (forthcoming). It would not have been possible for us, within the context of this report, to do justice to the vast amount that has now been written on this subject. From the point of view of policy-makers, so long as the environment has *any* effect, efforts should be made to improve it and arguments over the relative influence is a somewhat sterile debate. Nicholson, in his review of *Bias in Mental Testing* (Jensen, 1980) argues that 'so long as even the smallest amount of individual variation in the quality (of intelligence) is under the control of environmental factors, it makes perfectly good sense to try and alter environments which seem to retard the development of intelligence' (Nicholson, 1980).

The material is organised into five chapters and Chapter 6 is a concluding discussion. Chapter 1 reviews the literature on the relationship between social class and educational attainment. Chapter 2 examines what are loosely termed 'home-based' factors, which may contribute to the association. These are material disadvantage, and cultural attitudes and experiences. Chapter 3 concentrates on the contribution of school and school-related factors to educational disadvantage. The areas discussed are the distribution of resources; the curriculum; the examination system; streaming; truancy; teacher quality and teacher expectation. Attempts mediated through the school at preventing social disadvantage from leading to educational disadvantage are discussed in Chapter 4. These include the post-Plowden policies; curriculum development; research into parental involvement and provision for school leavers. Chapter 5 is concerned with policies which have been implemented outside the provision of statutory schooling. The areas covered include home-visiting schemes for families with pre-school children; financial support of various kinds, for example uniform grants and educational maintenance awards for sixteen to nineteen year olds; and policies for disadvantaged school leavers. Finally, although in no sense attempting to produce a policy 'blueprint', the concluding Chapter 6 suggests areas towards which policy might usefully be directed.

Rutter and Madge (1976), in their SSRC review, suggest that the word 'deprivation' is not only overworked, but means different things to different people. The authors consider that the term 'deprivation' acts as a 'projective test in which each person reads into the concept his own biases and confusions'. They suggest instead that the broader term 'disadvantage' be used, implying unfavourable conditions or circumstances, detriment or prejudice. Accordingly the term 'disadvantage' will be used in this report. Although the source of funds for this review is an SSRC panel on 'transmitted' deprivation we have not been able to find much research which has investigated *inter-generational* aspects of educational disadvantage. This is mainly because of the intrinsic difficulty of carrying out such research. It is also partly, we suspect, because of doubts about the concept of a cycle of deprivation or transmitted deprivation which earlier work on conceptual issues for the SSRC panel raised. We do not, however, doubt that many of the educational difficulties suffered by children in certain social groups today were also suffered by their parents, possibly even more acutely.

Despite undoubted improvements in standards of living since the development of the welfare state, there is considerable evidence of widespread social disadvantage in Britain today. Social disadvantage is not easy to define partly because it is a relative concept, tied to the social context of time and place. Thus, circumstances that are considered to put people at a social disadvantage today might not have been considered in the same light ten years ago. Similarly, what is considered an inadequate wage or an unacceptable environment in one part of Britain may be perceived differently in another area. Wedge and Prosser (1973) considered three criteria were important constituents of social disadvantage. They were certain types of family composition (one parent or large families), low income and poor housing. They defined socially disadvantaged children as those who were in *all three* categories. Among those studied 6 per cent, or one child in sixteen, met all three criteria. In our discussion of social disadvantage in Chapter 2 we include additional material factors (such as unsatisfactory conditions at work, unemployment, poor health and adverse environment) and certain cultural aspects of mother–child interactions and parental attitudes.

When the term 'disadvantage' is used in relation to education, the following groups can be described as 'educationally disadvantaged':

(i)   Those who are denied equal access to educational opportunity in terms of type of school, resources, teachers or curriculum.

(ii)   Those who, despite performing well in school, leave at the earliest opportunity.

(iii)   Those who underachieve or who perform less well than they might because a variety of social and environmental factors result in their being unable to take advantage of educational opportunities.

These groups are not, of course, mutually exclusive, but they do represent a proportion of each age group of young people. A further group of pupils, who may not be considered disadvantaged on social or economic criteria, perform badly at school and leave having achieved little after eleven years of compulsory schooling. In addition, it can be argued that pupils whose aspirations have been raised by their experience of school, but who are unable to realise those aspirations in the labour market, are more disadvantaged than if their ambitions had not been raised in the first place. However, it is our view that those with few or no formal qualifications are the most disadvantaged. The greatest over-supply of manpower is in the area of unskilled labour. The raising of aspirations and skill levels improves opportunities in the labour market, both in the long and the short term.

1 Social Class and Educational Attainment

In order to understand the relationship between disadvantage and educational performance account must be taken of the broader context of the relationship between social class, educational performance and equality of opportunity. This must include some study of educational systems and institutions. A great deal of attention has focussed on the relationship between education and equality of opportunity. This includes the complex question of equality of access to education. To understand it in the British context it is necessary to examine educational change and developments since 1944 (see Silver, 1973; Rubenstein and Simon, 1969, and Fenwick, 1976).

The proponents of the tripartite system, which developed after the 1944 Act, aimed to treat children of the same measured ability in the same way and to provide groups of children with an 'equal but different' education according to their measured ability and assumed needs. Children were tested at eleven and assigned to the type of school, grammar, technical or 'modern', which was deemed most suitable for them. It was intended that there would be 'parity of esteem' between the three types of school. In effect, the grammar schools remained the most sought after, providing the route to higher education and higher status occupations. Few local authorities developed technical schools and the secondary modern schools became the 'cinderellas' of the education system, though catering for the majority of the secondary-school population. The rationale for this organisation was to be found in the then current psychological theories of intelligence which were, it was believed, able to predict future attainment at a relatively early age, and it was thought that this arrangement served each child according to his or her needs and was fair (see Burt, 1943 and Fenwick, 1976).

Almost from its inception this system of secondary education was criticised both on grounds of social justice and efficiency (Blackburn, 1945). The work of Floud, Halsey and Martin (1956) demonstrated that local authorities varied considerably in the proportion of grammar-school places which they provided, and that grammar-school places were disproportionately allocated to children of middle-class parents. Critics, some convinced of a culture bias in the IQ selection tests, argued that selection was not according to ability but according to environment and, since many talented children of working-class parents were being denied access to grammar schools or, having gained a place, left at the earliest opportunity, it was a socially wasteful system. There was condemnation of a system which labelled children as 'failures' at such an early age. The 'parity of esteem' which was to be earned by the technical and modern schools was hampered by inferior resources and the initial ban on pupils in modern schools being entered for public examinations, (Lady Simon of Wythenshawe, 1948 and Simon, 1953).

A series of government reports, *Early leaving* (1954) and the Reports by Crowther (1959), Newsom (1963) and Robbins (1963) demonstrated the waste of undeveloped talent badly needed in a technological society and demolished a long-held notion that a 'pool of ability' was limited within each age group. Halsey (1972) argues that the liberal policies of equality of opportunity failed because they were based 'on an inadequate theory of learning. They (the liberal policy-makers) failed to notice that the major determinants of educational attainment were not schoolmasters but social situations, not curriculum but motivation, not formal access to school but support in the family and community.'

During the 1950s and early 1960s the concept of equality changed from what Crosland (1961) called 'the weak version', the chance for all to compete by objective methods, to 'the strong version'. The weak version assumes that access to elite education is based not on birth or wealth but on measured intelligence so that 'all children of the same measured intelligence at the appropriate age have completely equal access'. The strong version acknowledges that measured intelligence is affected by such factors as environment, poverty and parental education, and that, therefore, 'every child should have the same opportunity for acquiring measured intelligence, so far as this can be controlled by social action' (Crosland). Two years later the Secretary of State for Education, Sir Edward Boyle, used the same phrase in his foreword to the Newsom Report, 'the essential point is that all children should have an equal opportunity of acquiring intelligence'.

In the early 1960s there was widespread optimism about the extent to which the education system could achieve equality of opportunity in the United Kingdom. By the early 1970s this had changed, partly as a result of the influence of American research on British thinking. Coleman (1966) conducted a large-scale survey of the achievement of some half a million students in some 4000 elementary and secondary schools. It was claimed that the results indicated that educational attainment was largely independent of the schooling a child received. Jencks (1973) re-analysed statistical data from several studies, including Coleman's and he argued that 'None of the evidence we have reviewed suggests that school reform can be expected to bring about significant social changes outside the schools.' Furthermore, Jencks estimated that equalising educational opportunity would do little to make adults more equal. It was argued that 'If all high schools were equally effective, cognitive inequality among twelfth graders would hardly decline at all, and disparities in their eventual attainment would decline by less than 1 per cent.' Family background was considered to have more influence than genetic inheritance on an individual's educational attainment but only a moderate influence on eventual occupation and income. The key measurable factor in an individual's mobility was the status of their families. A further element was 'luck' which might be described as all the other elements social science could not measure. Jencks concluded that equality was best promoted by the redistribution of income. In Jencks' recent work he argues even more strongly that being born into the 'right family' and getting a college degree are both extremely important for occupational and economic success, that variations in intelligence have surprisingly little effect and non-cognitive personality traits are just as important for career success as academic ability or cognitive skills (Jencks, 1979).

Other writers, such as Bowles and Gintis (1976) argue that 'educational inequality is rooted in the basic institutions of our economy . . . (its sources are to be found) in the mutual re-inforcement of class sub-cultures and social class biases in the operation of the school system itself.' The education system, it is argued, corresponds to the stratified division of labour of a capitalist economy and prepares children for their place in the economic hierarchy. Jencks *et al*. (1973) and Boudon (1973) have also argued in different ways that class inequalities are generated and maintained by forces too strong to be influenced by egalitarian educational reform.

Whilst maintaining a more optimistic view of what could still be done to further equality, Halsey (1975) maintains that the 'liberal' reforms failed owing to a lack of appreciation of the social and economic factors. There has been, Halsey argues, a 'trivialisation' of the concept of class which, for example, conceives of parental attitudes as separate factors rather than formed by a parent's position in the social structure. Whilst acknowledging the varying levels of ambition and aspiration at any given economic or income level, Halsey argues that 'a theory which explains educational achievement as the outcome of a set of individual attributes has lost the meaning of those structural forces which we know as class. An adequate theory must also attend to those structural inequalities of resource allocation which are integral to a class society' (Halsey, 1975). The relationship between these 'structural inequalities' and attainment are discussed in this and the following chapter.

Numerous studies demonstrate the differential attainment of children from different social groups. In discussing them they will be grouped together according to the age of the pupils studied.

Attainment at Primary-School Age

In the study of an age group of children born within one week in March 1948, Douglas examined attainment at different stages (Douglas, 1964). He divided the children into four groups: the children of parents in the upper middle class; the lower middle class; the upper working class and the lower working class. He found that at age eight the children of parents in non-manual occupations performed better than the children whose parents followed manual occupations. The difference between the two groups, at this age, was 7.59 points. When Douglas followed up these two groups three years later he found that this initial difference of 7.59 points had risen to 9.44, a rise of 12 per cent. The relative deterioration on norm-referenced tests shown by the children of manual workers was most marked in their performance on non-verbal intelligence tests, whilst it was relatively small on reading and vocabulary tests. The same tests were used at both ages.

In 1963 the Central Advisory Council for Education (England) was asked by the then Minister of Education (Sir Edward Boyle) to 'consider the whole subject of primary education and the transition to secondary education'. Under the Chairmanship of Lady Plowden it set out both to explore why some primary schools achieve well in apparently adverse circumstances and what it was about the home that mattered so much for a child's education. The Plowden Committee commissioned a survey of schools and parents in an attempt to relate what they learnt about home and school to the attainment of the children. The survey stressed the importance of parental attitudes for their child's education. Interestingly, in many respects the parents thought alike, irrespective of occupational background. For example, 75 per cent of parents interviewed wanted their child to stay on at school beyond the minimum leaving age, and there was little difference between the socio-economic groups in the number of evenings when some time was claimed to be spent in a joint activity with the child or in the number of parents who wanted the school to give the child work to do at home. There were, however, some marked differences between those in professional and managerial occupations and those in semi- and unskilled occupations. The most noticeable difference was in the part claimed to be played by fathers in their children's education – in the choice of school, meetings with the head or attendance at school functions. The survey's author concluded that the contribution to children's education made by variations in parental attitudes was stronger than that made by variations in home circumstances, although the attitudes were possibly, to some extent, conditioned by the circumstances (Peaker, 1967). Acland (1980) has queried this finding in a critique of the Plowden research, which is discussed in the next chapter.

Another study of a cohort of children was begun ten years after that of Douglas. The National Child Development Study took as its sample all the children in England, Scotland and Wales who were born in the week 3–9 March 1958. In their report on the progress of those children from birth up until the age of seven, the authors, Davie, Butler and Goldstein (1972), found social class was the variable with the strongest association with attainment in reading and arithmetic at seven years of age. The authors found that 50 per cent of seven year olds in social class V had 'poor' reading scores compared with 7 per cent in social class I, which leads to the claim that the chances of an unskilled manual worker's child being a poor reader are six times greater than those of a professional worker's child. The results for social class II and III non-manual, were similar to those of social class I, but then there was a considerable gap between the scores for social class III manual whose results were closer to those of social class IV and V. Davie *et al*. maintain that 'Social class V children appear to be at a particular disadvantage in respect of poor ability and attainment at school.'

Wedge and Prosser (1973) looked at the incidence of social disadvantage among the children in the National Child Development Study and at the attainment of those children considered to be 'disadvantaged'. Three criteria were considered to be crucial to disadvantage: family composition (five or more children or only one parent figure); low income; and poor housing. Wedge and Prosser not only found that considerable numbers of children fell into each category but that 'more than one child in every three (36 per cent) was in either a one-parent-figure family or a large family, a low income family or had been badly housed. Nearly one in three (30 per cent) of all children was from a low income or poorly housed family.' The children who formed the most extreme group of socially disadvantaged, those who were in a one-parent or large family *and* were badly housed *and* were in a low-income family amounted to one in sixteen or 6 per cent.

When the authors considered educational provision for this extremely disadvantaged sample they found that one in six was receiving special help within the normal school for educational backwardness compared with one in sixteen in non-disadvantaged groups. On average, disadvantaged children were three-and-a-half years behind other children in their reading scores, over half of them were backward in reading and a similar proportion were behind in arithmetic. However, it is also important to point out that one in seven did better on the mathematics and reading tests than half the non-disadvantaged group. The single factor most strongly associated with high attainment was social class. Only one in twenty-five of the disadvantaged was middle class. The small group (one in seven) of high achieving children among the sample of disadvantaged were the subject of further analysis by Wedge and Prosser. An attempt was made to ascertain whether differences in the attainment of the disadvantaged children were associated with the factors which are known to be associated with attainment amongst children in general or whether there were factors specific to the disadvantaged group. Forty variables concerned with birth, housing, school, health and family circumstances were considered but no single factor showed differences among the disadvantaged group alone and where an association was found in both groups of children it was never greater among the disadvantaged. The group of high-achieving disadvantaged children are being followed up by the National Children's Bureau (NCB) as part of the DHSS/SSRC Transmitted Deprivation Programme. Drawing on data relating to the secondary-school experience and examination results of the sample until the age of sixteen, an attempt is being made to discover if the group is different in any way, for example in terms of family or housing circumstances, from the low-achieving disadvantaged group.

It is also important to try to ascertain how far those who are most disadvantaged outside school are also most disadvantaged at school, and how this is manifested. They may not be more disadvantaged in terms of resources but in length of schooling, teachers' attitudes or curriculum. These questions are dealt with in Chapter 3.

Children's attainment in reading was one of the factors examined by Rutter, Tizard and Whitmore (1970) when they carried out an epidemiological study on the Isle of Wight. A series of related surveys were carried out on complete age groups of children. The main objective of the studies was to give a comprehensive picture of 'handicap' in a total population of children living in a defined geographical area. The age groups were in the middle years of their schooling at eight, nine and ten years. The children were given a verbal and non-verbal test of intelligence, a mechanical arithmetic test and a group reading test. The findings showed that children whose fathers were in manual occupations were over-represented amongst those who performed least well on intelligence tests. These children were also over-represented in the reading-retardation group. (This group consisted of children who were not necessarily those who performed least well on the reading test but were those whose reading performance was poorer than was predicted from their reading scores.) A similar study was carried out in an Inner London Borough, where although it was found that reading retardation was not associated with unskilled parental occupation, it was less common in the families of non-manual workers with clerical, managerial or professional jobs (Berger et al., 1975).

In the report on London Educational Priority Area (EPA) schools, Barnes and Lucas (1975) studied the relationship to social class of various home background factors or characteristics of family circumstance, considered to be indicators of disadvantage. They found that 'as children's objective circumstances become more disadvantaged, so their reading performance tends to be lower.' The range of average scores, when all the factors had been controlled for, was twenty-six points of reading score. This represented more than two years reading age, between the average score for the children of professional and managerial families, who were born in Britain, who did not receive free school meals and who came from small families, and the average score of the children of West Indian immigrant unskilled workers, whether or not they received free school meals and irrespective of the size of their families.

When they were eleven years old the children in the National Child Development Study were tested again in reading and mathematics. Fogelman and Goldstein (1976) point out that the tests at seven and eleven were not the same and did not elicit the same kinds of behaviour so that they are in effect 'comparing one component of performance with another at the different ages'.

Kellmer-Pringle, Butler and Davie (1966) claim that there is clear evidence that the lower the occupational status of the father, the poorer the attainment of the child at age seven. In reading 56.2 per cent of children of parents in social class I were considered to be good readers compared with 23.3 per cent of children of parents in social class V. Attainment did not decrease by uniform amounts from social class I to V. The non-manual groups had similar scores but there was a considerable gap between them and the manual groups. In their analysis of the data Fogelman and Goldstein estimate that the children whose fathers were in social class I, II and III non-manual were, at age eleven, about 1.0 year ahead of social class III manual and social class IV, who, in turn, were about 0.4 years ahead of those from social class V. Moreover, the results showed that the differences between the same groups of 0.9 years and 0.7 years, found when the children were seven years old (Davie et al., 1972) had increased to 1.9 years in reading and

1.1 years respectively. The results of the mathematics tests were in a similar direction. At age seven the proportion of children with 'good arithmetical ability' fell from about 28 per cent in social class I to about 14 per cent in social class V, although the decline was not uniform (Kellmer-Pringle *et al*.). By age eleven similar results amounted to an average difference associated with each seven-year score of 1.1 years between the results in social class I, II and III non-manual and the results in social class III manual and IV, and a further difference of 0.6 years between the latter group and social class V (Fogelman and Goldstein 1976). When the effects of family social mobility were also examined the authors found, as did Douglas, that children from 'upwardly mobile' families improved their attainment scores in comparison with static families, who, in turn, improved their scores relative to the 'downwardly mobile' families. Although different statistical methods were used to analyse the information from the two cohort studies the evidence suggests that the gap in the measured attainment between different social groups in primary school has not narrowed and may even have widened. This despite the fact that, as Fogelman and Goldstein point out, the twelve years between their cohort and the children in Douglas' study 'have seen an increased apparent egalitarianism in educational provision'. The removal of the 11+ examination in many areas might have been expected to lead to a reduction in social class divergence. In their later study Douglas *et al*. (1968) suggest that the divergence in scores at age eleven may be due to the pressure of the 11+ examination, since the divergence was not found in Scotland where secondary selection takes place at 12+.

These studies have been carried out by different researchers, at different times and have used quite different techniques. Yet they have all found remarkably similar results; that there is a strong and persistent relationship between social class and attainment in primary school, and, in particular, between socio-economic disadvantage and low attainment.

Attainment at the 11+ Examination

The different chances of boys from various social classes and geographical regions being selected for grammar school have been well documented. The first study to do so was carried out by Floud, Halsey and Martin (1956). Although the chances varied between the two geographical areas of their study (Hertfordshire and Middlesbrough) and, to some extent, from year to year, they found overall that in Middlesbrough the son of a professional or businessman had more than seven times the chance of a son of an unskilled worker and about five times the chance of a skilled worker's son of receiving a grammar-school education. In Hertfordshire he had three times the chance of the skilled worker's son and six times the chance of the unskilled worker's son of doing so. In a later paper, drawing on the Crowther Report (Central Advisory Council for Education, 1959), Floud argues that ability to pass the 11+ examination was socially differentiated, but that ability itself appeared to be far less so and 'that there is a substantial reserve of uneducated ability in the offspring of working-class fathers cannot be doubted' (Floud, 1961).

Marked social-class differences were also noted by Douglas (1964). He found that 54 per cent of upper-middle-class children, but only 11 per cent of lower manual working-class children went to grammar schools. According to Douglas, the middle-class children were consistently at an advantage until very high levels of individual performance were reached, 'with children in the top 2 per cent ability, social background is unimportant, but below this it has a considerable influence on their chance of going to grammar schools'. In a later study Douglas et al. (1968) suggested that part of the divergence of intelligence test results between children from different social classes may have been a temporary artefact of the stresses of secondary selection. They also argue that the social inequalities in selection are most apparent for those of 'borderline' ability.

Children from the lower socio-economic group then, in addition to lower attainment in primary school, had to contend with an assessment procedure which, according to these research studies, was biased against them. Today, few authorities retain the 11+ and the majority of secondary-school children attend comprehensive schools. However, Caroline Benn (1980) disputes claims by both the present Conservative and the previous Labour Government that 83 per cent of secondary-school children attend comprehensives. The real figure, she claims, is about 67 per cent which includes schools which may be organised on comprehensive lines but which do not provide a genuine comprehensive education. Benn cites the examples of 'the misuse of voluntary comprehensive status for selective purposes . . . and selection within the comprehensive system itself – like closed access sixth forms'. Furthermore, in the most recent report of the progress of the cohort in the NCDS Steedman (1980) found that, although in 1974 53 per cent of the sample were in comprehensive schools, over half of them had started off in a secondary modern or a grammar school which became comprehensive while they were there between 1970 and 1974. Despite comprehensive reorganisation she claims that 'selection continued to influence the social class composition of school intakes in 1969'. Of those children entering grammar schools 53 per cent had fathers in non-manual occupations, twice the proportion for children entering comprehensive or secondary modern schools. The two groups entering comprehensive and secondary modern schools also achieved similar average scores (around 40 per cent) on verbal and non-verbal tests whilst the group entering grammar school had a higher average score of 60 per cent. The difference was similar for mathematical attainment and, to a lesser extent, for reading comprehension. Steedman points out that, although it might have been expected that the intake of the comprehensive schools would resemble the combined intake of grammar and secondary moderns in terms of ability and social class, this was not the case.

Attainment in Secondary School
Several studies have looked at the progress of children from different socio-economic groups in the secondary school. Many of the groups of children studied have been at selective schools.

At secondary level Douglas *et al*. (1968) found that middle-class children had higher intelligence and attainment scores than did their working-class counterparts, but the findings for fifteen year olds were more complicated than for eight and eleven year olds. Although the social classes continued to diverge in educational attainment, the social class variation in intelligence was reduced so that the gap was less at fifteen years than at eight years. Douglas *et al*. subdivided both the middle-class and working-class cohorts into upper and lower sections according to the education and social origins of the parents. Between the ages of eleven and fifteen the divergence noted earlier continued for reading and mathematics. The upper-middle-class group made considerably more progress in mathematics than the rest and they also had the highest attainment in reading. The manual working class had the lowest achievement in reading and mathematics. However, the non-verbal intelligence scores for the four groups were nearer to each other at fifteen than they were at eight or eleven and the verbal intelligence scores also converged between eleven and fifteen. When Acland (1973) re-analysed the Plowden longitudinal data he found the class differential did not appreciably increase as the children grew older. This conclusion is at odds with Fogelman *et al*. (1978), who claim that the pattern over the three ages at which the NCDS sample was tested (seven, eleven and sixteen) is of a widening gap between children of different social classes. Their data on sixteen year olds show large average differences between the social class groups, although the standard deviations within each class are also fairly large. Even so, their figures imply that 'at sixteen only about 15 per cent of social class V children could be expected to score above the mean of the non-manual children'. Interestingly, in the mathematics test the relationships among the regions are markedly different according to the social class of the children. In the reading test each social class group in the South of England made relatively good progress between the ages of eleven and sixteen, while the opposite was true for Scotland. At the age of seven, Scottish children were, on average, ahead of other areas of the community in their reading scores (Davie *et al*., 1972) but at sixteen they had been overtaken by children in England. Thus, the question of whether there is an increasing or decreasing gap between groups of pupils from different social classes is unresolved. Research findings exist to support both claims. The evidence, however, does not give much ground for optimism about the success of the educational system in removing these class differences; they may, indeed, increase with greater exposure to schooling.

Some further indication of able working-class pupils who do not achieve their potential can be gained from the Crowther Report (Central Advisory Council for Education, 1959) in which it is claimed that 48 per cent of children with a measured IQ of 120+ leave school by the age of sixteen as do 87 per cent of those with an IQ of between 108 and 120. All of these pupils are above average ability and, Crowther claimed, the ones who leave are predominantly working class. The wastage of talent in the existing system was also emphasised in the Robbins Report (Committee on Higher Education, 1963). Drawing on data from the Crowther Report the Robbins committee found that half the national service recruits to the Army, who were rated in the two highest ability groups, had left school at fifteen. Douglas found that inequality of opportunity increased in secondary schools, even at the highest ability levels so that 'able boys and girls from working class families . . . have been heavily handicapped in their later secondary school careers through relatively early leaving and poor examination results' (Douglas *et al*., 1968). Boys from manual working-class backgrounds who had been in the bottom stream in primary school improved their test performance between the ages of eleven and fifteen, although they left their secondary modern schools early. Of the high ability boys from the lower manual working class who went to a selective secondary school, nearly half had left school by the time they were sixteen-and-a-half. This finding leads Douglas *et al*, to claim that 'early leaving and low job aspirations make it probable that as many as 5 per cent of the next generation of manual workers could have been qualified for administrative or professional occupations'.

The pressures on working-class boys at grammar schools to leave school at the earliest opportunity have been described by Willmott (1969) in his study of adolescents in the East End. Yet in the NCD study of eleven year olds, parents were asked whether they wanted their child to leave school at the minimum age or not. Even among those considered to be disadvantaged only one in six said they wanted their child to leave as soon as possible (compared with one in thirty among the non-disadvantaged group). Sixty-six per cent of 'disadvantaged' parents, compared with 85 per cent of other parents said they would like their child to continue with some form of further education after leaving school (Wedge and Prosser, 1973). The reality is clearly different when their children reach the age at which they can leave. The NCDS sample were part of the first cohort of children to stay in full-time compulsory education until the age of sixteen. In 1974, in the third follow-up, the parents were interviewed and for the first time the children, then aged sixteen, were asked to complete an individual questionnaire. The sixteen year olds were asked about their post-school intentions. Sixty-two per cent of the cohort thought they were likely to leave school when they were sixteen, 7 per cent thought they would do so at seventeen and 23 per cent envisaged staying on until they were eighteen (8 per cent were uncertain) (Fogelman, 1976). In the study of the progress of the NCDS sample through different types of secondary schools, Steedman found that comprehensive pupils were the group most keen on staying on at sixteen, particularly in well-established, purpose-built comprehensive schools. This was mainly due to girls and children from working-class families (less rather than more advantaged categories) wanting to stay on longer.

Fogelman found that there was a gap between what parents expected of them and what the young people expected to do at sixteen – and a larger gap between what the parents would have liked them to do – and the sixteen year olds' intentions. Only 52 per cent of parents expected the children to leave school at sixteen and only 36 per cent wanted them to leave at the minimum age. Nineteen per cent expected them to stay on until eighteen, although 25 per cent would have liked them to do so. Twenty-four per cent expected them to continue their full-time education beyond eighteen, but 33 per cent would have liked them to do so. The young people's aspirations and expectations were lower than their parents'. Fogelman does not discuss possible explanations for these differences between the interviews at eleven and sixteen and between the parents and the children. It may be that parents hold more realistic expectations of their child's capabilities when that child is nearing the end of his or her experience of secondary school than at the beginning. The parents' expectations may also have been affected by the changing economic climate and employment prospects between 1969 when the children were eleven and 1974 when the cohort was sixteen. Donnison and Soto (1980) have suggested that the general character of the town of residence will exert an influence on the pupil's motivation for educational success. They speculate that 'unless they are unusually confident about their future, economic insecurity may well make the children of manual workers more cautious about taking their education further and, thereby, missing immediate opportunities for work'. It is paradoxical that poor employment prospects locally (and nationally) may result in a smaller rather than larger proportion of young people staying on at school.

Almost half the young people in the NCDS wanted to leave as soon as possible in order to earn some money and be independent; 12 per cent said their families needed the money and 22 per cent thought they were not good enough to stay on. It is probable that some pupils who said they were leaving school in order to start earning would stay on at school if there was some financial incentive to do so. This point will be discussed in a later chapter. The large number of working-class pupils who leave school at the earliest opportunity reduces the proportion of such pupils in the group who will take public examinations at sixteen. In addition, this number is reduced still further by those who then leave and do not go into the sixth form.

Attainment in Public Examinations

In any discussion of examination results there are two separate but related measures to be considered: the number of examinations taken and the grades received. Research by Brimer *et al*. (1977) examined the relationship between pupils and school characteristics and pupils' achievement in public examinations at 'Ordinary' and 'Advanced' levels. The sample was, therefore, as the authors admit, highly selective and consisted of children who were 'likely to be in the top 50 per cent of achievers in their cohort'. This seems to be an overestimate since GCE examinations are only designed for the top 20 per cent of the ability range. Questionnaire data from schools, teachers and pupils and examination results were collected for schools in four local authorities. The findings indicate that family influence factors (which include inherited factors and the influence of early child-rearing) were most effective in the early stages of education in relation to the child's readiness to learn to read. Family influences, along with previous school, continued to be important for the choice of and admission to secondary school, but, it is argued, by the time 'O' levels were taken 'most of the selective variables arising from family background and prior educational background will already have taken effect'. This is supported by evidence from the Oxford Mobility Study (Halsey, Heath and Ridge, 1980). The authors state that 'for those who survive to enter public examinations, class similarities rather than class differences describe the success rates'. Brimer further maintains that 'when the level of education offered is such that the learner's prior history (familial and school) determines those who will be admitted to it, then social class of family will cease to exert an important influence amongst the survivors'. Differences in achievement at the secondary stage of education, it is considered, are more to do with individual factors such as personality and motivation and the quality of school instruction and resources. For example, in mathematics 'O' level results Brimer *et al*. found 'the lack of a strong social class influence is confirmed by the low correlation with father's job'. But many pupils from disadvantaged backgrounds do not even get as far as taking 'O' level mathematics. Brimer's interpretation of the results is that 'higher achieving schools are those which maximise the interaction between ability of pupils in mathematics and expert teaching'. In chemistry 'O' level it is argued that the higher achievement rates were associated with 'a preference for staying on at school and with time spent in private study', both of which would be less likely for disadvantaged pupils. The social class of father's job was positively correlated with good chemistry results, although negatively correlated with help given at home. The authors suggest, and it seems possible, that school effects are likely to be stronger for subjects which rely on specialised instructions and on specialist equipment which would militate against help being given at home. Whereas in subjects like English literature or social studies, learning from television, from books at home or from family discussions are all likely to play a part.

Rutter *et al*. (1979) in their study of twelve London secondary schools found significant associations between parents' occupation and examination success. Using a scoring system which assigned one point to an 'O' level grade A, B or C or a CSE grade one, and half a point to an 'O' level grade D or E or a CSE grade two or three, it was found that in the middle-ability band the average examination score was 2.1 for children whose fathers held clerical or professional jobs, compared with 1.1 for children of unskilled manual workers. The differences were significant for this band, less so for the upper band and were not statistically significant for the lower band.[1]

A recent analysis carried out by the Department of Education and Science (DES) related the participation of sixteen to nineteen years olds in education to socio-economic factors and it was found that 65 per cent of the variation between local authorities in full-time participation in CSE or GCE courses in schools and further education colleges could be accounted for by socio-economic indicators (DES, 1979c).

The Sixth Form
The Crowther Report found that in 1957 70 per cent of the army

recruits who had been in a sixth form had come from non-manual backgrounds. During the 1960s it was widely hoped that the expansion of the sixth form would benefit pupils from lower socio-economic groups. However, a national survey of sixth-formers in 1968 for the Schools Council showed that 67 per cent were from non-manual backgrounds. Despite the 50 per cent increase in numbers of pupils in sixth forms since the mid-1950s, the social class composition had hardly changed and over half of those previously in the two top ability groups had left school at fifteen (Morton-Williams and Finch, 1968). Halsey *et al.* (1980) argue that there is a high loss of pupils from working-class families at entry into the sixth form. Over four times as many middle-class as working-class boys were still at school at sixteen, but nearly ten times as many stayed on until eighteen. Once there, the working-class boy has almost as good a chance of completing the course as a middle-class boy. Working-class boys who stayed on in the sixth form and took Higher School Certificate – or in the case of the younger cohorts – 'A' level examinations, gained results similar to those obtained by middle-class boys. Halsey *et al.* claim that the differentials in examination success 'can almost wholly be explained by the differentials in staying on at secondary school'. It is argued that 'family climate appears to be a far more important determinant of success or failure in the eleven plus than the pupil's own measured ability', but having passed the 11+ examination 'it is the character of the school which is crucial'. This seems to imply that once the hurdle of the 11+ examination was cleared the ethos of the secondary school exerted a strong socialising influence on pupils to conform to academic values and to perform well accordingly.

Further and Higher Education
Some pupils who leave school at sixteen continue their education on a part-time basis through day-release courses and apprenticeship schemes. Glennerster (1972) has documented the inadequacy of the day-release provision for school leavers during the period of the birth rate bulge, from 1963 to 1969. The number of young people under eighteen who were granted day release by their employer hardly rose at all, from 250,000 in 1961 to 255,000 in 1969. In 1969 only 10 per cent of girls and 39 per cent of boys under eighteen, in employment, were allowed time off work for education and Cohen and Nixon (1981) quote a recent working paper which stated figures of 15 per cent and 30 per cent respectively. The majority, many of whom come from socially disadvantaged backgrounds; receive no further education after leaving school, a right envisaged in the 1944 Act.

It is well known that working-class young people, particularly those whose fathers are in semi- or unskilled occupations, are under-represented in higher education. Glennerster has calculated that in the 1960s there was a significant increase in the proportion of university places taken by children whose parents belonged to the clerical occupation group, and a slight increase in the proportion of places taken by children whose parents belonged to the manual group (from 27 per cent in 1961 to 31 per cent in 1968). However, he concludes that these groups were still substantially under-represented, since in 1966 they formed 63 per cent of all parents in the relevant age band. The small changes can be seen in the table compiled by Glennerster from Robbins figures and University Central Council of Admissions (UCCA) Reports for 1967/68.

Table 1.1   Percentage of 18 year olds entering university by social class 1961 and 1968

Social class		1961 (undergraduates)	1968 (entrants)
I	Professional, managerial	19	19
II	Intermediate	42	32
IIIa	Clerical	12	18
IIIb	Skilled manual	20	19
IV	Semi-skilled manual	6	10
V	Unskilled	1	2
Total		100	100

Westergaard and Resler (1975) estimated that in the early 1970s 'manual workers' children were less likely to enter university than children of professional and technical fathers by a factor of nearly nine times'. The late 1960s and the early 1970s saw a considerable expansion of higher education provision. However, the following table from UCCA shows that class inequalities remain.

College of education closures during the last decade may have contributed to smaller proportions of working-class students in higher education overall, since they have traditionally recruited more students of working-class origin. (In the Robbins Survey of training colleges in 1963 42 per cent of students came from manual class homes.)

Social Class Trends
From around 1950 until the mid-1970s there was increased government investment in education (see Glennerster, 1972 and Blackstone and Crispin, 1980). This is reflected in the trend towards greater

Table 1.2   Home candidates and acceptances by social class

Social class		Accepted candidates		
		1977	1978	1979
I	Professional, managerial	20.9	21.7	21.9
II	Intermediate	41.2	41.5	42.3
IIIa	Clerical	14.8	14.4	13.4
IIIb	Skilled manual	16.6	16.1	16.3
IV	Semi-skilled manual	5.2	5.2	5.0
V	Unskilled	1.2	1.2	1.0
Total		100	100	100

Source: UCCA Statistical Supplement to the Seventeenth Report 1978/79.

attainment (measured by pupils voluntarily staying on past the statutory school-leaving age) and achievement (measured in terms of success in public examinations (see Klein, 1975, and Halsey *et al.*, 1980). Klein states that between 1952 and 1973 the proportion of pupils staying on for one year beyond compulsory education increased from 26.1 per cent to 58.6 per cent. The figure for those staying on for two years rose from 12.4 per cent to 34 per cent. It should perhaps be added that the increase in the numbers staying on beyond compulsory schooling slowed down considerably in the mid and late 1970s).

Between 1961 and 1973 the proportion of school leavers obtaining at least one 'A' level rose from 8.2 per cent to 16.2 per cent; for one 'O' level the increase was from 19.2 per cent to 27.6 per cent. In 1965 the CSE was introduced and between 1966 and 1972 the proportion obtaining a basic CSE grade increased from 15.8 per cent to 36.3 per cent. Halsey's data show comparable increases.

To what extent social class differentials have been reduced or maintained over the same period is harder to assess. On length of schooling, Halsey *et al.* found no evidence of 'simple linear progress towards meritocracy'. Rather, they suggest, 'the service class has set a pattern of increasingly extended secondary schooling, following a path towards saturation . . . which is trodden later first by the intermediate and finally by the working class.' In considering class differentials in examination success Halsey *et al.* consider that the 11+ examination was the 'branching point' that was decisive for class selection. For those that survived and went on to enter public examinations class similarities were stronger than class differences. It should be noted, however, that only the younger of Halsey's cohorts (those born between 1933 and 1942 and between 1943 and 1952) would have been passing through secondary and higher education during the period from 1950 onwards and only relatively few of the youngest cohort would have experienced comprehensive secondary education.

The post-Robbins expansion of higher education improved the chances of all social classes of going to universities. However, 'the fastest *rates* of growth went to the working class but the largest *absolute* gains to the service class' (Halsey *et al*).

Conclusion

This chapter has reviewed evidence concerning the attainment of pupils coming from different social backgrounds at various stages of education. In summary, during the primary years of schooling there are clear group differences in attainment with children from families where the wage-earner works at a manual occupation achieving at a consistently lower level than other groups. The phasing out of selection has removed an obvious opportunity for this initial handicap to be institutionalised by the tripartite system. Whilst the 11+ was in existence, clear evidence exists to show that children from the most favoured socio-economic groups were disproportionately placed in grammar schools.

Much of the evidence quoted belongs to the period of selective education, but even the most recent studies demonstrate that in the early years of secondary education there are consistent group differences in attainment. Towards the end of secondary education the literature is less clear and conflicting claims have been noted. Some researchers have argued that the group differences diminish, perhaps as a function of the much higher early-leaving rate of children from social classes IV and V. Others maintain that no such convergence takes place, at least until 'A' level. In post-statutory schooling and further and higher education all the evidence reviewed has shown that children of manual workers are seriously under-represented even though, for brief spells owing to the availability of extra places, this balance has been altered slightly.

The manual working class make up some 65 per cent of the population. Clearly the majority are not 'disadvantaged' and it would be an over-simplification to extrapolate from the disadvantaged group to the entire working class. However, the broad social class differences in educational achievement which have been noted increase considerably when the disadvantaged are compared with the advantaged group. This is true of many of the research findings in Chapters 2 and 3. In writing about educational disadvantage throughout this review we discuss both social class differences in attainment and the educational problems of the most materially disadvantaged children in society. It is often difficult to separate the two issues. Moreover, the literature often does not make a clear distinction. Although the two groups are not necessarily the same, the disadvantaged find themselves in those circumstances at least in part because of their social class position. How to operationalise the concept of disadvantage and how to assess the size of the group is a problem. The issues of the minority of low achievers and the more general issue of inequality in education become blurred. This is the background against which we examine studies of educational policies (see Chapters 4 and 5) which might help disadvantaged children and young people.

Note
1 The NCDS is in the process of analysing its data on the examination results of their sixteen-year-old cohort, who would have taken public examinations in 1974. Results of the analysis are not yet available.

2 Home-based Factors

The previous chapter reviewed evidence on the relationship between social class and educational attainment with special reference to disadvantage. A strong association was found between attainment and socio-economic status. This chapter will discuss the particular home background factors which may be related to this differential attainment in an attempt to elucidate some of the contributory factors in the association between disadvantage and low attainment. It is unlikely that causal links between disadvantage and low attainment will be identified. The evidence is not available and in its absence it is not possible to establish how, or the degree to which, circumstances or processes actually affect attainment. The possible potential consequences of certain home-based factors for educational disadvantage are noted where appropriate. The evidence will be reviewed under two headings: material disadvantages and cultural factors in child-rearing and attitudes to education.

Material Disadvantages
It has already been noted that the term 'disadvantage' is a relative concept which varies over time and also between societies. Here, the evidence concerning poverty, conditions at work, unemployment, health, housing, family size, one-parent families and environment is reviewed.

Poverty
A recent major study which throws light on the extent of disadvantage in Britain today is the study of poverty in the United Kingdom, carried out by Townsend (1979). It aimed to estimate the numbers of the population living in or on the margins of poverty, to study their characteristics and problems and, in doing so, to contribute to the development of an explanation of poverty. The theme of Townsend's report is that 'Poverty can be defined objectively and applied consistently only in terms of the concept of relative deprivation'.[1] It is argued that it is inappropriate and misleading to discuss poverty in absolute

terms since societies vary according to their culturally defined needs. Moreover, what are considered 'necessities' and 'luxuries' also change over time. Townsend suggests that living standards should be judged not only on cash income but on four other resources: capital assets, employment benefits, receipt of public social services and benefits in kind, such as gifts. All these factors need to be taken into account when the extent of poverty is considered. Townsend found that for every one of the five types of resource, the 20 per cent of households with the highest net income received the greatest amount of the other four resources. The Royal Commission on the Distribution of Income and Wealth (1977) estimated that accumulated wealth probably accounted for some 60 per cent of personal wealth although the figure was lower at higher income levels. Their report argues that 'Family circumstances affect the ability to accumulate wealth' and that owner occupation of houses and life assurance policies both increase in value as mortgages are paid off and policy premiums are paid.

Three measures of poverty were used in Townsend's study:

(i)   The State's standard: that is, the level at which people become eligible for supplementary benefits.

(ii)   The relative income standard: this is defined both in terms of a number of types of household (e.g. one parent or childless couple) and the mean income for each type.

(iii) The deprivation standard: the level below which people experience deprivation disproportionately to their resources.

In the study deprivation is defined 'relatively to the community's current style of living, as established in the survey'. Townsend points out that there is not any simple and consistent relationship between poverty and income – 'the population is not divided cleanly into the deprived and non-deprived. Many people are deprived in some respects, but not in others . . . for part but not all of their lives.' With this caveat in mind, the three measures of poverty were applied to the sample and it was estimated that by the State's standard 7 per cent of households were in poverty and 24 per cent were on the margins of poverty; by the relative income standard 10.5 per cent, and by the deprivation standard 25 per cent of households were in poverty. Poverty was closely correlated with occupational status, the highest incidence being among unskilled manual workers and their dependants. Nearly half those people whose husband's or father's occupations were in unskilled manual work were below, or on, the margin of the State's standard of poverty. This was in contrast to the figure of one-third of those in other manual occupations, and one-tenth of those in professional and managerial occupations. The deprivation suffered by those families living in or on the margins of poverty is graphically illustrated in the case studies in Townsend's report. The cameos portray a bleak picture of comfortless housing, inadequate diet, lack of social life and holidays, no birthday parties or pocket money for the children and constant worry over unemployment and making ends meet.

Taking as their criteria families who were receiving free school meals and supplementary benefit, Wedge and Prosser (1973) estimated that in their sample about one child in seven (14 per cent) was living in poverty at eleven. This was likely to be an underestimate as, like Townsend, they found families who failed to take up benefits for which they were eligible. Since the needs and resources of families varied over time it was also likely that more than one in seven children had lived in low-income families at some time in their life.

Low income may mean that parents have to spend more time at their job or on household tasks which leaves less time to spend with their children. They will have less money to spend on books, crayons, puzzles or outings to help their child's development and to develop the skills which the school rewards.

Conditions at Work
Townsend uses the term deprivation at work to show that 'further privileges conferred upon, or gained by, non-manual groups may maintain their advantage over manual groups, despite general advances in the number and scale of employee rights.' Townsend developed several indices of the concept of deprivation at work, which included such items as the hours of work, length of notice and amount of sick pay to which employees were entitled, holidays, welfare and fringe benefits, and physical conditions of work. In each instance, manual workers were found to be at a marked disadvantage to other workers. Wedderburn (1970) has discussed the fact that improvements, in terms of employment, redundancy rights, etc. have usually been accompanied by parallel improvements in the employment conditions of non-manual workers, thus maintaining the differential between occupational groups. In considering the disadvantaged position of manual workers relative to the position of non-manual workers, both in terms of conditions of work and levels of pay, Townsend and Wedderburn state that complacency over progress is misplaced. The same points are made by Routh *et al*. (1980).

Poor conditions at work may have an indirect effect on employees' children and their educational experience. Long hours and short holidays reduce the amount of time parents have available for their children. Heavy physical work, which gives rise to severe fatigue may mean they are frequently too tired to meet some of their children's needs. More indirectly a sense of powerlessness at the work place may carry over into other aspects of life. When this happens parents may passively accept low standards of educational provision or decisions made about their children at school about which they are unhappy.

Unemployment

Unemployment too was strongly related to occupational class in Townsend's study. Unskilled manual labourers accounted for only 9 per cent of males experiencing no unemployment during the preceding year, but they accounted for 17 per cent of those experiencing one to nine weeks' unemployment and 39 per cent of those with ten or more weeks of unemployment. This contrasts with the professional and managerial group, who experienced virtually no unemployment during the same year. Townsend suggests that there are not two states of 'employed' and 'unemployed' but five gradations from full-time secure employment to continuous unemployment. The relationship found, in his study, between poverty and unemployment exists not only during the period of unemployment but for a long time afterwards. The situation is similar for those who experience recurrent unemployment. Either they do not earn enough to raise their families above the poverty line, or they are never in work long enough to establish a standard of living above that level. The case histories described in Field (1977a) confirm this.

A recent report by the Central Policy Review Staff (CPRS) entitled *People and their Families* (CPRS/CSO, 1980) claims that the unemployed tend to be predominantly the young or the old. But the rise in unemployment has resulted in an increase among those with families to support. The CPRS state that 'in January, 1979, 151,000 men between twenty-five and forty-four had been unemployed for over six months, compared with 75,000 in 1973. In November, 1977, 270,000 men with 630,000 dependent children were receiving unemployment benefits'. This compared with 120,000 and 280,000 respectively in 1973. Sinfield (1977) has argued that the extent of poverty in unemployment is closely related to the length of time out of work and the need to support a family. 'The largest families had the smallest resources and the greatest difficulty in making ends meet – and these problems were clearly exacerbated by length of unemployment.' Sinfield also cites evidence from Showler which supports the view that unemployment is a cause of disadvantage in the labour market and of subsequent poverty since the long-term unemployed may become labelled as 'unemployables', be viewed with suspicion by potential employers or be referred less often for jobs by employment officers. Moreover, recurring unemployment does not allow time for resources to be built up to cushion the effects of further periods out of work. The effects of long-term unemployment, and of poverty which frequently accompanies it, on family life, are illustrated by some of Townsend's case histories. These document children sharing beds in damp, verminous houses, existing on an inadequate diet and subject to frequent minor illnesses and with 'nowhere to play indoors and nowhere safe near by'. Although not drawn out by Townsend the implications for educational disadvantage are clear.

Unemployment can have effects on the community as well as on the individuals and their families. Sinfield describes how the 'impoverishing' effects of unemployment on a community can be seen 'in both public and private services: poor schools with insufficient or less qualified staff . . . limited shopping facilities forcing the poor to pay more . . .'

During the 1950s when Douglas carried out his cohort study, unemployment among the fathers was far lower than would be the case today. Most of the prolonged unemployment was the result of physical or mental illness or handicap. Seventy-nine per cent of the reported instances of unemployment through illness were in the lower manual working class, nearly twice as many as would be expected. The children whose fathers were unemployed through illness had scores on attainment tests that were 1.7 points below the expected average when allowances were made for social class, family size and housing conditions. The families concerned showed other signs of poverty, such as overcrowded or adverse housing conditions. Douglas (1964) found that the children in these families did considerably worse than children from similarly disadvantaged homes where the father was employed. They had lower test scores at both eight and eleven and their teachers reported they were lazy and inattentive at school and that parents took little interest in their progress. Wedge and Prosser (1973) found one in twelve of the disadvantaged children in their cohort had a father who was unemployed for the whole year preceding the interview compared with one in 3000 of the rest of the sample.

To summarise so far, material disadvantage in terms of poverty and unemployment may have direct implications for educational disadvantage. There will be less money to spend on books, materials or outings. There is likely to be increased stress which may mean that parents are able to show less interest or encouragement for their children. There may also be more pressure on older children to leave school at the earliest opportunity in order to earn money to help support the family (although in a time of severe youth unemployment in parts of the country this may be futile). Older children may be more likely to take evening or weekend jobs to earn extra money which means they have less time and energy for their studies either at home or at school.

Health

One indicator of a nation's health is infant mortality. Whilst, since the turn of the century, the rate has fallen, the gap between the social classes remains. Data from the Office of Population and Censuses and Surveys indicate that in the United Kingdom deaths among infants under one year old have fallen from 22 per 1000 live births in 1961 to fourteen per 1000 in 1976. Perinatal mortality rates (deaths in the first week of life) have fallen even more, from around thirty-seven per 1000 births in the mid-1950s to around twenty per 1000 in the mid-1970s. However, there are considerable differences in child mortality rates between socio-economic groups. The CPRS, drawing on 1971 Census data, state that perinatal death rates for social class V are four times higher than for social class I. But even more striking is the disparity between different social groups in childhood deaths due to accidents. For example, 'the rate for deaths among boys due to falls, fires and drowning is more than ten times greater for social class V than for social class I' (CPRS, 1980).

The hazards of childbearing tend to be associated with social disadvantage. Baird and Illsley (1953) found that low socio-economic status was related to low birth weight babies and perinatal deaths. Birch and Gussow (1970) have described the interweaving of factors which contribute to the adverse ante-natal and post-natal conditions of socially disadvantaged mothers. These mothers tend to be physically less sturdy, to have children earlier, more frequently and until a later age. They are less likely to receive pre-natal care and more likely to be delivered in inadequate conditions. These findings are supported by those of Wedge and Prosser (1973) who considered that, compared with other children, the disadvantaged group whom they identified at eleven by their social circumstances, were 'at the time of birth already facing substantially diminished prospects of normal development of their chances in life'. Drillien (1964) and Illsley (1966) suggest that among low socio-economic groups there is an association between low birth weight and a depressed IQ score. The report commissioned by the DHSS and recently presented by Black and others on inequalities in health (Black *et al.*, 1980) suggests that, on the basis of international evidence, much could be done to improve ante-natal care and its uptake. The research group found that only 4.5 per cent of babies of social class I and II weigh less than $5\frac{1}{2}$lb at birth compared with 8.2 per cent of babies of social class IV and V.

The incidence of poor vision, impaired hearing and dental decay has also been found to be more common among low income families (Bloom, 1964; Wedge and Prosser, 1973). All of these conditions are likely to affect educational performance. If the children concerned are not able to see the blackboard or printed page clearly, or are not able to hear what the teachers say, or if they are in discomfort with toothache they are not likely to perform in school to the best of their ability. Yet Davie *et al*., Wedge and Prosser and Black *et al*. all found that families in social class V and, to a lesser extent in social class IV, made *less* use of the health services (as measured by attendance at clinics or take-up of immunisation programmes) than did other families.

Another indicator of inequalities in health is suggested by the findings in the National Child Development Study that social class differences in the height of children had hardly changed between 1953 and the mid-1960s. This confirms Tanner's (1969) and Tizard's (1976) findings that although children are tending to get taller each decade, the differences between the classes are not narrowing. A study of urban children aged fifteen, in Newcastle-upon-Tyne, found that children in social class I and II were, on average, 4.4 kg heavier than children in social class IV and V (Miller *et al*., 1960). In an earlier related study of 1000 families in Newcastle-upon-Tyne Spence *et al*. (1954) found that, even in adverse circumstances, most parents provided adequate care for their children. However, where ill health, either mental or physical, of one or both parents were combined with a poor environment and a low income, then the health of the children was at risk.

Douglas *et al*. (1968) found that self-reports of father's and mother's health were less favourable in the manual working class than among the middle class. In addition, when either parent was in poor health the children's school attendance became worse, except in the case of middle-class boys. This tendency occurred for both boys and girls, although it was more marked for girls. Where there was little illness in the family middle-class girls lost considerably less time from school than manual working-class girls, but as the amount of illness increased, this gap narrowed. Absence from either primary or secondary school was found by Douglas *et al*. to be associated with poor performance in tests, with early leaving and few 'O' level passes. However, children from middle-class families and/or those who attended primary schools with good academic records did not fall behind in test scores even after fairly frequent absence. It was the children from the lower manual working-class families, especially if they attended academically poorer schools, whose work suffered as a result of absence. During the early years of schooling middle-class children tended to be absent more than the manual working class, but later the position reversed. There were, however, differences according to sex and type of school.

It is claimed by Douglas *et al*. that even severe illness in childhood had little effect on school progress and led to only a slight depression on test performance. This is in contradiction to the claim by Rutter *et al.* that chronic physical illness in childhood has been shown to be associated with an increased rate of reading difficulties (Rutter, Tizard and Whitmore, 1970). Evidence from the Isle of Wight Survey suggests that, of children with chronic physical handicaps, 14 per cent were at least twenty-eight months retarded in reading compared with 6 per cent in the general population control group.

In 1976 a government study of children's health and the School Health Service (DHSS, 1976, The Court Report) concluded that 'there is now extensive evidence that an adverse family and social environment can retard physical, emotional and intellectual growth, lead to more frequent and more serious illness and adversely affect educational achievement and personal behaviour.' Referring to what the Court Report called the 'long shadows' cast by inadequately treated childhood illness, Black and his colleagues put forward several suggestions for taking the services to the people who have most need of them but who, for various reasons, such as inequality in provision and the services being geared towards middle-class consumers, make less use of them. They argue that early childhood is the period at which intervention and prevention could do most to break the association between health and socio-economic status. The report suggests an experimental district action programme be set up in ten areas of high mortality and adverse social conditions. As part of the programme a range of improvements such as free milk, ante-natal and child health clinics and day care facilities for children would be offered and their effects monitored.

Townsend mentions a Government Nutrition Survey of pre-school children in 1967/68 (DHSS, 1975) in which he claims 'disturbing findings have not been fully published'. Although the report had no detailed data on individual intake according to occupational class Townsend claims that 'a scatter diagram at the end of the report showed that a very large number of children had less than 80 per cent of the recommended daily energy intake'. The diet of some children is inadequate. The problem, however, is more often one of balance rather than quantity. It is a paradox that war-time rationing had a positive effect on the overall nutritional balance of the population's diet (Greaves and Hollingsworth, 1966). Greater affluence in the 1950s and 1960s does not seem to have improved matters. Lambert (1964) considered that there had been less improvement since the 1950s than might have been expected and a review by the Office of Health Economics (1967) indicated concern over families who did not take in the recommended allowances of protein and calcium.

Smoking and pregnancy

There are certain circumstances of pregnancy and birth which are known to be associated with low birth weight and infant mortality (Butler and Alberman, 1969). One of these circumstances is smoking during pregnancy. Davie *et al*. (1972) found, in the NCD study, that children whose mothers had smoked during their pregnancy were shorter and read less well at the age of seven than children whose mothers did not smoke. At age eleven the children whose mothers had smoked during pregnancy were, on average, three months behind other children in general intelligence, four months behind in reading and 1 cm shorter in height. Moreover, Wedge and Prosser (1973) found that mothers who did smoke were more likely to be disadvantaged in terms of housing, income and family composition. One in five of their disadvantaged sample had mothers who smoked heavily during pregnancy (ten or more cigarettes a day) compared with one in ten of the ordinary group.

Fogelman (1980) has analysed the follow-up data of the NCDS sample at the age of sixteen in order to investigate a possible relationship between mothers smoking during pregnancy and the development of the adolescent. He found that, even after allowing for related background factors, the children of mothers who had smoked ten or more cigarettes per day after the fourth month of pregnancy achieved lower scores on tests of reading and mathematics than other children. Children whose mothers smoked less heavily did less well on the tests than children whose mothers had not smoked at all. The results for children's height and the proportion said to suffer from asthma or bronchitis were less clear. For boys a relationship was found with height but for girls the relationship was not statistically significant and daughters of moderate smokers (less than ten cigarettes per day) were slightly taller than daughters of non-smokers. Although children whose mothers had smoked heavily during pregnancy were the most likely to have suffered from asthma or bronchitis there were more reports about the children of non-smokers than the children of moderate smokers. Although Fogelman expresses doubts about the direct causality of the relationships he suggests that, given what is known about the possible effect of smoking on children's development 'there is every reason to continue to persuade all those who are pregnant not to smoke'. Follow-up work currently being carried out on the disadvantaged sub-sample of the NCDS may shed more light on this issue.

Family size

In Townsend's study the proportion of people in poverty increases with size of family. It was found that 'there were 21 per cent of men and women with one child, 30 per cent with two children, 31 per cent with three and 69 per cent with four or more who had a net disposable income in the previous year of less than the (State's) standard,[2] or up to 40 per cent higher.' Families with children were found to have more fluctuating incomes and families with children under fifteen accounted for over half the population in poverty. Among the several studies which show that individuals from large families tend to have a lower level of intelligence and inferior reading attainment are those of Anastasi, 1956, Douglas, 1964, Davie et al., 1972, Rutter, Tizard and Whitmore, 1970, and Douglas et al., 1968. The association is less marked for mathematical attainment but remains even when birth order and social class are controlled for. It occurs in all social groups although it is less evident in individuals from middle-class homes. Thus, Douglas (1964) found that the impact of family size on educational performance was greater among the manual than the middle-class children. In the middle classes it is children, more particularly boys, from a family of four or more offspring who may be educationally disadvantaged, whereas in the manual working classes the children are progressively handicapped with every increase in family size. Large families also tend to have the worst housing conditions and amenities and to spend less per head on food. Douglas states that 'the children from large families are at a disadvantage in these respects in each social class, but most of all when their parents come from the lower manual working-class.' Wedge and Prosser found that at the age of seven or eleven more than one in six 'disadvantaged' children (18 per cent) lived in a family where there were five or more children.

One-parent families
Considerable concern is currently expressed over the position of children who are growing up in one-parent families and over the effects this may have on their educational attainment. It is a commonly held view that a secure home environment with two parents is needed for the satisfactory normal development of children, and that where family relations are disrupted emotional and/or educational development may suffer. Thus, children not living with two parents are often regarded as being at a disadvantage. Of course, satisfactory relations are possible where there is only one parent and the presence of two parents does not, by itself, ensure harmony and security. Although some of the evidence is inconclusive, on the whole studies seem to show that, by themselves, one-parent families, as a result of either death or divorce, show little association with educational disadvantage.

In the Isle of Wight study Rutter et al. (1970) found that about one in seven of the ten year olds in their sample were not living with their two natural parents. However, a 'broken home' showed no association with intellectual or educational retardation, whereas it did with delinquency and child psychiatric disorder.

Douglas et al. (1968) showed that, whilst the sudden death of a father did not appear to affect academic performance, his death after a prolonged illness seemed to result in poor attainment. This suggests that the preceding stress and the possible disruption involved in caring for or visiting the sick father might contribute to the poorer attainment, rather than the one-parent situation which ensued.

In the National Child Development Study, Davie et al. (1972) found that 2.8 per cent of their sample, at the age of seven, were living in households with no male head and 7.8 per cent were not living with both natural parents. This 'atypical' family situation was associated with poor reading ability, and the association was stronger for boys than for girls. But the children living in an 'atypical' family contained more working-class children. When the comparison was carried out within each social class group, the children from atypical situations in the middle-class or skilled manual families were still shown to be at a disadvantage, but there was no difference in the reading performance between children in social class IV and V, whether they were in normal or atypical families. It can be assumed from the NCDS findings and from a study by Edwards and Thompson (1971) that although children from atypical family situations achieve less well overall at school, the difference may be due to differences in socio-economic status and the material disadvantage associated with one-parent families in certain occupational groups. Wedge and Prosser (1973) found one child in sixteen was living with one parent only at either seven or eleven years of age.

Several other reports have drawn on the NCDS data. These have variously shown that one-parent families were over-represented in the lower socio-economic groups, were more likely to live in poor housing and to be at a financial disadvantage (Essen, 1978). The children were more likely to have attended more than one school by the age of eleven (Ferri, 1976). They were also more likely to have spent some time in local authority care (Essen et al., 1976) and, when the children were sixteen, their parents were more likely to have lower educational aspirations for them (Lambert, 1978).

Ferri, drawing on the NCDS data on eleven year olds, found that the family situation in which the children were living at the age of eleven was related to their performance in reading and arithmetic and to their progress at school, from the age of seven. However, the cause of the family situation was found to be important in relation to the different attainment within the subgroups of one-parent families. In addition, most, but not all, of the difference could be accounted for by disadvantaging factors such as low income, poor housing and low socio-economic status. For example, the children of single mothers, cared for by their mothers, appeared to be doing less well than their peers in two-parent families when 'raw' scores were compared. But most of the difference was attributable to other adverse economic conditions associated with being fatherless. Ferri warns that the findings can only be tentative since the members in the sub-sample were small.

When the NCDS sample was followed up again at the age of sixteen Essen (1979) looked at the school attainment of children in their final year of compulsory schooling, who were living in one and two-parent families. Essen's purpose was to investigate which differences emerged and which remained when the groups were compared with children in similar material and social circumstances. Children were defined as having lived in a one-parent family if, at the time of any of the follow-up interviews, they were living with one natural parent but no other parent figure, or if, at birth, their mother was single, widowed, separated or divorced. Some of the latter group of children had subsequently gained a substitute parent figure. The 'motherless' subgroup of the 'one-parent' group was small, but the larger 'fatherless' group was further divided into those who were without their father before they were seven, after they were seven, still fatherless at sixteen or who had a substitute parent by that age. Essen found that the children who had spent any time living in a one-parent family had statistically significantly lower mean scores in both mathematics and reading than children who had always lived with two parents. However, allowance was made for the background factors associated with parental situation which are themselves independently associated with poorer school attainment. These included social class, family size, amenities in the home, tenure of home and space in which to do homework. When this allowance was made the differences between the groups were greatly reduced and they were no longer statistically significant. Moreover, the adjustment effect was such that the two-parent children no longer had the highest score for reading, but retained their advantage in mathematics. The results for the fatherless and motherless groups were close. Children who had gained a substitute father tended to have a slightly lower score than those who remained fatherless. Essen offers no comment on this finding but it may be that the presence of a step-father produces certain emotional tensions in the child which effect performance at school. Alternatively the mothers who remained single may have devoted more time and attention to their children and included them in adult activities. This finding supports Murchison's contribution to the Finer Report (1974) which indicated that children brought up by mothers on their own had slightly better attainment than those whose mothers remarried after widowhood or divorce. Essen found that low income was a substantial part of the social disadvantage, particularly for those families who remained fatherless, but surprisingly housing (amenities, tenure and private space) did not emerge from the analysis as an important factor. Essen concludes that 'although children in one-parent families have relatively low test scores overall, to a large extent this reflects their poor material circumstances, rather than the absence of one parent *per se*'.

The National Children's Bureau have recently published the follow-up study of the 640 children in their sample who were born illegitimate (Lambert and Streather, 1980). In the report, which deals with the children when they were eleven years old, the children are studied in three groups: those remaining illegitimate, those who have been adopted and those legitimated by marriage. One-third of the children born illegitimate in 1958 were living in poverty. The report argues that it is the poverty, not the lack of legitimacy, which matters and that the benefits of adoption result from the straightforward change from a working-class to a middle-class household with the attendant material benefits.

From the evidence available it would appear that it is not usually the family disruption by itself which is important, but the longer-term social and economic adversities which are often associated with the disruption, which have implications for educational disadvantage. However, to a considerable extent, teachers judge children in the classroom by their actual performance on academic tasks, although the pupils' language, appearance and personality will also have a bearing on their judgements. Teachers do not 'control' for disadvantageous conditions when making their assessments. In terms of 'raw' scores children from one-parent families do tend to score less well than their two-parent peers. But teachers may, ironically, consider the atypical family situation with or without associated economic factors as irremediably limiting the potential performance of children. Teachers may, as a consequence, have correspondingly lower expectations for these children, and these expectations may create a further disadvantage for the children. Teacher expectations and their effects will be discussed further in the next chapter.

Housing

Townsend's study makes use of several indicators of poor housing. These included structural defects, inadequate facilities and insufficient bedrooms or play space. In his sample 61 per cent experienced at least one type of poor housing and 11 per cent experienced three or more indices of poor housing. Townsend states 'much the most important structural factor to be associated with housing deprivation was occupational class'. This was in part explained by the type of housing tenure. Fewer owner-occupiers or tenants of unfurnished rented accommodation experienced poor housing.

Several studies show that overcrowded housing conditions and poor household amenities are associated with lower ability and attainment (Douglas, 1964, Davie et al., 1972, Murray, 1974, Rutter et al., 1970 and Fogelman, 1975). Douglas (1964) classified the homes of the children in his study as 'satisfactory' and 'unsatisfactory'. The former had not more than one adverse condition (e.g. overcrowding, bed-sharing or lack of amenities) and the latter had two or more adverse conditions. Douglas sought to establish whether children from adverse housing conditions would be handicapped in their test performance and whether the effects of such an environment would be cumulative. His evidence indicates that children from 'unsatisfactory' manual working-class homes had lower scores in the eleven-year tests than when tested at eight, whereas those from 'satisfactory' homes improved their test score during the same period. The position for children from middle-class homes was reversed; at eleven children from 'unsatisfactory' homes had made up their earlier lag in scores. Douglas suggests that for the middle-class children, the adverse housing circumstances had exerted their full influence by the time the children were eight 'and then the influence is off-set by other favourable factors in the homes or in the schools'. Simpson (1964) carried out an analysis of Douglas' data which separated out the overlapping effects of family size, parental interest and academic record of the school from housing conditions. The results reduced the effect of housing on school performance but increased the gap between the middle-class and manual working-class children.

In the National Child Development Study Davie et al. collected information on overcrowding and amenities in the home. 'Overcrowding' was defined as more than 1.5 persons to a room. The three 'basic' amenities were a hot water supply, a bathroom and an indoor lavatory. They found that 15 per cent of the study children, in 1965, were living in overcrowded conditions at home. The figures showed a marked social class trend. In social class I the figure was 1 per cent, in social class V it was 37 per cent. Approximately 93 per cent of children from social class I and II had the sole use of the above amenities compared with less than 66 per cent of children in social class V. Davie et al. consider that these conditions were important correlates of school attainment. They estimated that overcrowding was the equivalent of two or three months' retardation in reading age and absence or shared use of basic amenities was equivalent to about nine months' retardation in reading age. The effects were smaller for attainment in arithmetic and were estimated to be one-and-a-half months and two months respectively. In the sub-sample of children from the NCDS who were considered to be disadvantaged, Wedge and Prosser found that one in six lived in a flat, maisonette, rooms or a caravan compared with one in fifteen of other children. Ninety per cent of them shared a room and 52 per cent shared a bed. One in twenty-two of the disadvantaged children shared and wet their bed at the age of eleven. Seventeen per cent of the disadvantaged children lived in families without the sole use of a water supply, 17 per cent had no bathroom and 25 per cent had no indoor lavatory (Wedge and Prosser, 1973).

Only one in twenty-five of the disadvantaged was middle class, the majority were working class. When they were tested at the age of eleven the disadvantaged group did less well than the other children. The averages of their reading and mathematics scores were lower; more of them scored in the lower ranges and fewer of them scored in the higher range. Overcrowding was found to be associated with aggression, lack of curiosity, impulsiveness and extraversion in nine-year-old Scottish children in Educational Priority Areas, (Murray, 1974).

Poor housing may well affect educational progress as a result of the difficulties of studying at home, the lack of quiet or privacy and an inadequate night's sleep. In one study (Dale and Griffiths, 1965) the grammar-school children who were moved from a high to a low stream were almost all from working-class families and almost half of them had poor facilities for homework.

Fogelman (1976), in the report on the NCDS children at sixteen, found that, at a time when adolescents value privacy, 39 per cent of the sample did not have their own bedroom and 8 per cent had to share a bed. Drawing on the same cohort of children, Essen et al. (1978) relate the housing conditions to attainment at sixteen and to progress in secondary school from the age of eleven. The relationship between housing conditions and attainment at sixteen was found to be similar whether the child experienced unsatisfactory housing at the age of seven, eleven or sixteen but there was no evidence that there was any particular age at which housing circumstances were crucial for educational attainment.

The view that poor housing is associated with low educational attainment seems well supported in the literature. However, Rutter and Madge (1976) point out that 'the associations are indirect and the mechanisms ill-understood'. It has also been suggested that poor housing is related to educational disadvantage because of the concentration of poor housing in areas with the poorest schools (Plowden, Central Advisory Council for Education, 1967).

Environment

Although Townsend extended the analysis of deprivation in housing to environmental deprivation this is fairly narrowly defined in terms of the *immediate* environment. He considers that 'the value assumptions upon which experimental indices of poor environmental conditions are based are usually neither expressed explicitly nor critically discussed. As a consequence, deficiencies short of some presumed social standard are listed without any very clear attempt to specify the mean or median or to show the kind of privileges enjoyed by those living in spacious and well-appointed amenities.' Whilst acknowledging the need for a concept of environmental deprivation which includes 'the lack of or difficulty of access to gardens, play spaces, parks, water, shopping facilities, health centres and so on, and exposure to noise and dirt' Townsend's study is restricted to three measures. These were the existence and size of garden, frequency of air pollution and whether or not children had a safe place in which to play. He found that as many as 22 per cent of the population lacked the sole use of a garden; 27 per cent experienced some degree of air pollution and over 33 per cent of children aged between one and ten had no safe place to play in near their house. As many as 11 per cent of children aged between one and four experienced all three kinds of deprivation.

Environmental deprivation was closely related to social class. Seventeen per cent of those in professional or managerial occupations, compared with 34 per cent of those in semi or unskilled occupations, experienced air pollution; 25 per cent of children aged one to four from the professional group but 44 per cent of children of the manual group had no safe place to play near the home. Townsend claims that over two-thirds of the families of manual workers with young children experienced 'a marked degree' of environmental deprivation.

Attention has focussed recently on the potentially harmful effects to children of lead poisoning. Children with high levels of lead in their bodies have often been found to have low IQ ratings or to show more signs of disturbance than others and are much more likely to live in a disadvantaged inner-city area. However, in a recent review of the research Rutter (1980) writes that much of the evidence is unreliable either because the indicators of psychological damage were too crude or because no allowance was made for other factors, such as a socially disadvantaged environment.

Many of the adverse social conditions in the inner city will overlap and may have a cumulative effect on children's lives but the relative effects of this 'seamless web of circumstance' are, as the Plowden Committee acknowledged, difficult, if not impossible, to isolate. Parents who are unskilled workers are likely to earn low pay and to have poor working conditions, and be subject to periods of unemployment. In addition they will often have large families, live in poor housing conditions, have an insufficiently nutritious diet, be prone to ill health and have low educational attainment. The Plowden Report admits that 'In a neighbourhood where the jobs people do and the status they hold owe little to their education, it is natural for children as they grow older to regard school as a brief prelude to work rather than an avenue to future opportunities.' It was to ameliorate such circumstances that the Plowden Committee recommended the setting up of Educational Priority Areas (EPAs) which are discussed in a later chapter.

The pattern of urban disadvantage and of the inter-correlation of social conditions has been well documented in studies of the inner city, where the highest incidence of disadvantage has been thought to be concentrated. Recent detailed accounts are to be found in the reports of the inner-area studies, sponsored by the Department of the Environment and carried out in London (Lambeth), Birmingham (Small Heath) and Liverpool (DOE, 1977 a, b and c.).

Since the late 1950s and early 1960s there have been changes in the nature of urban development (see Harrison and Whitehead, 1978). The development boom and the resulting congestion in terms of office space, housing and traffic which led to movement from inner areas to overspill and development areas changed to one of economic decline, decay and unemployment. The White Paper (1977) noted not only the decline in population in the cities between the mid-1960s and the mid-1970s, but the greater numbers of skilled workers leaving, relative to unskilled. Allnutt and Gerlardi (1980) state that 'The provincial inner areas have double the national proportion of unskilled workers, and in each case have a higher proportion than in the authority as a whole. Conversely, the proportion of non-manual workers, especially in the professional and managerial groups, is lower in the inner areas than in the conurbations.' Those who remain in the centre of inner cities tend to be the semi or unskilled, who face a situation of declining employment opportunities. For example, the inner area study of Liverpool found that one in three men living in the most affected areas of the city were unemployed in 1975 and many of these had young children. Those who can move do, leaving behind the least mobile, who are usually the poorest and the least skilled.

The educational progress of children in such areas was studied by Chazan *et al.* (1976) who carried out a longitudinal study of children in infant schools in areas where the population was defined as 'deprived'. 'Middle class' or 'settled working class' schools were used as controls. Compared with controls the deprived area children were poorer in oral language, reading and related skills and mathematics. They were also considered to be not so well adjusted in school and to have lower levels of concentration. The differences remained but were less striking when the deprived group were compared with the settled working class group. The differences became evident early on in the child's career in the infant school and were maintained over the three years spent there but there was no evidence of a widening gap in achievement and adjustment. Chazan *et al.* consider that the difference in favour of the control group child 'no doubt reflects the more adequate preparation of these children for the demands of schooling by their parents' and the finding that their gain is maintained is probably due in some measure 'to relatively greater parental support and interest in their educational achievement'. Evidence on parental interest and support, some of which conflicts with Chazan's view, is discussed later in the chapter.

Wedge and Prosser found that although overall one eleven-year-old child in sixteen in Britain was disadvantaged the regional distribution was not uniform. In the south of England the figure was one in forty-seven, in Wales and the north it was one in twelve, but in Scotland the figure was one in ten. The authors state that '11 per cent of the eleven year old British children lived in Scotland, but 19 per cent of the disadvantaged children lived there'. The teachers of the children in the NCDS sample rated just under half of the 'disadvantaged children' as 'well-adjusted' compared with almost three-quarters of the 'ordinary' group, whilst one in four of the 'disadvantaged' was considered to be 'maladjusted', but only one in eleven of the other group.

Coates and Silburn's (1973) study of St Ann's, a disadvantaged area in Nottingham, found that nearly 50 per cent of the seven-year-old children had reading ages of between four and five years, only 4 per cent were up to two years ahead of their peer group. This contrasted with almost 60 per cent of seven-year-olds in a commuter suburb of Nottingham, who had reading ages of between one and five years in advance of normal standards. In the Birmingham inner area study only 3 per cent of males in Small Heath had qualifications of 'A' level or above, compared with 13 per cent nationally, and only 13 per cent had 'O' levels or CSE, compared with 22 per cent nationally. The Liverpool inner area study found, in 1974, that inner Liverpool had 7 per cent of the secondary-school population but only 5 per cent of those in the city taking CSE examinations. Over 50 per cent of school leavers had not taken CSE or 'O' levels (DOE, 1977b, 1977c).

Although the majority of people living in inner-city areas are not unemployed and do not live in overcrowded homes or lack basic amenities they are affected by the dereliction and vandalism and may find, as did some Small Heath residents, that their address made it harder to get jobs or mortgages. 'The concentration of poor homes, unskilled population and high unemployment can have an indirect effect,' state Allnutt and Gerlardi. They maintain that the proportion of inner-city residents expressing dissatisfaction with the area was two or three times higher than the proportion for England as a whole.

The concentration of disadvantage in a few inner-city areas has recently been questioned (Harrison and Whitehead); and it has been suggested that such disadvantages may be a question of social location rather than geographical location (Hall, 1980, Webber, 1977, and Berthoud, 1976). Whilst acknowledging that inner-city areas do suffer disadvantage, Blackstone (1980b) has suggested 'positive aspects of inner city life on which to try to build'. A wider range of local, hence accessible, public facilities and specialised services can be offered in areas where consumers are concentrated; the multicultural nature of the inner city can be reflected in the variety of shops and restaurants and the stability of many inner urban communities can permit community development.

Many people in rural areas are also disadvantaged. Their geographical isolation results in higher costs for transport and goods and services, restricted opportunities for employment and leisure, and more thinly stretched social services. Most of the research evidence on children has been on those in urban areas. But children in rural areas may have to travel to small schools where they mix with few children of their own age and where facilities and curricular opportunities may be limited (see Boulter, 1979, Boulter and Crispin, 1978 and Chazan *et al.*, 1976).

Cultural Factors in Child-Rearing and Attitudes to Education

The 'cultural deprivation' thesis
In America during the 1960s a widely accepted explanation for the school failure of disadvantaged children was embodied in the concept of 'cultural deprivation'. The term was widely used after the publication of *The Culturally Deprived Child* (Riessman, 1962). The development of the concept of cultural deprivation has been traced by Friedman (1967) and Becker (1963). Adherents of this notion maintained that low achievement could be attributed to early environmental experiences and different child-rearing practices which resulted in cognitive and linguistic deficits (Krugman, 1956, Wrightstone, 1958

and Brooks, 1966). Interest grew after 1963 because of the Federal Government's 'War on Poverty'. Education was seen as a means of countering these deficits, thereby improving the conditions and life chances of poor people and ethnic minority groups.

'Culturally deprived' children were considered to come from homes which were both materially and intellectually inadequate. These were often graphically described. For example, Brooks writes of a culturally deprived child as having 'taken few trips, perhaps his only one the cramped, uncomfortable trip from the lonely shack on the tenant farm to the teeming, filthy slum dwelling and he probably knows nothing of poetry, music, painting or even indoor plumbing'. Psychologists such as Hunt (1964) went so far as to state that 'the difference between the culturally deprived and the culturally privileged is, for children, analogous to the difference between cage-reared and pet-reared rats and dogs'. Deutsch (1964) stressed the importance of the pre-school years as the most effective age at which to administer 'compensatory' enrichment programmes. There arose a plethora of such programmes, many of them aimed at alleviating material, as well as supposed cultural disadvantage. Some were aimed at helping pre-school children (Operation Head Start) others were aimed at the older age groups (Higher Horizons Program, Project Upward Bound). The success of these compensatory programmes will be discussed in a later chapter.

In Britain the notion of cultural deprivation was accepted by the Plowden Committee, who wrote, 'Cultural deprivation can also have disastrous results . . . a child brought up in a family which, because of poverty, missing parents or the low intelligence of parents, cannot provide security or sufficient emotional or intellectual stimulation, may miss a significant stage in his early social development.' Whilst acknowledging that a child from an impoverished background may have a normal, satisfactory emotional life, the committee considered that 'what he often lacks is the opportunity to develop intellectual interests. This shows in his poor command of language.' The lack of intellectual stimulation, and inadequately developed language skills were seen as contributing to the cultural deprivation which undermined the disadvantaged child's chances of educational achievement. The root of these failings was considered to lie in poor motivation; in the quality of mother–child interactions during the formative years, which were crucial for intellectual development; in the lack of language skills and literary experiences offered by parents who possessed few books and rarely read to their children and in the lack of parental interest in and knowledge of the child's education. The evidence in support of these views and some of the counter arguments will be considered next.

Mother–child interactions

During the 1950s and 1960s the belief in the importance of the first five years of life for intellectual development was strengthened by research findings. Early mother–child interactions were said to bear directly on later mental health (Bowlby, 1953). Animal research suggested that imprinting had permanent effects (Connolly, 1974) and studies of the development of IQ indicated that, although IQ varies in the early years, by the age of four it has stabilised (Bloom, 1964). However, research findings on social class differences in parenting during early childhood are not consistent. It has been claimed that in the early months of a baby's life the amount of physical contact and stimulation received by the child is related to his mental development (Lewis and Goldberg, 1969, Yarrow, 1963, cited in Pilling and Pringle, 1978). There is evidence to suggest that, if anything, working class children, particularly girls, are at an advantage at this time (Moss *et al.*, 1969). Lewis and Wilson (1972) found that there were no social class differences in the mother's verbal contacts with the child but women from lower social class groups had more physical contact with their infant. During these early months infants whose parents came from the lower socio-economic groups tended to be ahead in mental development. However, Tulkin and Kagan (1972) claim that their sample of middle-class mothers of ten-month-old, first-born girls spent less time in physical contact but more time in verbal interaction and cognitive stimulation with their children. These differences are considered to be important since it is thought that verbal, not physical, stimulation and the mother's involvement in the child's play, rather than the number of toys, fosters mental development during the child's second year of life (Clarke-Stewart, 1973, cited in Pilling and Pringle).

Active, as opposed to passive, learning and goal-directed behaviour has been the subject of much research by psychologists (Held and Hein, 1958, Piaget, 1955). It will not be discussed in detail here. However, some of the research findings have implications for the discussion of disadvantage and under-achievement. Greenfield (1969, cited in Bruner, 1974) has noted the importance of the environment and the sequence of goals set for the child by the parent in the development of cognitive growth. Schoggen (1969, cited in Bruner) found social class differences in the emphasis on goal-directed behaviour which adults attempted to elicit from the children in the two groups. Middle-class children received more stimulation towards attaining a goal than did working-class children. Similar trends emerged from studies on how mothers from upper and lower socio-economic groups teach their children. Hess and Shipman (1965) and Bee (1969) found that the middle-class mothers paid more attention to goal-directed action, they allowed their children to set their own pace and to make more decisions, they used questioning as a strategy for structuring problem-solving and praised successful efforts rather than criticising failure.

Research based on observations and/or interviews with the mothers of slightly older children of four to seven years, has shown social class differences in control techniques (Hess and Shipman, 1965 and 1967, Newson and Newson, 1972 and 1976). In a study carried out by Cook-Gumperz (1973) it was found that in a hypothetical social control situation, middle-class mothers used strategies which included more information about consequences of an action, whilst working-class mothers used more imperatives. Follow-up data from Hess *et al.* (1968) and Hess *et al.* (1969) showed that the more a mother felt externally controlled and less in command of her everyday life, when her child was four years old, the more likely the child was to have a low IQ and poor academic achievement at the age of six or seven. This view is supported by Greenfield (1969) who asks, 'If a mother believes her fate is controlled by external forces, that she does not control the means necessary to achieve her goals, what does this mean for her children?' One possible answer is suggested by Robinson and Robinson (1968), who concluded that 'children with a high degree of achievement motivation tend to become brighter as they grow older, those with a more passive outlook tend to fall behind . . . the degree of achievement motivation is related to the socio-cultural background of the child; middle-class children are more strongly motivated towards achievement than are lower-class children.'

The incidence of depression and neurotic disorder is higher among working-class women. They are, however, less likely than middle-class women to seek medical help (Rutter, 1976). Furthermore, Brown *et al.* (1975) showed that working-class women with young children experienced far more acute stress than middle-class women with young children. Phillips (1968) also found that stress was more frequent in the lowest social groups and that disturbance was more likely if there was a lack of positive experience. He suggests that the balance between positive and negative experiences is important. Rutter *et al.* (1970), in their study on the Isle of Wight and in an Inner London Borough, found that emotional disorders were more common in London, both in ten-year-old children and their parents. In both areas child psychiatric disorder was associated with family disruption, parental illness or criminality and social disadvantage (measured by family size, overcrowding and type of accommodation). On the Isle of Wight depression in women was strongly associated with personal and family problems and in London with low social status. It should be recognised, however, that many of the studies cited in this section have not examined the relationship of these factors to educational outcomes.

Few specifically educational policies would do much to alleviate depression and neuroticism among mothers in situations of social disadvantage. Broader changes in social and economic policies would be needed. However, improved day-care and pre-school provision and parental and community involvement programmes would help some women. It is argued that such programmes may also help *children* from disadvantaged backgrounds with problems of poor motivation. When Zigler and Butterfield (1968) administered the Stanford Binet Intelligence Test in a way which was intended to increase the child's motivation by giving him or her a feeling of success then disadvantaged pre-school children increased their test competence.

Language

A series of experiments by Kirk, Hunt and others found that four-year-old children enrolled on a Headstart Programme, whose parents were mainly unskilled or unemployed, were less competent at a series of naming tasks than middle-class children (Hunt *et al.*, 1975, Kirk and Hunt, 1975). Kirk and Hunt suggest that if the children do not know some of the words that are used during their early years in school, the resulting confusion may contribute to their cognitive disadvantage. As Pilling and Pringle point out, this may not mean that socially disadvantaged children have smaller vocabularies. They may know as many words as middle-class children but some of them may be from their own culture and not incorporated in any cognitive demands. Pilling and Pringle have reviewed the evidence suggesting that language is a major contributor to differences in intellectual performance between middle-class and working-class children. They conclude that there is evidence of social class differences in the *mastery* of language. Social class differences in *understanding* are not always found (Bruck and Tucker, 1974) and where they are found, Nurss and Day (1971) and Labov (1973) consider that they may be due to dialect difficulties. However, there have been claims that middle-class children are better at using syntactic knowledge (Frasure and Entwisle, 1973), using more complex speech at infant school age (Tough, 1970, Hawkins, 1969, Brandis and Henderson, 1970) and at secondary-school age (Bernstein, 1962; Lawton, 1968).

While socially and educationally disadvantaged children tend to score low on psychometric tests it has not been established that this failure is *caused* by linguistic and intellectual deficits as supporters of the notion of cultural deprivation maintain. Advocates of the 'cultural difference' theory argue that most socially disadvantaged children do not have language or cognitive defects and that they come to school with the same ability to reason and the same language structure as middle-class children (Labov, 1973, Baratz and Baratz, 1969 and 1970, Ginsburg, 1972). It is argued that every human society provides experiences sufficient for normal cognitive and linguistic development and that lower working-class and ethnic minority children come from cultures which are different, rather than deficient.

There may, however, be differences in the ease with which children from different social class backgrounds approach school demands. Cole *et al*. (1972), Bruner (1974) and Blank (1973) consider that, although working-class and middle class children have the same range and distribution of linguistic and cognitive ability, working-class children fail to use their ability in the classroom, partly because they are not sufficiently motivated and partly because they have difficulty in transferring skills acquired elsewhere to the classroom. Whereas the middle-class child uses his intellectual skills in a variety of situations, the working-class child might only use his when specifically required to do so.

Bernstein has suggested that differences in early childhood socialisation and in ways of communicating have implications for how children from different backgrounds respond to school. Bernstein maintains that the middle-class child learns to use an 'elaborated' communication code which 'orientates the child early towards the significance of relatively context independent meanings' (Bernstein, 1977). The middle-class mother is a 'powerful and crucial agent of reproduction who provides access to symbolic forms and who shapes the disposition of her children so that they are better able to exploit the possibilities of education'. Disadvantaged children are often said to arrive at school with poorly developed language and lacking basic concepts (AMMA Report, 1979). Tough (1974, 1977) maintains that disadvantaged children are not linguistically deficient but that lack of practice, opportunities and encouragement contribute to their apparent unwillingness to use language in a manner appropriate to the educational environment. However, there is some evidence that the great majority of working-class children both talk and are talked to a good deal at home, and only a small minority may suffer deprivation in this respect (Wootton, 1974). A study by Tizard *et al*. (1980) of children's language at home and at school suggests that both middle-class and working-class children talked and were talked to a good deal at home but that school provided fewer occasions for adult–child conversations than is normally supposed. In addition, research by Francis (1975) with children with reading difficulties suggests that they have sufficient knowledge of the language structure and vocabulary to master reading. Poor test scores or reading failure in the socially disadvantaged may not be due to language or cognitive defects but to the lack of motivation or interest discussed earlier.

Ginsburg (1972) considers that the lower-class environment *may* be deficient in that the parents provide fewer reading experiences for the pre-school child but he maintains that this does not warrant compensatory education, but rather an adaptation by the school to the language and ways of thinking of disadvantaged children. Similarly, in their Report, the Plowden Committee accepted the recommendation by the National Association for the Teaching of English that research be carried out into the types of reading schemes and library books which would be most effective with children of different backgrounds and abilities. (Research commissioned by the Plowden Committee (Morton-Williams, 1967) found that 60 per cent of unskilled workers had five books or less in the home apart from children's books and magazines compared with 5 per cent of professional workers and that the children of unskilled workers borrowed fewer library books.)

There are no clear-cut conclusions on the linguistic competence of disadvantaged children. The position is complicated by claims about dialect or cultural differences. However, it seems likely that certain children may experience difficulty in responding to school demands. Teachers and policy-makers need to be aware of this and attempt to develop strategies for eliciting in the classroom the language skills learned outside school.

Parental attitudes
The importance of parent's attitudes for children's achievement emerged some years ago in studies by Fraser (1959), and Floud, Halsey and Martin (1956). In Douglas' study (1964) the level of parental interest in their children's work was based on reports made by the class teachers and on records of parents' visits to school. This 'second-hand' reported information may have biased the results in favour of middle-class parents. However, on the face of it, the evidence supported the view that the working-class child was disadvantaged at school largely because of his parents' lack of interest in his educational progress. Parental interest and attitudes to education outweighed the effects of social class, size of family, quality of housing and academic record of the school. The effect of parental interest was partly explained by social class, a larger proportion of middle-class than working-class children having interested parents. But within each social class those children whose parents were interested in their education scored higher on achievement tests than those with uninterested parents.

The Plowden Committee commissioned their own survey of primary-school children, teachers and parents and found, like Douglas, that parental attitudes to school were more strongly associated with educational achievement than any other factor. As measures of parental interest in and attitude towards their child's education the Plowden researchers took parents' answers to questions about the age at which they wanted their children to leave school and the secondary school they preferred. (A selective system still operated in many areas in 1967.) Account was taken of parental initiative in visiting the school and making contact with the head and teachers and in asking for work for the children to do at home. Questions were asked about the amount of time parents spent with children at home in the evening and whether they helped them with school work. The 'literacy' of the home was assessed by what the parents and children read, whether they belonged to a library and how many books there were in the home (Morton-Williams, 1967).

The survey found evidence of an association between social class and the responsibility and initiative taken by parents over the children's education, in the interest and support shown by fathers over education and upbringing, in the time and attention devoted to children's development and their interest in and knowledge of their children's school work. For all of these factors the situation was likely to be more favourable the better the social circumstances of the home. There were, however, noticeable differences in the part played by the father in the child's education. Over 40 per cent of manual workers but only 25 per cent of non-manual workers had left the choice of school to their wives. Almost half of the manual, but less than a quarter of the non-manual workers, had not been to their child's present school. There was little class difference in the parents wanting the school to give their child work to do at home in the evenings, yet far fewer children of manual workers were, in fact, given work to do. More recently Newson and Newson (1977) found that in their study in Nottingham 82 per cent of working-class parents of seven year olds helped their child with reading. The Plowden Committee concluded that 'a strengthening of parental encouragement may produce better performance in school'. However, Bernstein and Davies (1969) argue that the Plowden measures of parental interest and attitudes were, in fact, measures of strongly class-linked behaviour patterns and it was these behaviour patterns that were associated with school achievement. Encouraging schools to increase their parent contacts would not necessarily, by itself, raise the achievements of working-class children.

Acland (1980) has criticised the way the findings of the national survey commissioned by the Plowden Committee were arrived at and used to support the key policy recommendations relating to parental involvement and Educational Priority Areas. He re-analysed the raw data obtained in the course of the national survey and maintains 'the independent effect of attitudes on achievement is weak and uncertain and so gives little support for the view that improved attitudes will lead to improved performance levels'. Acland claims that in the original analysis data for some subgroups showed attitudes to be considerably less important than circumstances or school variables and that sometimes attitude variables had been incorrectly identified as circumstance variables and vice versa. His re-calculations suggest that circumstances were of almost equal importance to attitudes. He also points out there there is an element of judgement in the classification of the variables. For example, one variable which the Plowden researchers identified as an 'attitude' variable was based on a question about whether or not the parents took their children on outings. Yet it can be argued that this is just as much a reflection of the families' financial resources and should have been included in the list of 'circumstance' variables. Acland regrouped the home background variables selection items which were 'intuitively most interesting and most clearly relevant to the parent involvement policy'. These were, the level of contact between home and school; parents' feelings of exclusion from school; level of parental help given at home; child's response to school; and measures of literacy of the home and parental aspiration. The findings indicate the importance of the variables measuring parental aspirations (no doubt affected by the 11+ examination) and literacy of the home. The variables most closely identified with parental involvement (for example, parental contact with the school) were only weakly related to achievement. Acland's re-analysis also included an examination of the association between variations in the school environment of the kind described in the parent involvement policy and the measures of parents' supportive behaviour and attitudes. The results showed firstly a relatively strong association between school factors and parental contact which suggest that the more schools provide opportunities for meetings with teachers the more parents will take up these opportunities although the direction of influence is uncertain. Acland suggests that it could be the more parents pressed for such provision the more likely the school would be to respond. Secondly, there was only a weak association between school provision and parents' attitudes. Though schools may make more provision, parents may still feel excluded or discouraged. It is possible that seeing what does go on in schools (for example, 'Fletcher' (Maths), 'Breakthrough' (reading) and 'Projects') will make them feel even less able to help their children.

Davie *et al.* (1972) used three measures of parental interest: the teacher's rating; whether or not the parents had visited the school to discuss their child; and the parents' aspirations for the child. Using these criteria it was found that social class differences on all three were large. For example, 76 per cent of children in social class I had parents who had initiated discussions with a member of staff, compared with 43 per cent of children in social class V. What social class differences do exist are likely to be greatest between disadvantaged and more privileged families. Thus, Wedge and Prosser found that neither parent of three out of every five of the children in the disadvantaged group had visited the school compared with one in three of the other group.

There is other research, however, which suggests that working-class and/or disadvantaged parents, do not lack interest in their child's education. For example, Halsey's research in Educational Priority Areas found considerable concern and interest in education (Halsey, 1972).

Although there may be some working-class parents uninterested in their children's education, possible explanations for what is sometimes assumed to be lack of support, need to be explored. One explanation may be the opportunities or lack of opportunities offered for parent–teacher contact. Davie *et al.* found that middle-class children were more likely to be at a school which had established parent–school contacts (89 per cent) than were working-class children (75 per cent). A second possibility may be that working class parents feel ill at ease or the subject of criticism when they visit school. Teachers represent authority and parents who have had unhappy experiences at school or with authority figures may be reluctant to meet them (Halsey, 1972). Moreover, interviews with parents have consistently shown that working-class parents tend to have less knowledge of the education system and of school practices. Midwinter (1977) asserts that the disadvantage of many working-class children at school is due to their parents' lack of educational knowledge. Jackson and Marsden (1962) found middle-class parents knew how to set about choosing a primary and secondary school with good academic records, whilst working-class parents often made the choice on quite trivial grounds. Many are ill-informed about the curriculum and even the smallest change in methods can be a source of confusion to working-class parents. Young and McGeeney (1968) wrote 'they could see the massive walls; they did not understand what went on behind them'. The difficulties of overcoming the communication gap between parents and nursery teachers is discussed by Tizard *et al.* (1981). They suggest the gap is not due to lack of interest nor just to differences in knowledge but also to differences in parents' and nursery teachers' respective interpretation of 'play', 'reading' and 'learning' and the values attached to such activities.

The evidence on parental interest, or lack of it, needs to be treated with caution. Sometimes at least part of the evidence is based on teachers' assessments which may tilt the balance in favour of more advantaged groups. Other evidence is based on indicators which may not be the most sensitive or even the most appropriate and which may be measuring something other than parental interest. For example, frequency of visits to their child's school may indicate more about the relatively flexible working hours of fathers in non-manual occupations than about their level of interest in their child's education. It seems likely that there are several possible explanations for behaviour which is often interpreted as lack of interest. Teachers need to be aware of the alternative possibilities.

Conclusion

This chapter has reviewed research concerning the home circumstances of children and young people, and explored their implications for educational disadvantage. Research findings indicate that material disadvantage may both limit access to education and make it more difficult for children to benefit from it. Poverty increases the possibility of family stress and may put pressure on children to take part-time jobs or leave school as soon as possible. Research also shows that inequalities in health, both in terms of incidence of illness and in quality and in take-up of services can lead to retarding effects on physical and intellectual growth amongst disadvantaged groups. This, in turn, may affect educational performance. There is, however, no firm evidence yet available that these processes and circumstances directly affect educational outcomes.

The factors in this section relate mostly, but not solely, to circumstances of social disadvantage. It is difficult to separate the issues of social class and social disadvantage. It has already been noted that the majority of the manual working class are not socially disadvantaged. However, much of the research evidence is concerned with social class differences in attainment. When the relationship between, for example, an unskilled background and attainment is considered, social class may be not an explanatory variable but a proxy variable, incorporating several dimensions (wealth, overcrowding, parental attitudes etc.). But there is very little evidence about the relative strength of the contribution made by the individual variables for which social class is intended to stand. Research methodology has not been sufficiently sophisticated to isolate crucial variables. Recently, however, Douglas, drawing on the data from the 1946 cohort, has carried out principal component analyses on environmental and parental factors (Douglas, personal communication). Three factors consistently emerged with a heavy loading. They were:

(i)   housing (overcrowding, completed family size);
(ii) parental interest, support and attitudes to their child's education (including an assessment of early child care);
(iii) the educational level of the parents and the occupation of the husband.

An attempt was made to estimate the relative importance of each factor for the children – for their future school (selective or non-selective), their ability (as measured by tests at different ages) and their later marriage patterns. These three factor scores were used to predict the final level of qualifications for the cohort members. 'Parental interest' makes the greatest contribution to this prediction, particularly for girls; 'home circumstances and family size' the least. For the cohort as a whole these factors provided good predictions of the group who gained high, medium or low qualifications; but they did not provide a set of satisfactory prediction of the level of qualifications of individuals. This is not surprising since each individual experiences some unique pressures and circumstances which influence his progress.

Cultural differences in child-rearing practices are outside the scope of strictly educational policies, but awareness by teachers of different techniques of care and control used by parents may enable them to structure tasks in ways which acknowledge differences whilst eliciting appropriate responses and sustaining motivation. Similar strategies are suggested in the discussion of language. Research evidence on parental attitudes should be treated with caution. Lack of interest has often been assumed from teachers' assessments of parents but direct evidence from parents suggests that most do not lack interest but are inhibited by lack of self-confidence or insufficient knowledge.

Whilst many of the 'home-based' factors in this chapter may contribute to educational disadvantage some of their effects may be countered by actual or suggested educational policies which are discussed in later chapters. However, some of the social disadvantages described here may be exacerbated by certain aspects of the education system.

Notes

1 The term 'relative deprivation' was coined by Stouffer (1949) and the concept was developed first by Merton (1957) and then by Runciman (1966) to denote feelings, rather than conditions of deprivation relative to others.

2 Townsend discusses the measures of poverty used in his study in Chapter 6 of *Poverty in the United Kingdom*. Broadly speaking the State's standard of poverty or the State's definition of a poverty line is the Supplementary Benefit Standard in any given year.

3 School Factors

This chapter is divided into eight sections. They are: the distribution of financial resources; the curriculum; public examinations; ability grouping; truancy; teacher provision and quality; and teacher expectation. Each of these areas is discussed with special reference to educational disadvantage. The final section is concerned with research into school differences and school effectiveness.

The Distribution of Educational Resources

Educational finance

This section is concerned with the relationship between educational disadvantage and the distribution of educational resources as indicated, in particular, by educational expenditure. In any discussion of educational finance it is important to distinguish between 'costs' and 'expenditure'. Fowler (1979) has illustrated how every expenditure involves cost to the person or institution paying it, but not every cost involves expenditure. At national level the most important instrument of government expenditure control is the review carried out by the Public Expenditure Survey Committee (PESC). The results of the PESC are crucially important for local authorities because they affect the size of the Rate Support Grant (RSG) and the extent of local authority spending. The money available to be spent on education comes from two principal sources, the amount raised by local authority rates and the Rate Support Grant. There is no identifiable educational component in the RSG which is a block unhypothecated grant.

Local authorities levy rates on domestic, commercial and industrial premises. The money thus raised funds recurrent expenditure on the public services and amenities for which the local authorities have responsibility. The amount raised by the local authority is a relatively small proportion of the authority's money. The largest proportion is gained from central government, from the Rate Support Grant.

In 1979/80 and 1980/81 the Grant accounted for 61 per cent of 'relevant' local authority expenditure which includes spending on personal social services, Home Office Services, Local Environmental Services, Employment Services, Local Transport Finance and Housing (Revenue Account) as well as on education. Once the total size of the RSG has been decided upon by central government in consultation with local authorities, it is allocated to each local authority. Some local authorities are wealthy and have rate resources above the national average. Such authorities have more scope for political and financial freedom since they are likely to have a development budget of excess financial resources. Byrne (1976) claims that an analysis of the product of a 1p rate for authorities shows that those with a high rate yield are predominantly middle-class areas with a good standard of housing and transport, a low school population and more than adequate provision of places in tertiary education (sixth form or further education). In other words, they are areas of low social need.

At the other extreme are areas of high social need where the LEA, with resources below the national average, is heavily dependent on the Rate Support Grant. Quite small fluctuations in the Grant can have serious consequences for poorer authorities, operating on a restricted budget. 'On one hand, local wealth can thus lead to greater security of planning; and conversely, local poverty can lead to annual incoherence and lack of control over provision of resources to match agreed objectives' (Byrne).

The Rate Support Grant has three elements: the 'needs' element, the 'resources' element and the 'domestic' element, although this may be changed in the near future (see p. 56). These elements are allocated as a block grant and authorities have discretion over how they allocate the money between and within their services. The distribution of the needs element between local authorities is calculated according to complex formulae based on multiple regression.

Although the distribution of the Rate Support Grant across local authorities has been described as 'perhaps the most important single act of territorial justice taking place in the economy' (Barnes, 1978), the grant can contribute to the uneven distribution of resources. For instance, it is argued that the system of a block grant increases local autonomy and provides incentives for responsible local decision-making, but Blackstone and Crispin (1980) question whether this autonomy is not bought at too high a price. In short, it may lead to an uneven distribution of educational expenditure between one authority and another and can deal only imperfectly with variation in educational costs across the country. For example, in an attempt to reduce variation, labour cost differentials in London have been included in the needs formula since 1977/78. Blackstone and Crispin urge that the priority for certain items of expenditure be made explicit, by means of earmarked grants, which would aid accountability between central and local government.

On the other hand, Tunley et al. (1979) question whether the system is sufficiently responsive to local needs. They declare that 'it is now officially admitted that the process is subject to hidden political decisions in the selection and suppression of factors to be tested', and in the words of the Layfield Commission (DOE, 1976), 'a good deal of subjective judgment' is also relied upon. Changes have been suggested by several writers, including Field et al. (1977), Burgess and Travers (1980) and Fowler, Jackman and Perlman (1980). For example, as a more appropriate basis for the calculation Field et al. suggest taking the average income of each area, 'thus relating the subsidy inversely to the ability to pay off the relevant population'.

These and other criticisms of the Rate Support Grant have contributed to pressures for change, and reforms in the Grant System were incorporated in the Local Government Planning and Land (No. 2) Bill.[1] The Bill makes proposals which alter the system of paying grants to local authorities. The needs and resources element of the RSG are replaced by a single block grant (see DOE, 1979, for details). It is the Government's view that this system will be less complex than the RSG, that it will improve the accountability of local councillors to their electorate, and that it may discourage authorities from overspending. Further, the Secretary of State is empowered to declare an area to be an 'urban development area' and to assume local government powers for that area. The Bill has been much criticised by both Labour and Conservative members of the local authority associations and the Labour Party. Opponents consider the proposals will lead to pressure on individual authorities to conform to the spending patterns of the average authorities and that large spenders, like the ILEA or Sheffield, would be handicapped as a result.[2] It is argued that central government, in particular the DES and the Department of the Environment, will gain greater control, particularly over education, which takes more than half local government spending (see Burgess and Travers, 1980).

The new Block Grant System included as part of its Grant Related Expenditure (GRE) estimate an allocation of special needs monies. This allocation included an amount for the provision of special education based on an estimate of 1.8 per cent children in Special schools. It also included in the 1980/81 settlement, an additional sum for the 13.2 per cent of children assumed to have additional needs but not to be in special schools. This money was allocated on the basis of six special needs indicators taken from the National Dwelling and Housing Survey (NHDS): these were measures of free school meals, large families, one-parent families, non-white or foreign families, low socio-economic group and lack of houshold amenities. However, not only is the grant unhypothecated and hence may be used for services other than education, but even within education, there is no requirement to serve the needs of disadvantaged children.

Educational expenditure

We now consider the amount of money allocated to education and how it is spent. Over the past twenty years actual expenditure in *cash* terms has increased from £950 million in 1960/61 to £8,430 million in 1978/79, representing a nine-fold increase. In *real* terms educational expenditure doubled. The most important factor contributing to the growth was the rise in the number of school children, from 6.9 million in 1960/61 to 8.9 million in 1978/79. Other factors include the greater numbers of students in full-time education beyond the statutory school years and the national trend to lower average pupil–teacher ratios.

Blackstone and Crispin have drawn together a considerable amount of information on educational expenditure since 1960 (see Tables in Appendix A and B). During the period from 1970/71 to 1977/78 local authority current and capital expenditure on education declined from the level of the early 1970s. This was followed by a period during which education expenditure, as a proportion of total local authority expenditure, remained stable. Recurrent expenditure from 1974/75 has remained at between 54–55 per cent and capital expenditure has remained at between 12–13 per cent of total local authority expenditure. Capital expenditure was considerably reduced during the 1970s (although the nursery sector share was increased in 1975/77). The consequent reduction in the school buildings programme meant that some pupils continue to be taught in low quality buildings with poor accommodation or facilities. The HMI Survey of Secondary Schools (DES, 1979a) found single sex schools, in particular, often lacked appropriate or sufficient specialist accommodation and the DES Building Survey (DES, 1977) found cause for concern over the medium and long-term effects of repeated cuts on capital programmes. The report suggests that no less than nine out of ten secondary schools were deficient in practical accommodation or library facilities.

In an Expenditure White Paper (March 1980) which details plans until 1983/4, it is stated that educational expenditure will be reduced by £820 million or 9 per cent, between 1978/79 and 1983/84. Since government overall expenditure is being reduced by 4 per cent this means that the education sector is being hard hit. The reason given is declining school rolls. Current expenditure on primary and secondary education is to be cut by 6½ per cent although pupil numbers are expected to decline by 13½ per cent. Provision for the under-fives is to be reduced by 5 per cent below the present £170 million, although a small nursery building programme will allow for surplus primary-school accommodation to be converted for nursery education. Between 1978/79 and 1983/84 the Government hopes to save £300 million on meals and milk. These reductions in expenditure are likely to disproportionately affect the disadvantaged who would otherwise benefit from nursery provision and free meals and milk. In contrast in 1981/2 £3 million pounds, rising to £12 million in 1983/84, is to be allocated to the assisted places scheme. Although ostensibly to help disadvantaged children from poor families to attend independent schools the upper limits of parental earnings have been raised to £11,000 for families with one child, which suggests the scheme is likely to subsidise many advantaged middle-class parents who want a private education for their child. Only small reductions are planned in higher education. Non-advanced further education will be increased in 1981/82 and then remain at that level. Adult education suffers the most in the White Paper, for provision is to be cut by one-third below the 1978/79 level and it is anticipated that the difference will be met by increased fees and enrolments.

Le Grand (1982) has attempted to estimate the relationship of public education and expenditure levels to the population divided into socio-economic groups. His data come from the 1973 General Household Survey (GHS) and DES statistics. The GHS data concern the number of people in six socio-economic groups (SEGs) attending different sectors of public education. Le Grand first compared the percentage distribution of expenditure with the percentage distribution of the 'client' population and then the expenditure per person in the client population for each SEG. On the basis of his calculations he estimated that children in the top two groups, professionals, employers and managers, who comprised 20 per cent of the population aged 0–49, received 24 per cent of education expenditure, whereas those families in the bottom two groups, semi and unskilled manual workers, who comprised 22 per cent of the population, received 20 per cent of expenditure. When education expenditure per person was considered, the top two groups received nearly 40 per cent more per person than the bottom two groups. When the figures were standardised for age and sex the picture hardly altered. Le Grand's analysis has been carried out using two variables: (i) the proportion of the population falling into socio-economic groups one to six and (ii) the average cost for each sector of the education system. For children of statutory school age, the proportion of total spending for each socio-economic group must equal the size of that group. There is no opportunity in the calculations for deviation to be introduced as the proportion spent equals the proportion of the population multiplied by the average per unit cost. Above and below the statutory school age, where there is differential take-up of provision between socio-economic groups (unlike the statutory age where all pupils of the relevant age are involved) there are likely to be disparities, as indeed Le Grand found. The figures, as Le Grand acknowledges, do not distinguish between grammar, modern and comprehensive schools. The costs in each type of school are averaged out. But because a higher proportion of middle-class than working-class children went to grammar schools in 1973, and because the grammar schools were more expensive to maintain (excluding the cost of the sixth form), middle-class children probably received a larger share than the figures suggest.

Le Grand relates his findings to calculations based on the Central Statistical Office's (CSO) estimates of the distribution of taxes and benefits by income group. He calculates the average 'original' income for households in each income group: that is, income before payment of taxes or receipt of any transfer from the State, and the education expenditure per household by the State. The distribution favours the higher income groups with the absolute amount increasing as the income increases. The CSO data is taken from the Family Expenditure Survey (FES) which presents results on a per household rather than a per person basis. There are large differences between the top and bottom groups, which Le Grand attributes to the fact that many of the households in the low income groups are composed of elderly people who are unlikely to benefit from education expenditure. However, this group will include one-parent families, large families and families with only one breadwinner, who *will* be using the education services.

Le Grand's study supports evidence put forward by Barnes (1978). Using data from the OPCS General Household Survey of 1973, Barnes illustrates the inequalities in access to educational resources on a national scale.

Variations between local authorities
In order to be able to compare the expenditure of different local authorities measures are needed which take account of the varying sizes of different areas since gross spending figures fail to do this. There are two measures commonly used. One is a breakdown of basic education expenditure divided by the numbers of pupils. This is customarily drawn up for each sector (nursery, primary, secondary and tertiary) and is published annually as 'unit costs'. The second measure is the pupil–teacher ratio, that is the number of full-time equivalent pupils to one qualified teacher.

Each year the Chartered Institute of Public Finance and Accountancy (CIPFA) publishes Education Statistics (Actuals), which give details of actual expenditure on education by local authorities in previous financial years and Education Statistics (Estimates) which detail the proposed expenditure for the coming financial year. By drawing on data from the Education Estimates 1980/81 we calculated the 'top ten' and 'bottom ten' authorities in terms of unit costs.

Table 3.1   Educational estimates 1980—81

Unit Costs – Net Expenditure*

"Top Ten"

Primary		Secondary	
ILEA	£703	ILEA	£959
Haringey	630	Brent	808
Brent	616	Haringey	796
Ealing	594	Harrow	790
Powys	583	Manchester	775
Newham	580	Powys	756
Dyfedd	572	Newham	744
Newcastle	537	Hounslow	744
Richmond	520	Barking	736
Wolverhampton	515	Ealing	735

'Bottom Ten"

Trafford	£395	Solihull	£565
Cornwall	394	Oldham	565
Stockport	393	Stockport	564
St. Helens	391	Hereford and Worcs	563
Tameside	388	Suffolk	551
Somerset	388	Kirklees	549
Lancashire	384	Northants	547
Northants	380	Bradford	536
Lincolnshire	379	Dudley	532
Dudley	362	Wakefield	524
Average for all LEAs	£436	Average for all LEAs	£629
SD	57.9	SD	67.9

* Excludes debt charges, RCCO and specific grants.
Source: CIPFA Education Estimates 1980/81.

There is considerable variation, even amongst the top-spending authorities. For instance, the ILEA, with a primary unit cost of £703, expects to spend 61 per cent more than the national average, whilst Wolverhampton, with an estimate of £515, expects to spend 18 per cent more. At the other end of the range there is less variation. Trafford, with an estimate of £395, expects to spend 9 per cent below the national average whilst Dudley, with the lowest estimate of £362, expects to spend 17 per cent less. Nine of the 'top ten' authorities are Metropolitan and six of these are in the Greater London area. Although five of the 'bottom ten' authorities are also Metropolitan, four of them are in the North West of England.

For secondary pupils a similar pattern was found, with more variation among the 'top ten' authorities. The ILEA and Ealing expect to spend 52 per cent and 17 per cent respectively above the national average, whilst Solihull and Wakefield expect to spend 10 per cent and 17 per cent respectively below. Nine of the 'top ten' authorities are Metropolitan boroughs and eight of these are in the Greater London area. Seven of the 'bottom ten' authorities are also Metropolitan boroughs and five are in the North or North West.

There is a considerable degree of overlap in expenditure patterns between the primary and secondary sectors. Six authorities are in both 'top ten' groups and three are in both 'bottom ten' groups. It should be noted, however, that variation in local authority expenditure on education is less than the variation in other social services – for example in health. Klein (1975) provides evidence that in 1971/72 there was a considerable range in the distribution of spending on hospitals. In the nine regions on which Klein provides information, the range of expenditure per head of population is from 62 per cent above the national average, to 69 per cent below it.

Pupil–teacher ratios
We also calculated the 'top ten' and 'bottom ten' authorities in terms of pupil–teacher ratios (PTRs). (See Table 3.2.)

The average primary PTR for England and Wales is 22.3. The standard deviation from the mean is 1.9. The variation in the 'top ten' authorities ranges from an average of 5.6 less pupils per teacher in the ILEA to an average of 3.1 less pupils per teacher in Gwynedd. As with the Unit Cost analysis we found less variation between the 'bottom ten' authorities. The three authorities with a PTR of 24.3 (Bromley, Stockport and West Sussex) have an average of two extra pupils per teacher whilst the three authorities with a PTR of 25.3 (Dudley, Somerset and Lincolnshire) have an average of three extra pupils.

Seven of the 'top ten' authorities are Metropolitan and four of these are in the Greater London area. Six of the 'bottom ten' authorities (there are actually twelve in this group) are Metropolitan, of which two are in Greater London and three are in the North West.

The average secondary PTR for England and Wales is 16.1. The standard deviation from the mean is 0.98. Brent, with the lowest PTR (13.0) has on average 3.1 pupils per teacher less than the national

Table 3.2   Pupil—teacher ratios

"Top Ten"			
Primary		Secondary	
ILEA	16.7	Brent	13.0
Wolverhampton	17.1	ILEA	13.5
Newham	17.4	Barking	13.5
Dyfedd	17.4	Waltham Forest	13.8
Powys	17.8	Newcastle	14.0
Bradford	17.9	Wolverhampton	14.2
Brent	18.0	Haringey	14.2
Haringey	18.3	Harrow	14.2
Newcastle	18.6	Rochdale	14.4
Gwynedd	19.2	Barnet	14.4
"Bottom Ten"			
Bromley	24.3	Kent	17.2
Stockport	24.3	Essex	17.2
West Sussex	24.3	Norfolk	17.2
Hampshire	24.4	Dyfedd	17.2
Tameside	24.4	Calderdale	17.3
Oxfordshire	24.5	Gloucestershire	17.3
Sutton	24.8	Devon	17.4
Wirral	24.8	Derby	17.4
Hereford and Worcs	25.0	Warwickshire	17.6
Dudley	25.3	Somerset	17.8
Somerset	25.3		
Lincolnshire	25.3		
Average for all LEAs	22.3	Average for all LEAs	16.1
SD	1.9	SD	0.98

Source: CIPFA Estimates 1980/81.

average, whilst Rochdale and Barnet, with a PTR of 14.4, have on average 1.7 pupils less. The ten authorities with the highest PTRs have a smaller range, from an average of 1.7 pupils per teacher more (Somerset) to an average of 1.1 pupils more (Kent, Essex, Norfolk and Dyfedd).

All the 'top ten' authorities are Metropolitan and seven of these are in the Greater London area, whilst eight of the 'bottom ten' authorities are counties. There does not appear to be any geographical pattern within this group. Five authorities are in both 'top ten' groups but only Somerset appears in both 'bottom ten' groups.

Although not all the high-spending authorities have the most favourable PTRs (Ealing and Richmond, in the primary sector, and Manchester, Powys, Newham, Hounslow and Ealing in the secondary sector, are in the 'top ten' group for Unit Costs but not for PTRs) the degree of overlap between the two measures is considerable. There is, however, much less overlap between the measures for the 'bottom ten' authorities. Only five authorities (Stockport, Tameside, Dudley, Somerset and Lincolnshire) are in both groups at primary level. There is no overlap at all at secondary level.

In examining pupil–teacher ratios it is important to note that a low ratio cannot automatically be taken as an indicator of educational quality. Evidence from research is inconclusive and conflicting. However, there is general agreement that although small classes may not necessarily aid learning, there may well be other advantages to both pupils and teachers. Many studies in both Britain and the United States indicate that variations between schools or between local authorities in the size of the school class shows no clear relationship to differences in academic achievement. Indeed, what trends exist seem to go in the opposite direction, for example Jencks *et al*. (1973), Averch *et al*. (1972), Pidgeon (1974), Rutter and Madge (1976), Summers and Wolfe (1977) and Little *et al*. (1971). The research on class size has been summarised by Burstall (1979) who raises issues which are taken up by Cullen (1979) and Kay (1980). Burstall notes the problems inherent in attempting to isolate one variable in the complex educational process. Kay and Burstall both suggest that the quality of classroom life, teachers' attitudes, teaching style and qualifications may be as, if not more, important than numbers of pupils.

Glennerster (1972) calculated the variations in expenditure and in PTRs in primary and secondary education between local authorities in 1961/62 and 1968/69 using the statistics collected by the Institute of Municipal Treasurers and Accountants (IMTA). We carried out comparable calculations using the CIPFA 1980/81 estimates. However, it is important to note that there may not be direct comparability between our calculations and those of Glennerster owing to boundary changes that have taken place between authorities and to the differences in the IMTA and CIPFA categorisation of expenditure.

The comparison between the 1961/62, 1968/69 and the 1980/81 calculations may be seen in Table 3.3. The larger the co-efficient the greater the variation between authorities. Between 1961/62 and 1968/69 the variation between authorities in both primary unit costs and primary PTR was reduced. At secondary level, where Glennerster does not provide figures for the PTR, the variation between authorities in unit costs does not alter. However, the variation in both primary measures and the secondary unit costs measure increased markedly by 1980/81.

There are several possible reasons for this increase. First, the quota limiting the number of teachers each authority could employ was removed in the early 1970s. Secondly, during the 1970s the changes in

Table 3.3   Variations in unit costs and pupil—teacher ratios between local authorities

	Primary		Secondary	
	Unit costs	PTR	Unit costs	PTR
1961/62	8.9	5.6	7.4	–
1968/69	6.4	4.7	7.3	–
1980/81	13.0	9.0	11.0	6.0

the rate support grant allocations favoured some areas, particularly inner cities. Thirdly, the political differences between authorities have probably sharpened.

The expenditure figures in Table 3.1 reflect different socio-economic or local demographic circumstances of authorities. The average cost of teachers may differ between local authorities since 'good' areas tend to hold staff for longer which means there are fewer new entrants to the teaching force in that authority and consequently a higher salary bill. Another explanation for different per capita expenditure is the difficulties facing authorities in sparsely populated areas. The greater spending of Welsh authorities reflects low population density (Rhodes and Moore, 1976). Education in rural areas is expensive because of high transport costs and the diseconomies of small scale. To some extent the higher unit costs in the London area are to be expected due to the higher costs of services and property and of teaching staff, who receive an additional London weighting on their salary. The higher labour costs in the London region might have been expected to result in higher pupil—teacher ratios, but this is not the case as Table 3.2 illustrates. A further possible explanation for differences in expenditure is the special problems of inner-city areas. These have been well documented by Marland (1980), Deakin (1980), Field (1977b) and Raynor and Harden (1973). These difficulties have been recognised by successive governments and have been reflected in special legislation providing aid to inner-city areas, which is discussed in Chapter 4.

Attempts to assess variation in educational expenditure by local authorities were made by Davies (1967) and its possible causes were the subject of a study by Boaden (1971). More recently Howick and Hassani (1979) have attempted to relate the expenditure, per *primary* pupil of English local authorities in 1976/77 to socio-economic features. These included the percentage of new commonwealth immigrants, households which were overcrowded, the proportion of unskilled workers, one-parent families and large families. All of these are associated with poor educational performance. The authors carried out analyses for all local authorities in England and Wales and for each type of authority (outer London, Metropolitan and shire county). They maintain that 'the results for all English authorities suggest that spending does tend to be higher in areas suffering from adverse conditions, and that such high spending is associated with inner-city deprivation (immigrants, overcrowding and one-parent families)' rather than with traditional working-class areas (unskilled workers and large families). They stress that the findings do not indicate that positive discrimination has been achieved nor do they indicate whether the amount of spending is adequate to compensate for adverse socio-economic conditions (and indeed this seems improbable) or whether the higher spending reflects greater costs.

When the same statistical exercise was carried out separately for each type of authority there were differences between each type. The higher levels of expenditure in the (outer) London area were highly correlated with adverse social conditions whilst the shire counties appeared to spend less; only 'overcrowding' was weakly correlated with expenditure. The Metropolitan districts fell between the two extremes. Howick and Hassani conclude that 'both general socio-economic needs factors and political affiliation are systematically related to expenditure in London and, to a lesser extent, in the Metropolitan districts, but not in the shire counties'.

When Howick and Hassani (1980) repeated the analyses for expenditure on secondary education, their findings were similar. When all English authorities were considered together, higher expenditure was found to be associated with unfavourable economic conditions, in particular those associated with inner-city stress. However, this association was largely due to the inclusion of London. When the same analysis was carried out for the shire counties and the Metropolitan districts, with London excluded, the results were much less conclusive. Again when the different types of authority were considered separately there was a correspondence between unfavourable conditions and high expenditure in London and the Metropolitan districts but no such tendency in the shire counties.

Howick and Hassani maintain that a higher proportion of spending in poor areas cannot necessarily be interpreted as an indicator of positive discrimination but may reflect a larger proportion of post-sixteen-year-old pupils on whom expenditure is higher than for younger pupils in these areas. This seems rather unlikely as staying-on rates are highly related to socio-economic status (DES, 1979c). Nevertheless, when Howick and Hassani considered the relationships between the percentage of over-sixteens and socio-economic variables they found that in the Metropolitan districts the proportion of pupils over sixteen was positively but weakly correlated with five of the seven social need variables. This result meant that the authors were not able to tell how far the slightly higher spending of socially disadvantaged districts was the result of educational disadvantage in these areas or the higher costs of educating the over-sixteens. They conclude that 'only in London is there convincing evidence that educationally disadvantaged pupils are likely to receive slightly higher expenditure.'

Another factor which may contribute to differences in local authority provision is the political composition of the authority. Boaden examined the political orientation of the county boroughs for 1965/66 and related it both to the socio-economic structure of the population and to the level of education expenditure. A positive association was found between expenditure and Labour Party representation and a negative association between expenditure and the proportion of the population in the higher socio-economic groups. Labour-controlled authorities tended to spend more than Conservative-controlled authorities and those county boroughs with a high proportion of working-class residents tended to spend more than those with a higher proportion of middle-class residents. The two variables are not independent in that areas with a high proportion of the population in the lower socio-economic groups may have greater social needs. However, Boaden attempted, by calculating partial correlation co-efficients, to estimate the extra effect of either variable. When the social class factor was held constant the partial correlation between Labour representation and expenditure was found to be both positive and significant. The higher levels of expenditure by Labour-controlled authorities was more than could be accounted for by their social class composition. It seemed likely, therefore, that it was related to conscious policy decisions, which gave a high priority to education.

Howick and Hassani also considered the average spending per pupil according to the political party with an overall majority in each authority. In the outer London boroughs Howick and Hassani found evidence of a relationship between differential expenditure on primary education and political control, with Labour councils tending to spend more than Conservative councils. But there were only seven shire counties under Labour control in 1976/77 and their expenditure was not significantly higher than that of other counties. In the Metropolitan districts the Labour-controlled authorities did spend more than the Conservative-controlled authorities but the difference was not statistically significant. When expenditure on secondary education was considered, a significant relationship between expenditure and political control was found only in London. Thus, ten years later the relationship between the two seems generally weaker than Boaden found for the earlier period.

It may be worthwhile to return at this stage to the point that costs and expenditure, although in some ways related, may reflect different factors. The discussion on socio-economic factors has shown that costs may be considerably higher either in rural or inner-city areas. However, the discussion of political factors has shown that expenditure may vary in accordance with commitment to education. Both Howick and Hassani and Bleddyn-Davies suggest that there is a 'traditional' element in expenditure patterns. Thus, even in areas where costs are not particularly high, spending may be generous. In a few cases, all these factors may coincide where an authority, for example the ILEA, has high costs and a high commitment to spending on education.

Byrne, Williamson and Fletcher (1975) examined the extent to which variations in local education authority policy and resources contribute to the variation in the educational attainment of children from different social class backgrounds. The theoretical framework for their enquiry was the notion of a socio-spatial system based on three propositions. These were that the concept of 'social class' refers to 'a relationship between groups differently placed in society to realise the main rewards of society'; that relationships between social class groups are characterised by control and domination; and that 'the rewards which accrue to different social groups in society are spatially distributed'. The rewards include 'real income' widely defined to include provision and quality of a range of public services and benefits. Byrne et al. then ask whether there is a significant degree of socio-spatial inequality in the education system of England and Wales and whether such inequality can be assessed in terms of differential outcomes (or life chances) for groups differently placed in relation to the system of inequality. Byrne et al. carried out a statistical analysis of LEAs in which they related measures of the 'socio-spatial system' (these included: the socio-economic status of the area's population; local environmental factors; local authority policy; resources; and provision) and related them to educational attainment (measured in terms of staying on rates after sixteen). They conclude that there is a clear inter-connection between measures of educational provision, measures of environmental condition and educational attainment and they emphasise the 'absence of territorial justice in education in this society'. They argue that 'school system in-puts are of considerable importance in explaining differences in attainment. In addition, there is a systematic relationship between the class background of an area and the educational resources available. In general, the higher the social-class composition of an area, the better the provision.' This is not entirely consistent with findings from other studies on variations in expenditure reported in this section.

Variations within authorities

Differences in education expenditure or resource allocation between local authorities may be too crude to indicate much about disadvantage, since they may mask disparities within local authorities or between individual schools. Little research appears to have been done on intra-authority provision but a recent study by Tunley, Travers and Pratt (1979) examined the allocation of resources between schools within the London borough of Newham between 1973/4 and 1976/7. The authors claim that the data indicate 'significant disparities of provision, and point to important relationships between these and social circumstances'.

Using, as far as possible, figures collected in the normal course of administration, the authors devised two sets of measures. The first set was concerned with teachers and had four related components: pupil–teacher ratios, pupils per Burnham point, percentage of staff on above scale posts and Burnham points per post. The pupil–teacher ratios are self-explanatory. The second element, 'pupils per Burnham point', was devised as follows. The local authority calculates a unit total for each school according to the age and number of pupils. This is translated into a points score which affects the number and seniority of the teaching posts in the school. 'Thus, the number of pupils divided by the number of Burnham points is a measure of the number of pupils sharing the more senior teacher resources in the school.' The basic pay scale for teachers is Scale 1. Thus, the third element of this measure is the percentage of staff who hold a post of responsibility at Scale 2 or above and is a measure of the proportion of senior staff in the school. The final component of this first set of measures is the number of posts in the school. This gives a measure of the level of teacher resources in the school. The second set of measures was concerned with expenditure and included spending on staff per pupil, maintenance and educational costs per pupil and total spending per pupil.

Tunley et al. take the first set of measures as an indicator of teacher quality, on the assumption that better teachers are usually considered to be able to attract better salaries and the Burnham system of points and scales encourages this. The individual schools were ranked on the two measures for the four years 1973/4 and 1976/7. In two of them the authors claim that over time there was a marked decline in the quality of staff and in their promotion prospects, whilst one school improved its position quite dramatically. Others experienced less change although overall the gap between best and worst provision narrowed over the four years. There were large increases in expenditure between 1973/4 and 1976/7. This was partly due to inflation but also reflected improvements in standards of provision. However, there was considerable variation in the rate of improvement between schools. In fact, 'the disparities of provision appear to coalesce in certain schools'.

Tunley *et al*. then identified levels of deprivation by area. They used census enumeration districts and six indices of deprivation: lack of amenities; shared amenities; proportion of unskilled manual workers; proportion of unemployed; overcrowding; and proportion of New Commonwealth immigrants. A system of measuring the relative deprivation of each enumeration district was devised. Although Newham as a whole is an area with many problems, there was considerable variation between districts on their score on the indices of deprivation. Newham operated fairly rigid catchment areas for each school so that several primary schools tended to feed the same secondary school. Thus, the deprivation score for the enumeration districts in each catchment area gave a crude measure of the social conditions of the children attending most of the schools in the borough. The authors related this to their information on schools and their quality in order to test the hypothesis that the poorest children attended the least well provided for schools.

They demonstrated that, although in 1973/4 there was little relationship between social conditions and provision at school, by 1976/7 the most socially advantaged children received the most favourable levels of resources, and children from more disadvantaged areas were more likely to find themselves in the less well provided for schools. The correlations were not, however, all that strong. The methodology also had the disadvantage of relying on the 1971 Census data. In an area such as Newham high mobility may affect the stability of the census data, even over a relatively short time. It may be that the increasing gap between resources and needs reflected also the ageing data. Newham, in fact, is consistently one of the ten authorities with the highest levels of expenditure on education; more resources overall were devoted to education between 1973/4 and 1976/7, and there was a reduction in the variation in provision between schools. However, if the authors' findings for 1976/7 are correct the use of some form of social index might have helped the local authority to implement more successfully a policy of positive discrimination.

Tunley *et al*. also suggest two ways in which policy exacerbates the situation and where there might be scope for alteration. One is the method by which 'communities' are identified and catchment areas drawn. However, if catchment areas are re-drawn to alter their class composition this may result in increased transport costs and to adverse reactions from, or effects on, Parent Associations. The other is the system of allocating finance to schools on the basis of the age of the pupils. Schools with a higher proportion of older pupils get more resources and since schools with higher staying on rates tend to be those with a lower proportion of children from disadvantaged areas, this system benefits the more advantaged pupils in what become the better resourced schools. However, local authorities' allocation procedure cannot stray too far from the national framework and, at present, the Burnham system is heavily based on pupil age-structure. Furthermore, sixth forms *are* more expensive to maintain. Their smaller classes, smaller pupil–teacher ratios and use of more costly materials are almost inevitably reflected in resource allocation policy. The solution lies in more radical reforms such as tertiary colleges or 'federations' of schools, and the abolition of small sixth forms, so that they are no longer a drain on resources which might otherwise be available to less advantaged pupils. Lastly Tunley *et al*. argue that the problems experienced by Newham were not helped by the complex system of national mechanisms for financial support and control of local authority expenditure. On one hand Newham had to cope with a succession of public expenditure cuts whilst on the other hand the authority received additional resources under the Rate Support Grant formulae which, during this period, favoured inner urban areas and 'as the borough responded to Government policies during this period, the more deprived children were worst affected.' Tunley *et al*. claim that over a period of several years Newham's budget estimates failed to take account of central government support and the authority underestimated what it would receive under the 'needs' element of the Rate Support Grant. Its budget had unduly large contingency allowances. The net result was that 'sums of money sufficient to eliminate the disparities of provision in schools have simply ended up in the bank.'

The Curriculum
In this section ways in which the curriculum presently adopted by many schools may contribute to educational disadvantage are discussed. Policies which have been introduced to provide 'special' curricula for pupils considered to be disadvantaged are dealt with in the following chapter. The discussion which follows is concerned with the curriculum of the secondary school, unless stated otherwise.

Local authority provision, buildings, equipment, resources, pupil–teacher ratios and in-service courses all have consequences for the curriculum which can be offered in schools. However, the curriculum is not independent of the society in which it is taught, but has to be seen as 'a selection from the culture of a society: certain aspects of our man-made world are thought of as so important that they should be passed on to the next generation' (Lawton, 1979). The curriculum is 'socially and historically located and culturally determined' (Hooper, 1971). A recurring dilemma for educationists, never satisfactorily resolved, is whether to teach all children the same curriculum or whether to offer different courses more 'suited' to their individual capabilities. If the first alternative is chosen there are problems of ability and motivation, but the second alternative has implications for social justice and future opportunities. It never has been the case that all children of a given age have been taught the same curriculum because until the relatively recent development of comprehensive schooling there were at least two different kinds of secondary school, each with their own curriculum. The historical aspects of the development of parallel curricula for elementary schools and grammar schools and the influence of the Hadow Report on the curriculum of the post 1944 secondary modern schools have been considered by several authors and will not be discussed here (Taylor, 1964, Glass, 1961, Smith et al., 1950, Lawton, 1979). While a dual system remained, dual curricula were the norm. However, the dilemma has been exacerbated with the growing proportion of young people, of all abilities, being educated together in comprehensive schools.

Keddie (1971) describes how teachers modify the curriculum to the benefit of the most able pupils, according to the teachers' perceptions of different types of secondary-school pupils. In the primary school, Nash (1973) shows how, even in an unstreamed class, 'not only is different knowledge made available to different students, who seem to have different intellectual and social characteristics, but also that the children are fully aware of it'. For Bowles and Gintis (1976) the education system allocates individuals to fixed positions reflecting the hierarchical class divisions in the wider society and 'the formal and hidden curriculum socialises people to accept as legitimate the limited roles they fill in society'. A similar view is held by Apple (1979) for whom the curriculum is 'symbolic property, which schools preserve and distribute'. Apple argues that 'curricular and more general educational research needs to have its roots in a theory of economic and social justice, one which has as its prime focus increasing the advantage and power of the least advantaged.' Some writers consider that much of the traditional curriculum is not accessible to those without the necessary 'cultural capital' (family attitudes, expectations and experiences, which enable the child to take advantage of the opportunities offered by schooling), which is not inherited by the disadvantaged members of society (Young, 1971, Bourdieu, 1973, Bernstein, 1977). Others draw parallels between Benjamin's (1939) satire on the 'eternal verities . . . (of the) saber-tooth curriculum' and the teaching of Latin and classical studies, in order to question the significance of such work for the less able, or indeed any pupil, in the latter decades of the twentieth century. Whatever the content of the curriculum there is some evidence that disadvantaged pupils may have their choices and hence their opportunities restricted. For instance, certain groups of pupils may be directed towards option courses which do or do not lead to public examinations. The somewhat 'tortuous' routes taken by teachers in attempts to ensure that pupils make the 'right choices' have been illustrated in Woods' (1979) ethnographic study of a secondary school. The teachers' criterion for allocating or re-allocating pupils to options is not solely that of past academic performance. Family background, with associated social class overtones, appears to be an important influence on teachers' decisions. Hopkins (1978) and Becher and Maclure (1978) have also discussed how the options system in secondary schools can lead to differentiation between pupils according to whether or not the options lead to examinations. Pupils are identified as 'academic' or 'non-academic' and the option courses likewise come to be seen as courses for the 'bright' or 'not bright' and 'curricular differences are institutionalised and used to reinforce the existing social divisions' (Becher and Maclure). But it is not solely the teachers who do the directing. Peer-culture and parental influences also operate. Pupils 'employ different interpretive models, distinguished by instrumentalism on one hand, and social and counter-institutional factors on the other' (Woods). Woods suggests that the different attitudes and values which underpin these models derive from positions in the social class structure. He emphasises that, for the low-stream third-year pupils, many of whom will be disadvantaged, the notion of subject 'choice' is a myth for 'if you are no good at anything there are no grounds for making a choice and you gravitate towards the non-examination subjects. Nobody selects those subjects for positive reasons.' (Curricula developments which have resulted from pursuing the second course of action, that of offering different courses, are discussed in more detail in the next chapter.) Here it will just be noted that the provision of a separate curriculum rests on the assumption that children can be sorted out early, an assumption which was frequently questioned when it underpinned selection by the 11+ examination. The teaching of separate courses allows little opportunity for transfer to examination courses since the prerequisite groundwork will not have been covered (see Ball, 1981). The dilemma for teachers is how to administer remedial help without blocking other opportunities. Remedial help given to the least able, in order to enable them to acquire basic skills may make it harder for the pupils to feed back into the mainstream of the school. Hopkins quotes the Senior Chief Inspector at the DES as saying 'you, therefore, have the strange situation that something which was intended to increase opportunities, limits them significantly' (Browne, quoted in Hopkins). Such courses, Hopkins suggests, implicitly encourage pupils to accept their situation rather than to exercise democratic rights to political participation which might lead to pressure for change. Furthermore, they feed both teachers' and pupils' expectations and are socially divisive.

The HMI Secondary Survey (DES, 1979a) found that where packaged courses were used for small groups of less-able pupils they reduced or, sometimes, eliminated subject or option choice and that in some cases the range of subject matter was so wide as to result in a fragmented timetable or what the HMI called 'timetable fillers'. The implications of the differential allocation of subject time to different groups of pupils even in a comprehensive school fully committed to the social as well as the academic aims of comprehensive education has been discussed by Welton (1979). In theory all pupils in the school he studied were given the opportunity to learn French in their first year but only sets in the upper ability band were taught French in the second year. However, whilst the first-year upper band pupils had five French lessons a week, Welton found that the lower band pupils had only two. Even if there had been much movement from the lower to the upper bands (in practice there was 4 per cent per year) the pupils from the lower ability band, having received much less language teaching, were unlikely to be promoted to the upper band.

Much recent debate has centred on the notion of a core curriculum which would involve all pupils, up to a certain age or standard, covering the same areas of knowledge. However, the Government's statement on the core curriculum (*Framework for the School Curriculum*, DES, 1980b) has been criticised by the Association of Metropolitan Authorities for taking a 'narrow and inappropriate view of the school curriculum as the collection of single subject disciplines', and for neglecting personal development (AMA, 1980). Lawton (1980) argues that if teachers are to forgo some of their control over the curriculum then the balance should be righted by their eventually becoming responsible for examining their own pupils. Examining boards would then fulfil only a moderating function and assist teachers with the preparation of examination papers. Becher and Maclure point out that, since curricular decisions are inevitably related to particular values, consensus is difficult. For instance, they ask how 'core' is core, who is to define the 'core', what is to be its constitution and who will decide upon it?

In proposing a core curriculum White (1973) asserts that it is important for every child to master the 'basic minimum' curriculum and that if a child has difficulties in learning he should not be shunted in a different direction but should have more time and energy spent on finding alternative ways of teaching him. Marland (1980) supports this, maintaining that 'too often in the inner city we have put down to "difficult backgrounds" problems that have been cognitive and which actual teaching can help pupils master.' In his view 'motivation' has been stressed at the expense of the teaching of skills 'yet "being able" is one of the best motivators'. Marland questions the view that there is a class culture conflict over the curriculum. Rather, he argues, 'the teacherlyness of school, that is many of the qualities labelled as "middle class" by observers, are among the qualities that pupils expect and want from school.' Other studies have found that the majority of pupils and their parents have quite 'instrumental' views of school goals, that they want to be taught and to gain qualifications which will help them to gain employment. This is particularly true of working-class pupils and parents, many of whom will be disadvantaged in relation to today's employment opportunities. Teachers, however, often have 'expressive' goals for their pupils (Rutter et al., 1979, Woods, 1979, Morton-Williams and Finch, 1968, Welton, 1979).

Other studies have shown that, for some reason, a number of pupils are alienated from school by the time they are half-way through their secondary education. What is taught either fails to interest them or they see little point in learning, or they are unable to meet the school's and society's criteria of success (see Willis, 1977 and Corrigan, 1979). The majority of this group of pupils are of lower ability and many will be disadvantaged in other respects. Hargreaves (1967), Lacey (1970) and Woods (1979) have all described the polarisation process which results in an anti-school group whose criteria for liking subjects and teachers are that they make few demands on them and allow them greater freedom to 'have a muck-about' (Woods).

There are no easy answers to these difficulties, one of the several school 'divides' noted by Woods, but some suggestions have been made. Whilst the school is seen to be primarily instrumental, with certification (in public examinations) being its main aim, then in a competitive society a proportion is going to fail. Yet it has been argued in this section that to segregate those considered to be actual or potential failures and, in the words of Becher and Maclure, feed them 'pulpy fare . . . designed for those with feeble powers of digestion' puts many pupils at a further disadvantage.

The work of Rutter et al. (1979) suggests that relatively minor reforms such as a conscious policy of participation and taking of responsibility by *all* pupils in non-academic areas of school life, such as assemblies, posts of responsibility and community involvement, may reduce pupil dissatisfaction. But direct curriculum change may be even more effective than these reforms.

Examinations

For most educationally disadvantaged pupils the present examination system is an irrelevance since many of them do not follow examination courses and leave school with nothing to show for their eleven years of compulsory schooling. Burgess and Adams (1980), Broadfoot (1980a) and Mortimore (1980b) summarise the various criticisms which have been levelled at the examination system from as long ago as 1911. These include the dominating effect they have on the curriculum and the limited achievement which examinations are able to measure. In addition, the HMI Report on Secondary Education maintained that the current form of examinations encouraged teaching which was unsound, unstimulating and ineffectual.

The fact that the examination system does not cater for all sixteen year olds has become more obvious with the advent of comprehensive schools and the raising of the school-leaving age than it was in the days of selective education, when only about a quarter of children went to examination-oriented grammar schools and most others left school at fifteen. Moreover, the public examination system was never intended to cater for more than about three-fifths of the population. The 'O' level GCE is considered suitable for the top 20 per cent of the ability range and the CSE is aimed at the next 40 per cent. Burgess and Adams calculate that at least one-fifth of the age group leave school without attempting either GCE or CSE, three-fifths leave without recognition of grade C or higher at 'O' level (or grade 1 at CSE) in any one subject and only one pupil in twelve receives a certificate 'which implied substantial performance in half or more of the range of subjects taken during their compulsory schooling'. This means that a sizeable proportion of the age range each year are likely to be considered, and to consider themselves, as educational failures since the examinations are, in the majority of cases, the only record of assessment used. The system thus reinforces educational disadvantage. Furthermore, this failure, as Broadfoot points out, is artificial since external examinations are 'norm-based' with limited proportions for each grade. Thus, 'the primary functions of public examinations, to provide for selection and maintain public confidence in standards, takes precedence over educational consequences.' Not only does the examination system place constraints upon the curriculum and label many pupils as failures, it can be argued that the constant competitive striving against each other for marks discourages co-operation and devalues the social and personal aspects of education since they are not formally assessed, although little evidence about this has been established.

The examination system is also expensive to operate and, in terms of consumer benefit, must be considered a resource that is disproportionately used by the middle classes and which benefits the disadvantaged hardly at all. Examinations consume financial and human resources some of which might be better directed towards the groups who derive no benefit from such a system. Schools vary considerably in their examination admission policies. Some enter weaker candidates who have only a slight chance of passing. Others attempt to maintain a high pass rate relative to their entry rate and only enter strong candidates with good chances of success. This means pupils who could, with good teaching and hard work, pass some examinations, are not given the opportunity to enter for them. There is also variation in the types of examinations for which pupils are entered. In some schools most pupils are candidates for the CSE examination and only a few pupils are encouraged to enter for the harder and more prestigious 'O' levels. In other schools the reverse is found. School policy will be affected by the goals of the staff, the courses taught and the balance of the academic intake to the school.

Britain lags behind other Western industrialised nations who are increasingly adopting some form of internal assessment or delaying formal assessment until the beginning of higher education. Some attempts, however, have been made to develop pupil profiles and methods of assessment for those who will leave school with no qualifications, containing information which would make them more attractive to prospective employers. Some of these schemes, such as the Swindon Record of Personal Achievement and the Scottish Pupil Profile System are described by Stansbury (1980) and Broadfoot (1979 and 1980b). Burgess and Adams suggest that much of the effort which has gone into attempts to 'increase the competences and to build the self-esteem' of the least able pupils could be equally relevant for all sixteen year olds. They outline proposals for a three-stage programme, nationally validated, for *all* pupils, from the end of the third year to the end of the fifth year. This would culminate in 'a statement giving a positive account of the young person's attributes, competences and interests, together with proposals for the future'. Such a scheme, if acceptable to employers, could benefit the disadvantaged group, who at present leave school with nothing. They would, at least, have some evidence of their skills, aptitudes and experiences which might help their transition to working life.

A study by Ashton and Maguire (1980) suggests that employers are more concerned with personality and motivation of job applicants than their educational qualifications. Ashton and Maguire studied employers' selection policies in three local labour markets. They found that although recruitment literature from large firms stressed educational qualifications employers often excluded any reference to qualifications, especially at the craft and clerical level. The authors conclude that it is important for careers officers and teachers to be familiar with local labour markets. Tomlinson, in the preface to Burgess and Adams, describes his observations of young people who have entered employment by way of job creation or work experience programmes and have proved so successful that they have been offered permanent jobs. Tomlinson states, 'Often the schools had recommended the youngster in the first place, but had nothing more tangible than their word with which to convince the employer. Had the youngster and his teachers been able to find a wider base for education and for the assessment and recording of it, perhaps the gap between what we can say we know about children after they have spent eleven years in the system and what they and their future employers need to know, will be narrowed' (Tomlinson, 1980).

If the present examination does not serve even bright pupils, by constraining their education, Mortimore (1980b) argues that 'those who start off with considerable educational disadvantage, stemming either from home or the school, are served appallingly'. He suggests that what is needed is a system of assessment which covers the entire age group who stay on at school until they are sixteen, which provides objective, but broadly based, information for pupils, parents and employers and forms the basis of further study either at school or in further education. This assessment could use a system of criterion-referenced tests, based not on set proportions gaining particular grades but on achievement of specified levels of skill, at different ages. This system is used widely in music examinations and is forming the basis of a new language course being promoted by the Schools Council (1980).

Initiatives such as this will not automatically alleviate the problems of disadvantaged pupils. They may, however, prevent the institutionalisation of that disadvantage by the structure of the examination system. Disadvantaged pupils entering criterion-based examinations will have a clearer knowledge of the skills needed to pass, preparation will be easier and if a candidate did not possess the necessary skills there would be advantage in delaying entry. Rather than entering for a norm-based examination with unspecified criteria with a high chance of failure disadvantaged pupils may take longer to prepare for a more explicit criterion-referenced one, and take it with an enhanced chance of success.

Ability Grouping

Streaming
This section examines what effects streaming or mixed-ability teaching have on educational disadvantage. Studies of the effects of streaming have consistently shown that children from high socio-economic status families are over-represented in upper streams and conversely, those from families of low socio-economic status are over-represented in lower streams (Jackson, 1964, Douglas, 1964, Lunn, 1970, Ford, 1970). Moreover, 'children who come from well-kept homes and who are themselves clean, well-clothed and shod stand a greater chance of being put in the upper streams than their measured ability would seem to justify' (Douglas). By implication, children who are socially disadvantaged are more likely to be in low streams than *their* measured ability would seem to justify. Studies of streaming have repeatedly shown this, but much of the research is now rather dated and there are few recent studies. Hargreaves (1972) argues that there is not *intentional* selective placement by the teachers but that it is a consequence of the allocation methods used, in which teachers' judgements and evaluation play an important part. In discussing Lunn's study of streaming in primary schools Hargreaves notes that 'intelligence tests were used for allocation to streams in less than half the schools and many used neither an IQ nor an attainment test'. When such tests are used middle-class children have the advantage in them. Moreover, when such tests are *not* used, and pupils are allocated according to teachers' subjective judgements alone, then middle class-children are likely to have an even greater advantage.

Teachers' judgement of childrens' academic ability may be influenced by what is known or inferred about the family background (see later section on teacher expectations) (Lacey, 1970 and 1974). Once pupils are placed in a low stream there is a likelihood that the process of labelling, teacher expectations and the self-fulfilling prophecy will operate with the result that they perform at the level expected of them, which may be below their capability. Both Douglas and Lunn make the point that once allocated to a stream pupils take on the characteristics expected of them and perform accordingly. Douglas found that the performance of children of similar initial measured ability who were placed in lower streams deteriorated between the ages of eight and eleven. At secondary level Lacey studied a selective grammar school when it was streamed and later when a new head introduced mixed-ability groups (Lacey, 1970, 1974). He found that under the streamed system the pupils of '5C' who 'knew they were the bottom stream and not highly regarded by teachers' did less well in 'O' levels than did the three mixed-ability fifth forms two years later, even though the measured IQ of '5C' was actually higher than two of those groups. Lacey attributes '5C's' lack of success to the students' view of themselves (as the 'throw-outs'), the teachers' view of '5C' ('low intelligence, bottom stream') and the difficult relationship between pupils and teachers.

There is some evidence that lower streams are disadvantaged by not getting a fair distribution of teaching skill. Both Hargreaves, in his participant observation study of a secondary modern school, and Lacey in his study of a grammar school, found that the lower streams tended to be taught by the younger, less experienced, less qualified teachers or those with weaker discipline. This was justified on the grounds that the 'A' and 'B' streams, preparing for public examinations, needed the better teachers. But both Marland (1980) and Shipman (1980) argue that disadvantaged, less-able pupils need more and better teaching if they are to acquire the necessary skills to equip them for working life.

There is also evidence that streaming affects pupils' attitudes and behaviour. Hargreaves found that sub-cultures developed and polarised between the 'A' and 'B' streams, which accepted the school's aims and co-operated, and the 'C' and 'D' streams, which rejected them (Hargreaves, 1967). Like Lacey, Hargreaves found that lower stream pupils were labelled as 'failures' by teachers and the more able pupils and came to consider themselves as such. Hargreaves' findings are supported by Woods' study (Woods, 1979).

Thus, streaming may contribute to educational disadvantage in several ways. Those pupils who are already socially disadvantaged, from the lowest socio-economic groups, are likely to be over-represented in the lower streams. Once placed there the possibilities of promotion are slight, an anti-school sub-culture may develop, pupils may perform according to the low expectations of them and they may be taught by the less experienced teachers. Feelings of failure and low self-esteem may cause pupils who are failing in the education system to become bored, apathetic or unmotivated, while others may become antagonistic to the education system.

Mixed-ability groups
Partly as an attempt to counter some of the negative aspects of streaming, particularly for the educationally disadvantaged, many secondary schools have introduced mixed-ability teaching in the first two or three years. Fewer schools maintain it throughout the school. The arguments put forward for mixed-ability working, summarised in an HMI discussion paper (DES, 1978c) fall into two groups: those concerned with social development and those which focus on more specifically educa-

tional reasons. The social development arguments are that mixed-ability grouping helps to prevent the rejection of the less able, and their subsequent feelings of low morale and inferiority; disperse 'behaviour problems' across each year; encourage co-operation rather than competition; and help to counteract social class differences and the continuation of a divided society. The educational arguments are that the poor motivation of the pupils in lower streams may be improved; the damaging effects of teacher expectation would be reduced; equal access to a common curriculum would increase educational opportunities; the 'streaming' of the most able *teachers* for the most able pupils would be avoided, as would the ranking of pupils and the underachievement of the less able. The HMI do not accept all of these arguments, not all of which have any empirical support, and they suggest that not all schools had sufficiently considered their objectives and the implication of adopting mixed-ability teaching.

The evidence indicates that the less able do achieve rather more in mixed-ability groups, whilst the able pupils do about the same in either form of organisation. Moreover, mixed-ability working seems to result in more positive attitudes towards school among all groups of pupils. In his follow-up study of a previously streamed grammar school, which changed to mixed-ability groups, Lacey notes that a single group of pupils could not be labelled academically in the same way as when they were divided into streams and the resources of the school (including teacher expertise) could not be differentially applied since the groups were of equal status. As already noted he also found that in mixed-ability groups all pupils improved their performance in 'O' levels, including the less-able pupils (who would still have been above average since the school was selective).

Lacey's findings, interesting though they are, refer to changes within a selective school, which is not the most representative environment for true mixed-ability teaching. However, the Banbury Enquiry studied the long-term effects of earlier streamed or mixed-ability teaching in a comprehensive school (Postlethwaite and Denton, 1978). The authors found evidence of a better overall performance in examinations on the part of the less able pupils from the mixed-ability group without any decline in the overall attainment levels of the more able pupils. Pupils who had previously been taught in mixed-ability groups had 'better attitudes to the school as a social community, whilst attitudes to the school as a working community seemed not to be significantly affected by earlier grouping differences'. Postlethwaite and Denton found an association (just short of significance) between favourable attitudes and low socio-economic status in the pupils from the mixed-ability background. They note, 'we might suppose that the off-spring of professional parents would have less favourable attitudes to school if they found themselves in a mixed ability system. This could be the result of the suspicion with which such parents might regard the mixed ability situation (for this would tend to be different from the environment in which they gained their own education).'

It appears that how schools organise their teaching, in streamed or mixed-ability groups, can have consequences for educational disadvantage. Easily measurable results, such as examination gains, indicate that mixed-ability teaching groups are more beneficial to the disadvantaged than streaming. Gains in terms of improved motivation, raised self-esteem and positive attitudes towards school are harder to gauge and there appears to be little empirical evidence in this area.

A recent case study of a large comprehensive school in Sussex, which initially had three broad ability 'bands' and later changed to mixed-ability teaching, suggests that friendship patterns remained within social class groups (Ball, 1981). Moreover, the author argues that working-class pupils may actually be worse off in the new system. Under the former system those in lower bands had a chance to do well within their band, but in mixed-ability classes this chance was reduced.

Truancy and Poor Performance

Poor attendance is one reason why any group of children might have poorer attainment than average. In particular where the school uses whole group teaching methods, rather than individual programmes, any pupil who is away from school frequently is likely to suffer educationally. Because of the association between disadvantage and poor attainment it is important to examine patterns of attendance to see if this relationship is modified to any extent by various forms of non-attendance. Information on different forms of non-attendance at schools is notoriously difficult to collect since the term includes both genuine illness and truancy (Cope and Gray, 1978). Furthermore, definitions of truancy vary. The definition used by the Association of Education Committees for their survey of attendance from 1968 to 1972, which is discussed in the Pack Report (1977) was 'absence from school without the parents' knowledge and without the school's permission'. But the Pack Report, which was concerned with truancy in Scotland, included non-attendance that was condoned by parents by, for example, the supplying of false excuses. The difficulty with this approach is that it relies on the subjective interpretation of register data by teachers or Educational Welfare Officers (EWOs), a procedure which Galloway (1976) has shown to be open to considerable bias. Such procedures also fail to include those pupils who, having registered, either abscond from school or, whilst remaining on the premises, do not attend lessons. How widespread a practice this is is difficult to estimate. Rutter *et al*. (1979) found a positive but not statistically significant correlation between fifth-year register data and self-reported absconding. In a study of attendance among second-year pupils in three London schools Davies (1980) found relatively few pupils were missing when spot checks were carried out, and several pupils were present who had failed to register.

Levels of attendance have been measured by the DES one-day survey (DES, 1974a) which reported an absence rate of 10.7 per cent for secondary pupils under twelve and 14.5 per cent for those above. More frequent measurement by Davies revealed differences of up to 5 per cent between attendance rates for morning school in the Spring Term and afternoon school in the Summer Term.

Evidence on stability of rates over time is available from the ILEA annual one-day surveys (ILEA, 1980). These show that in primary schools over the last ten years the absence rate has remained remarkably constant and has stabilised at about 8 per cent for the last six years. At secondary level (apart from a rise to 15 per cent in the year following the raising of the school leaving age), the rate has remained around the 14 per cent level for the past ten years. The secondary school rates, however, mask considerable differences between ages. The youngest pupils have attendance rates much like pupils in primary school but absence increases with age, up to a peak at fifteen when approximately one in four pupils can be absent on any one day. Galloway notes in his study the six-fold increase in persistent unjustified absenteeism between primary school and the fifth year of secondary school.

In the sixteen-year-old follow-up of the NCDS sample Fogelman (1976) found that teachers considered that 20 per cent of the study children had truanted to some extent in the preceding year and that 8 per cent did so fairly frequently. Fogelman notes that the pupils were part of the first year-group required to stay at school until they were sixteen. The findings might be different for subsequent year-groups. When parents were asked about their child's truancy 88 per cent said their child had not truanted during the year, 10 per cent said they had done so occasionally and 3 per cent said they had done so at least once a week. The different attendance rates which emerge from 'official' one-day surveys of registers, from teachers' reports and parents' recollections over a year indicate some of the problems of collecting evidence in this area.

Various factors thought to influence truancy have been discussed in the literature and have been summarised by Mortimore (1980c). They include individual, family, socio-economic and school influences.

Cooper (1966) and Tyerman (1974) have described truants as being lonely, insecure, maladjusted and unhappy. Chazan (1962) and Denney (1973) have argued that, in extreme cases, long-term absence can develop into school phobia. However, Billington (1979) found only slight differences in personality ratings between good attenders and known truants. In Woods' study of absenteeism, which forms part of the ILEA Literacy Survey, pupils considered by teachers to have worse behaviour also had lower attendance rates (Woods, 1980). Davies found that attendance rates were correlated with ability, as measured by transfer tests taken at age eleven; band one pupils had an absence rate of 12 per cent, band two had a rate of 15 per cent and band three, 20 per cent. In a study of attendance rates in the fifth form of secondary school and the first year of employment, Gray *et al.* (1980) found that poor attendance was not significantly associated with non-verbal intelligence, although there was a slight trend for the less intelligent children to include more poor attenders.

The association between poor school attendance and certain family factors has been well documented. Both Woods and Fogelman found that having four or more siblings or an unemployed father were all associated with truancy. Moreover, truancy was seven times higher among pupils whose parents wanted them to leave school at the earliest opportunity than for others. Davies found that mothers in full-time paid employment had children whose absence rates were low, possibly because of the disincentive to keep all but the genuinely unwell at home.

In Woods' study children who lived with both parents (or guardians) had lower absence rates, as did children whose parents were considered, by the teachers, to be 'very interested' in their child's education. Children thought to have 'stress in the home' had higher absence rates, as did those considered to have a 'poor attitude' to teachers, other pupils and to school work. Woods points out that information on parents' and children's attitudes and on domestic stress is subjective. Moreover, the data do not allow for a distinction to be drawn between justified and unjustified absence (truancy).

The studies by Gray *et al.*, Davies and Woods (all of which are concerned with London secondary schools) all found that pupils of West Indian origin had much higher levels of attendance than their indigenous peers or pupils with parents from other ethnic groups. Although Rutter *et al.* found that pupils of below average ability or from families of low occupational status were most likely to have poor records of attendance, after controlling for intake variation in verbal reasoning and parental occupation, significant school differences remained. These findings are similar to those of Reynolds (1974).

Several reasons have been advanced for why pupils do or do not truant. Fogelman reports that 20 per cent of those young people completing the questionnaire (nearly two-thirds of the original sample) said they had stayed away because they were 'fed up with school', 10 per cent because they 'had to help at home', 12 per cent because they 'wanted to do something special away from school' and 23 per cent for some other unexplained reason. Some adolescents possibly absent themselves from school because they feel school is offering them little they consider useful or relevant. Thus, Millham *et al.* (1978b) state 'it is the failure of schools to measure up to (their) expectations which produces high levels of truancy among vulnerable adolescents in the year before leaving'. Rutter *et al.* suggest that some schools are more successful than others in reducing truancy. This may be because of a positive school ethos which encourages pupils to attend regularly or a conscious policy of following up unexplained absence.

The research on truancy has several implications for the educationally disadvantaged. Cherry (1976) optimistically argues that the apparent disadvantage of serious absence at a young age can be overcome by regular attendance at a later stage. This view is not supported by Davies' study in which a bad record of attendance at primary school was a poor predictor for secondary-school attendance. Gray *et al.* provide some information on the short-term effects of prolonged absence from school by relating it to early leaving and employment patterns. By law children are compelled to remain in school until they are sixteen. Those whose birthdays come between September 1st and February 1st may leave school at Easter of the fifth year; the rest are supposed to remain until the public examinations take place in the summer term whether or not they intend taking any examinations. When Gray *et al.* studied the effects of attendance in relation to early leaving they found that three-quarters of poor attenders left at Easter compared with a third of good attenders. The early leavers tended to be of significantly lower intelligence than those who remained in school. There was a tendency for the children of non-manual workers to be less likely to leave early.

However, it appeared that school characteristics identified in an earlier study (Rutter *et al.*, 1979, see below) were associated with school leaving date. In the group of schools with the highest 'school process' scores (see p. 97) 25 per cent left early compared with over 50 per cent in the schools with the lowest school process score. Gray *et al.* show that poor school attendance has relatively little direct effect on the ex-pupil's chances of gaining employment, at least in the London region between 1978 and 1980. The Easter leavers also managed to find jobs in a shorter time than those who left school in the summer.

This may have been because there were fewer school leavers looking for jobs at that time. Alternatively, some of the young people may have obtained their jobs whilst still at school. This may even have influenced their early leaving. They were, however, more likely to be in unskilled employment. This was partly because they had left school with no examination qualifications but even in comparison with their peers who later left school with no success in examination the Easter leavers still had lower level jobs. Furthermore, 'Easter leavers had a generally worse employment record in terms of . . . unemployment and dismissal'. Finally, Gray *et al.* suggest that school attendance had an important indirect effect through the association of poor attendance with poor attainment and the consequent ineligibility of some young people for jobs that required higher qualifications.

To conclude, pupils with poor attendance records are likely to suffer as a result of having received less direct instruction and may well end up with gaps in key areas of learning. Few schools are able systematically to monitor patterns of attendance and to ensure that vital topics are not ignored if the teaching of them coincides with a particular pupil's absence. The crucial question remains, why, when education permits some opportunity of social advancement, are the children of the disadvantaged most prone to non-attendance? Perhaps the education route, as currently organised, presents too many hurdles. Perhaps, for the disadvantaged, the opportunities which education might offer are not apparent. Willis' ethnographic study of a group of working-class boys describes their 'entrenched general and personalised opposition to authority', the struggle to defeat organisational aims such as 'to make them work' and the importance attached to 'having a laff' (Willis, 1977). Willis's study suggests that, for those boys at least, the influence of the schools is subservient to that of the peer culture. There have been few good studies of peer influence, mainly because of the difficulties of studying the private interactions of a social subgroup. The studies there have been have emphasised the general youth culture (Sugarman, 1967) or delinquency. Both West and Farrington (1973) and Belsen (1975) have interviewed young boys about the influence of their peers in their delinquent activities. There are considerable problems of reliability of information with these studies, since they use self-report methods, although Farrington (1973) found reasonably good reliability when he compared the self-report data with more objective police records. A more unusual approach was adopted by Patrick (1973) in his participant observation study of a Glasgow gang in which he took part in the gang's activities.

Clearly the influence of peers extends beyond delinquency and some school pupils, especially during their teens, will be subject to pressures from their peers more powerful than from their families or from the school. Rutter (1979) suggests that during this period friendships intensify and there is more confiding in their age group. However he also argues that, for some major life decisions, adolescents still value family guidance.

Because of the lack of research evidence in this area, particularly for girls, it is not possible to say more than that it seems likely that different young people react to adolescence in different ways. Some will draw on the family, some on the school and some on the peer group to different degrees and this may change over time. The delinquescent sub-cultures which Hargreaves (1967) describes suggest that for those disadvantaged pupils, for whom school is not a place where they experience success, the peer culture will be especially important.

The school, Willis argues, has built up resistance to intellectual work and, although manual employment has the 'aura of the real world', the boys suspect that all work ('grafting') is unpleasant. In their view it is to be undertaken only for the financial rewards it offers and it is made bearable only by the opportunities for the cultural diversions of mas-culine self-expression and 'having a laff' with their peers. Corrigan (1979) found similar low expectations of work which, to the 'smash street kids' he talked to, resembled school in that 'you have to go and it's boring'. But work did not have the direct teaching and the control-ling function of school, against which the boys reacted, even though they may have led to examination success and improved job oppor-tunities.

Teacher Turnover and Teacher Quality

Turnover

This section deals with the relationship between teacher turnover and teacher quality and educational disadvantage. Declining pupil num-bers leading to school closures or amalgamations have resulted in a need for fewer teachers, reduced promotion opportunities and dramat-ically improved staff-stability. This situation is, however, relatively recent and many children now in secondary schools, particularly in inner-city areas, have experienced crises of teacher provision. For example, Rutter *et al.* (1979) state that during the period that their 'cohort' children went through their schooling, 43 per cent of the primary-school teachers had been teaching at their present school for three years or less compared with 26 per cent in the Isle of Wight Study (Rutter *et al*; 1975).

The problem of teacher turnover is discussed by Little (in Field, 1977b). Little draws on an ILEA study which indicated that in 1971 the authority had an annual teacher turnover of around 23 per cent. During the early 1970s the overall turnover level amongst primary-school teachers in the ILEA was 33.4 per cent and in secondary schools it was 25.9 per cent. This contrasts with the turnover for all LEAs at that time of 17.6 per cent and 15.3 per cent respectively (DES, 1974b). The ILEA had nearly twice as high a turnover rate as the rest of the country; but other inner-city areas also suffered high turnover rates. The difficulty of retaining experienced teachers is illustrated by an earlier ILEA Survey in which it was found that 77 per cent of the men and 87 per cent of the women had been teaching in their last school for less than five years. This means that many individual schools were faced with the joint problem of high staff turnover and a high proportion of inexperienced teachers. The measure of teacher turnover is one criteria on the ILEA index of educational priority (see Chapter 4). The measure used was the percentage of teachers who had been in the school for less than three years. In the ILEA school which was ranked first (i.e. the most disadvantaged) 75 per cent of the staff had been at the school for less than a year. For the school ranked fiftieth, the figure was 66 per cent and for the school ranked 100th, it was nearly half. The national average figure at that time was around 25 per cent.

The conditions of stress under which many urban teachers work and the phenomenon of the 'middle income flight from the cities' is graphically described by Thornbury (1978). Rutter *et al.* (1979) point out that the period of secondary schooling for their cohort was a difficult time for London teachers and children: 'Teacher shortages and industrial disputes led to part-time schooling for some children.' Yet within just a couple of years the decline in pupil numbers was affecting teaching turnover. The position was similar in other inner-city areas. For example, by 1974/75 the Inner Area Study team in Birmingham found that in primary schools the proportion of staff leaving at the end of 1974 and 1975 summer terms was respectively 8 per cent and 4 per cent and for secondary schools the figures were 11 per cent and 8 per cent (DOE, 1977b).

Although common sense suggests that high staff turnover contributes to educational disadvantage, that may be too simplistic a view. Rutter *et al.* looked at teacher continuity in terms of the number of teachers of English and the number of form (or set) teachers experienced by the fifth-form pupils in the twelve schools in their study. Although there were considerable differences in continuity between the schools the measure showed no association with academic outcome, attendance or delinquency although there was a negative association with pupil behaviour which was just significant. The authors state that 'it was perhaps surprising that such association as there was indicated that schools with the *least* continuity tended to have the *best* behaviour'. The results for third-year pupils were similar. The authors warn against attaching too much weight to this finding since, at a time of high teacher turnover, few of the children would have experienced much teacher continuity but it does seem to indicate that 'there were no observable academic advantages in striving to ensure that children were always taught by the same teacher, and indeed there may have been behavioural disadvantages.' The fact that a child may be taught one subject by several teachers over successive years does not necessarily mean there is high teacher turnover in the school. Also, whether or not it is a good thing to be taught by the same teacher for several years will depend for the individual child on how well he or she gets on with the teacher. Rutter *et al*. suggest that perhaps what is more important than having the same teacher is continuity of teaching by joint planning; an approach also strongly advocated by Shipman (1980). A consistent school policy must be harder to achieve with high staff turnover, where new staff are constantly having to be initiated into, and kept informed about, the school's aims and objectives. Teacher turnover is hardly a 'problem' which merits much attention now. Falling rolls and the changing economic climate have contributed to far greater stability than in the previous decade. The DES Survey of Secondary School Staffing in 1977 (DES, 1980a) based on information from a sample of 505 maintained secondary schools in England and Wales, found that 23 per cent of teachers had between ten-and-a-half and twenty-and-a-half years of service and the average length of experience was eleven-and-a-half years. The ILEA staffing survey for the same year indicates the extent of continuity currently being experienced in London schools (Mortimore, 1980a). The proportion of teachers with the same amount of experience (ten-and-a-half and twenty-and-a-half years) within the ILEA was just under 19 per cent and the average experience for all full-time teachers was just over nine years. The ILEA Survey also looked at experience within the current school. This is perhaps a better indicator of stability in London, where, due to the diversity of the population and the proximity of schools, there can be considerable movement within the authority. It was found that London teachers were slightly less likely than teachers nationally to stay in one school for a long time. Just under 14 per cent had been in their current school for more than ten-and-a-half years compared with 16 per cent of the national sample. However, the proportion of teachers in that school for less than two-and-a-half years was 37 per cent, the same as in the national sample.

Teacher quality

Little research has been carried out into what makes a 'good' teacher. As a research area it presents a veritable minefield, fraught with problems of political sensitivity and methodological objectivity. With reference to educational disadvantage some writers consider that teachers, in their concern for their pupils, can be too soft-hearted and concerned with 'social work' aspects of their relationship with pupils at the expense of teaching. Jones (1976) and Marland (1980) put forward a view similar to Shipman (1980) who considers that inner cities attract 'idealistic teachers willing to face the adverse social conditions and anxious to help deprived children'. Yet the ways in which the teachers try to help their disadvantaged pupils, by trying to 'soften the hard conditions they face' and by insulating them from competitive pressures, may handicap them further. Grace (1978) has shown how, in the majority of the ten inner-city comprehensive schools in his study, the 'good' teachers of contemporary urban working-class pupils were typified by 'an individualistic welfare commitment to the various distresses of inner-city pupils . . . in only a minority of the schools was the emphasis in typification of good teachers strongly based upon the quality of classroom teaching, or pedagogic skills as such'. The danger, Shipman argues, in this approach is that disadvantaged inner-city pupils may be fed a diluted curriculum and be 'confirmed into the working class by kindness'.

The amount of time spent in actual instruction is subject to variation. Time spent in actual teaching was one of the school processes studied by Rutter *et al*. They found the average time per school spent on the lesson topic varied from 65 per cent to 85 per cent and that behaviour was better in the latter schools. Between 2 per cent and 13 per cent of teachers' time was spent in dealing with equipment, materials and pupil behaviour, and behaviour was worse where the proportion was high. The amount of time spent 'on topic' was not, however, significantly associated with academic success. The authors state that although 'an attentive and well-behaved class provides the opportunity for effective teaching and productive learning' the crucial factor is the *use* that is made of such conditions. Better behaviour and academic outcomes were both associated with finishing lessons on time as opposed to finishing them several minutes early. Harnischfeger and Wiley (1975) suggest a model of factors affecting successful school learning in which they argue that 'the total amount of active learning time on a particular instructional topic is *the* most important determinant of pupil achievement on that topic'. Unlike Rutter *et al*. the authors dispute the assumption that teaching behaviour directly influences pupil achievement but it could be argued that although the active engagement of the pupil may be the most crucial factor, the necessary level of concentration may only be possible in the kind of well-behaved, learning-oriented atmosphere which the teacher plays a crucial part in creating.

On a more general level the HMI Secondary Survey (DES, 1979a) observed a tendency for the percentage of total teaching time which was allocated to designated remedial teaching to decrease in each successive school year to the extent that it had virtually disappeared by the fourth year. The DES Secondary School Staffing Survey (DES, 1980a) showed that remedial work took up 2.1 per cent of pupil time in year one but had dropped to 0.5 per cent in year five. This could be because the need for it had diminished but this does not seem likely. It seems more probable that as the public examinations approach more demands are made of teacher time by the timetabling of options and examination classes, leaving less time for remedial work.

To the extent that graduate status and teaching experience are considered to be indicators of 'teacher quality' there seems to be an uneven distribution of this resource between different types of school. Whilst some 47 per cent of all the teachers in the sample schools in the HMI Secondary Survey were graduates, they were distributed unevenly among the different types of schools. Fifty-nine per cent of teachers in grammar schools were graduates compared with 36 per cent in comprehensives offering a full range of subjects, 28 per cent in comprehensives offering a restricted range and 20 per cent in secondary modern schools. Teachers in grammar schools, and to a lesser extent in secondary modern schools, tended to be older and to have had longer teaching experience than teachers in comprehensive schools. Moreover, there tended to be a good match between the subject taught and the subject of qualification in grammar schools apart from the 'vocational' subjects such as metalwork and home economics. The correspondence was slightly less for the comprehensive and less for the modern schools, although the differences were not great (DES, 1979a).

Bates et al. (1974) suggest that if a school is situated in a predominantly working-class neighbourhood, particularly if it is 'creamed' by a grammar or independent school, it is likely to have fewer pupils staying on past the statutory age of sixteen. This has become less likely with the increase of comprehensives, but is a possibility in some areas with the survival of some grammar schools. As a result the school has fewer responsibility points and there may be pressure to use these for pupil welfare and practical subjects. It is then harder for the school to attract staff to provide adequate academic teaching and there may be less time spent on an academic curriculum. Similarly, Rutter et al. (1979) suggest that 'schools which put a great deal of emphasis on pastoral care did not have sufficient resources left to put an equal emphasis into the academic side of the school'. Disadvantaged pupils may suffer as a consequence.

The distribution of 'competent' teachers has been discussed by Gray (1977) who has re-analysed Morris' (1966) study of *Standards and Progress in Reading*. Gray concludes that children who are disadvantaged in terms of reading attainment or home background receive less 'competent' teaching. Teacher 'competence', Gray suggests, is a subtle but crucial aspect of educational resources. He argues that if fewer competent teachers are to be found in socially deprived areas then the positive discrimination policies by which teachers in EPA areas are paid an extra allowance could result in maintaining the existing inequalities since incompetent teachers will remain – and will be paid more for doing so. Gray suggests that a more effective policy would be to attract competent teachers into disadvantaged schools before implementing means of keeping them there. However, it is worth noting that Morris' study, published in 1966, referred to a sample of teachers between 1955 and 1957 so that the data re-analysed by Gray are now twenty years old.

Teacher Expectations

The idea that teachers' attitudes towards their pupils, their beliefs in the pupils' ability and their expectations of their performance could be affected by the social and economic circumstances of the pupil has obvious educational implications for the disadvantaged. The idea of a self-fulfilling prophecy was first introduced by Merton (1948) who described it as an expectation or prediction, originally false, which initiates a series of events that cause the original expectation or prediction to come true. Although suggested in studies by Douglas (1964) and Goodacre (1967) the first claim of experimental evidence for this phenomenon came from America, from Rosenthal and Jacobson (1968). Their study tested the hypothesis that teachers' expectations of pupils' achievement would function as a 'self-fulfilling prophecy' inasmuch as the teachers would treat the pupils in ways likely to make the expectations come true.

Rosenthal and Jacobson told the teachers in their study that certain children, whom they had in fact selected at random, were 'late bloomers' who would make considerable intellectual gains within the coming year. They claimed these predictions were fulfilled. In drawing the educational implications from their study Rosenthal and Jacobson suggested that disadvantaged pupils might do less well at school not only because of their home background or lack of motivation, but because of the adverse effect of teachers' attitudes and behaviour. The study attracted wide publicity, considerable hostility and methodological criticism. Many of the criticisms, which are discussed in detail in Brophy and Good (1974) and Pilling and Pringle (1978) would appear to be justified. However, Brophy and Good consider that the potential for self-fulfilling prophecy effects of teacher expectations exists when teacher expectations are inaccurate or inflexible, so that the teacher begins to treat a student consistently as if he were somewhat different from what he or she actually is. If, indeed, inaccurate predictions and expectations lead teachers to treat disadvantaged pupils differently this could have damaging consequences for the pupils' educational performance.

Several American studies have tried to replicate Rosenthal and Jacobson, avoiding those aspects which attracted most criticism. The studies have largely negative findings but Pilling and Pringle argue that in some of them the attempts at experimentally altering teacher expectation were 'feeble' and could hardly have been expected to do other than disprove the findings of Rosenthal and Jacobson. Fielder et al. (1971) carried out a study in thirty-six classes of three schools randomly selected, one in a middle class area and two in socially disadvantaged areas with a high proportion of Mexican-Americans. Nineteen per cent of the pupils were randomly selected and tested and at the beginning of term their teachers were told the children showed exceptional potential for intellectual development. When they were re-tested four months later this experimental group showed no evidence of 'expectancy advantage'. Fielder et al. admit that by the Spring Term teachers had probably already formulated opinions on the pupils' ability and it was too late to introduce new, possibly conflicting, expectations. Also one term may have been too short a period in which to achieve results. Mendels and Flanders (1973) attempted a replication study using 108 six- to seven-year-old children attending classes for the 'educationally deprived' in ten schools. The 'favourable-expectancy' children made slightly greater gain in IQ than the control children over a period of six months.

A study conducted by Beez (1970) provides some indication of the effects of labelling children. Sixty teachers were randomly assigned as individual tutors to children enrolled on a Head Start programme. Half the children were randomly presented as being of 'high ability' and half of 'low ability'. The teachers were given information on the IQ levels of the child assigned to them. This information was false and, in addition, the information on the 'low ability' group emphasised the adverse effects of their 'cultural deprivation' and predicted poor school achievement. Teachers worked individually with children on a

word-learning task and a puzzle. There were notable diff.
teachers' behaviour towards the two groups and in their res
word-learning task. Teachers with high expectations attem,
teach nearly twice as many words as those with low expectations. .
result their group scored almost twice as highly as the group labelle
'low ability'. The 'high ability' children were rated significantly higher
on achievement, social competence and intelligence and those ratings
were retained, even though all the children successfully completed the
puzzle task. Of course, in a 'real life' classroom the labelling effects
may well have been modified by the teachers' greater knowledge of the
children.

The mixed findings in experimental studies which have attempted to
replicate Rosenthal and Jacobson indicate that teachers are not easily
taken in by 'fixed' test results, when these results conflict with their
own opinions of the children. It is probably naive to expect teachers'
views to be so malleable. However, because these experimental studies
are inconclusive it does not mean that teachers' expectations about the
abilities of disadvantaged children have no effect on pupils' actual
attainment. Some studies of naturally occurring, rather than experimentally induced, teacher expectation have shown significant, though
small, effects on pupil progress. For example, Seaver (1973) found
that knowledge of an older sibling appeared to influence teacher
expectations. Seaver divided pairs of siblings into two groups according to whether the same teacher taught both siblings or whether the
siblings were taught by different teachers. Using IQ achievement data
he classified the older siblings as 'good' or 'bad'. Seaver hypothesised
that experience with the older sibling would induce teachers to expect
similar performances from the younger sibling. His prediction that
evidence of teacher expectation effects would show up in the group
where older siblings had been taught by the same teacher was confirmed.

Some observational studies of classrooms have found that teachers'
expectations, partly based on non-intellectual criteria, have affected
the teachers' behaviour and the ways in which the children are
grouped. Rist (1970) made periodic observations over three years of
ghetto children in the USA from when they started kindergarten
through to the second grade. From the beginning the children were
divided into three groups, seated at different tables and treated differently by the teacher. The initial groups were formed on the basis of the
children's socio-economic status, using information from registration
forms and interviews with mothers and social workers. The higher
status children were seated nearer the teacher, were labelled as 'fast
learners' and received more frequent and positive contact with the

teacher. This differential treatment continued when the children moved up into first and second grade since the teachers of those classes accepted the assessment of the children made by the kindergarten teacher, regardless of the children's performance. The high-status group received more instruction than did the low-status group, who received more discipline. However, different teachers will respond in different ways. Some will give more praise and attention to those for whom they have high expectations but others will give it to the less able because they may be considered to be more in need of it. Wernstein (1976) (cited in Pilling and Pringle) found that teachers gave children in the lowest ability reading group more praise for correct answers and more feedback than children in other groups.

It has been suggested that knowledge of low socio-economic status and a 'deprived' background may subtly affect teachers' assessments (Sharp and Green, 1975). Lunn (1970) found that in both streamed and unstreamed classes the reading performance of working class children tended to decline in relation to that of middle-class children between the ages of seven and ten years. Although teacher ratings of ability were, in most cases, closely related to test scores, where there were discrepancies teachers tended to underrate the ability of working-class children and to overrate the ability of middle-class children. Lunn suggests that the deterioration in the children's performance may be partly due to the negative teacher expectations of them. A further influence on teacher attitudes and expectations will be the views communicated by other teachers. Fuchs (1968) discusses how the belief that 'social conditions outside the school make such failures inevitable *does* make such failures inevitable.' She describes how an inexperienced but well-intentioned teacher is socialised by other members of staff to accept the prevailing rationale 'that in the slum it is the child and the family who fail, but never the school'.

In their study of twelve London secondary schools, Rutter *et al*. (1979) included teachers' expectations in their assessment of the 'academic emphasis' as one of their school 'process' measures. Teachers of the third year, middle-ability classes on which systematic observations had been carried out were asked how many of the children they expected to get either 'O' level passes or CSE grade ones in each subject. The researchers found the proportion of children in the third-year class expected to gain these qualifications varied from 2.5 per cent in one school to 45 per cent in another. The school scores on this measure correlated significantly with both attendance and academic 'outcome'. To test whether this was a reflection of the teachers' skill in judging children's abilities, the expectations were compared with the intake data on the schools. It was found that 'two of the schools in the *bottom* third with respect to academic expectations were in the *top* third with respect to the children's measured abilities at intake.' Rutter *et al*. acknowledge that it may be difficult for teachers to know how their children rate in comparison with children at similar schools and consequently they may develop 'inappropriate expectations as to what children can achieve . . . it seems probable that these expectations will be transmitted to the children who will then show some tendency to conform to their teachers' views of their expected attainment.' Rutter *et al*. found that children achieved higher levels of academic success in schools where the teachers made it obvious that they expected a high proportion to do well in public examinations. The authors point out that children are likely to work better 'if taught in an atmosphere of confidence that they can and will succeed in the tasks they are set . . . in turn, the children's good work will tend to reinforce and support the teachers' high expectations of them'.

Teachers of disadvantaged children need to be aware of the non-intellectual factors which may bias their judgement of pupils, their expectation for them and their treatment of them. Marland argues that even the humane, good intentions of inner-city teachers towards their disadvantaged pupils may 'mask dangerous attitudes which belittle the possibilities of educational growth for pupils'. Such intentions and attitudes may lead to an over-emphasis on social aspects of the teacher's role which leads to 'major underteaching justified by the pointlessness of aiming high in the face of such immense difficulties of background' (Marland, 1980).

Differences in the Effectiveness of Secondary Schools

The potentially damaging effects of teacher expectations, the self-fulfilling prophecy on pupil attainment and the ways in which teachers may socialise new colleagues into their own negative attitudes towards pupils have been discussed above. Some of those negative attitudes stem from the belief that schools in certain areas are working against insuperable odds and cannot hope to achieve academic success with such a disadvantaged pupil intake. Furthermore, it has been argued, by for example, Jensen (1969) and Jencks (1973), that compensatory education has failed and that the personal characteristics of pupils such as intelligence, social class and ethnic origins are more likely to be of greater importance for achievement and life-chances than schooling. However, recent research on school differences and school effectiveness suggests that not only are schools in similar areas, with similar intakes, very different from each other, but that the differences may have powerful implications for pupil success. Recent studies by Rutter *et al*. (1979) and Reynolds and Murgatroyd (1977) suggest that the pessimism of Jensen (1969) and Jencks (1973) is misplaced and that schooling can be effective for disadvantaged groups.

Rutter *et al*. carried out a comparative study of twelve inner London comprehensive schools. Having identified and controlled for any intake differences between the schools their aim was to examine a group of educational outcomes. If systematic differences should be found between schools, a second phase of the research would search for these process factors which were systematically related to the outcomes. Such a research design, based on statistical associations, would not be able to demonstrate causality, yet if the associations were strong and the pattern of findings was clear, it was hoped that the study might illuminate the search for what makes successful schools. Four measures of concurrent student outcome and one long-term measure were chosen. These were not seen as the only goals of schooling, but they represented areas which both parents and children consider important. The measures were academic results, student behaviour, attendance and delinquency. The long-term outcome was employment two years after leaving school, which is still being analysed and will be reported in due course by Gray and Rutter. Significant differences between schools emerged on the four main measures. For example, although in general pupils who appeared more academically able at age ten achieved better grades in examinations at age sixteen than those who at ten appeared average or below average, there was marked variation between schools. In some, all the pupils performed better than average; in others, all the pupils achieved less.

The examination scores were adjusted to take account of the academic difference in the intake and, in addition, differences in the occupational level of the parents. The adjusted academic results for the schools showed that the school with the best academic scores had 70 per cent more high grades than the expected level, whilst the school with the worst results had nearly 60 per cent below it. The other outcomes concerned with attendance, behaviour and delinquency were dealt with in a similar way, so that relevant background factors could also be taken into account. Like the academic measure there were stable differences between schools in these outcomes even after allowing for initial differences in intake to the schools. When the individual schools' performance on these outcome measures were compared, it was found that, with one or two exceptions, schools appeared to be remarkably consistent; those that had high levels of attendance and good behaviour also had good academic attainment.

Many of the administrative and physical features of school life did not appear to be related to the outcomes, whereas factors which were concerned with the processes and quality of life of the students did. In addition, the balance of particular types of students within a school appeared to have a marked effect on the outcomes. This means that the academic balance of the intake was more important than the social or ethnic mix.

The features of school life that were reflected in the process measures were:

(i) academic emphasis;
(ii) the classroom strategies of teachers;
(iii) rewards rather than punishments, although the latter were much more common;
(iv) the conditions and facilities enjoyed by students;
(v) opportunities for participation and responsibility.

The findings also showed the importance of a consistent approach by teachers to behaviour or standards of work, of effective leadership by senior staff, and of channels through which all teachers could have their views represented. The authors consider that the processes were a product of school 'ethos'. In schools where the ethos was positive, towards the students in general and towards the fostering of effective learning by the students, positive indicators were found. In other schools, where the ethos is negative, some of the more negative indicators may be found. The authors suggest that there are likely to be a number of ways in which a positive ethos is created and maintained in a school. The goals and expectations of the teachers, the models provided for the students, the efficiency of the feedback for both staff and students and the sensitivity of the leadership are all possible mechanisms.

The study carried out by Rutter et al. aroused more interest and controversy than possibly any other educational study in the past decade. Some of the criticisms of the study have been collected together in reviews in Wragg (1980), Tizard et al. (1980a) and Reynolds et al. (1980). Some of the criticisms are statistical, for example, the inadequacy of the intake measures. Others suggest the study lacks a base in sociological theory and that it neglects the curriculum. The authors have replied to some of their critics in Wragg (1980), Tizard et al. (1980a), Rutter et al. (1980) and Mortimore (1980d).

Goldstein (1980), Reynolds (1980) and Hargreaves (1980) all criticise the intake measures. Hargreaves' contention is that of the four intake variables, two (verbal reasoning scores at ten and a behavioural rating by teachers) are part of the school process and not solely input measures. The other two input measures (parental occupation and whether or not the parents were immigrants) are both too inclusive (only three broad categories of occupation are used and no allowance is made for cultural differences between immigrant groups) and too exclusive (the mother's influence is neglected). Reynolds considers that the intake measures are inadequate, ignoring as they do type of housing tenure and level of parental income. Goldstein makes a further criticism on statistical grounds, arguing that too much reliance is placed on tests of significance, and Heath and Clifford (1980) point out that two-thirds of the variance between schools is unexplained. They also suggest that too little account is taken of parental interest and encouragement.

Reynolds also claims that the book 'lacks a sociological imagination' which might have enabled the authors to link the structural factors of the school with the consciousness of the pupil. Similar criticisms are made by Hargreaves (1980) and Blackstone (1980a).

Some critics question how typical the schools were and thus how valid it is to generalise the results. For example, Wragg (1980) points out that the twelve schools are all in an inner city area with an above average level of social problems (for example, mothers with psychiatric disorders) and adverse living conditions, yet a below average pupil–teacher ratio, all of which imply that the inner-London schools are not typical. Acton (1980) considers that the researchers overemphasise the 'success' of their effective schools and underemphasise how relative it was since 'knowing middle-class parents' did not send their children to these inner-city comprehensive schools. However, this does not invalidate the findings by Rutter et al. that there were marked differences in behaviour and attainment between the twelve schools and that the pupils in the lowest ability group (band three) in the 'best' school did as well as pupils in the top ability group (band one) in the 'worst' school.

Reynolds (1974) has carried out a study of truancy in Welsh schools drawing students from a relatively homogeneous, economically deprived community. Using data based on measures of attainment, attendance and delinquency the researchers found systematic variation which remained over time. Reynolds states how existing research tends to see truancy as the result of family or personality problems and quotes Tyerman (1968) who concluded from his work on truancy that 'in general, the parents set poor examples and were unsatisfactory characters'. Reynolds, however, asks whether schools which are run in certain ways, with particular staff attitudes may prevent truancy, and vice versa. In studying intake over seven years with nine secondary modern schools Reynolds and Murgatroyd (1977) found that 'apparently similar schools with the same ability range from similar social backgrounds have very different levels of absenteeism, which cannot be accounted for by differing amounts of illness in the individual schools'.

Reynolds suggests that if schools do influence truancy the accepted solution of transferring the problem, for example by setting up alternative institutions such as truancy centres, needs to be reconsidered. If some schools are preventing the problem developing in the first place then other schools may learn from their experience. Reynolds' findings indicate that certain features of the school, such as size, levels of corporal punishment, rules and organisation, may cause truancy, which can be seen as a rational response. Reynolds suggests that although research has indicated that children from 'disadvantaged' homes have a greater risk of being truants, whether, or to what extent, the school regime may ameliorate or exacerbate the situation is a neglected question. If some schools are more effective than others, what can be done to bring the least effective up to the standards of the most effective? Whilst this would not solve the problems of educational disadvantage it might go some way towards alleviating them.

Rutter *et al.* are carrying out an intervention study working with teachers in the introduction of planned change in a small number of secondary schools. The study has three stages, based on translating earlier findings into well-defined educational aims, actions and objectives; developing a plan for implementing these actions by changes in school functioning; and evaluating the effect of these changes in bringing about improved behaviour and attainment.

Brophy and Good (1974), who have extensively reviewed predominantly American literature on pupil–teacher relationships, suggest that, hard-pressed though they are, teachers need to learn to monitor their own behaviour or at least receive some degree of feedback, if they are to shape the pattern of classroom interactions in a positive way. The authors describe a teacher-treatment study and present a model for intervention. In the treatment study teachers were given individual feedback about groups of pupils whom they were considered to be treating inappropriately and contrast groups of pupils whom, in similar situations, were being treated differently. Judgement about 'appropriateness' was made on the basis of behavioural data gathered in the classroom. Brophy and Good claim that after the 'treatment' feedback teachers called on 'low participants' more often and initiated more contacts with them, asked them more difficult questions, praised them more often and criticised them less often. Although the target pupils achieved less correct responses (not surprising since they were being asked more and harder questions) they were better behaved, initiated more contacts and made more requests for help from the teacher.

Brophy and Good present an intervention model which has influenced a study being carried out at the Massachusetts Institute of Technology which is attempting to improve classroom interaction between teachers and high-school students (Terry *et al.*, 1979). The Student/Teacher Interactive Learning Environment (STILE) project arose out of the Upward Bound compensatory education project which gave summer tutorial assistance to low achievers with, it is claimed, very successful results (95 per cent of the students entered college and 75 per cent remained until graduation). The project is designed to meet the needs of students, teachers and parents. It is considered that confident or low-achieving students need help in developing their confidence as learners in order to participate more fully in the classroom; teachers need help in developing skills and techniques to help such students who need feedback on their own performance; parents need to understand the educational process better and in particular how their own and teachers' expectations can affect their children. The project aims to develop 'peer observation and feedback' methods so that teachers can help other teachers to analyse classroom interactions. The quality and quantity of teacher–student interactions are observed and strategies devised for actively engaging students having difficulty. The STILE teachers then work with project staff to train other teachers in their techniques. The STILE teachers have identified several common 'negative messages' which teachers frequently give to pupils and they suggest remedies. Their techniques include ways of enabling students to answer difficult questions and of communicating the teacher's positive expectations so that the student is more likely to achieve the correct answer. The project is also working with parents on how expectations are communicated.

The research cited in this section suggests that schools with similar intakes, similar levels of resources, operating in relatively homogeneous districts vary in their effectiveness and that teachers can be helped to assess and improve their effectiveness in teaching disadvantaged pupils. It is probable that more emphasis needs to be placed in teacher-training on the effect of teacher expectation and on the stereotyped view noted by Fuchs that in the slums it is always the children who fail. But the experience of training is removed from the reality of the classroom and there is also scope for more in-service school and teacher evaluation.

Conclusion

The evidence reviewed in this chapter suggests that what goes on in school may, unintentionally, contribute to educational disadvantage, although this may be less likely in particular schools. Despite attempts at the equitable distribution of resources, inequalities remain whereby those pupils from higher socio-economic groups benefit disproportionately from the provision. What is taught in school may be differentiated according to pupils' perceived ability and curricula differences tend to reinforce existing social divisions and inequalities. For many disadvantaged pupils the present examination system is irrelevant because they are not entered or leave prior to examinations. Where the form of school organisation is streaming by ability there is some evidence, although it is somewhat dated, that socially disadvantaged pupils are over-represented in the lower streams from which the chances of 'promotion' are slight and the possibility of anti-school sub-cultures developing are considerable. Teacher turnover, less of a problem in present circumstances, may contribute to educational disadvantage but to a far smaller extent than inadequate teaching. Lastly, an undue emphasis on pupil 'welfare' at the expense of teaching, and the cyclical process of low teacher expectations leading to low pupil expectations and poor performance may exacerbate the educational disadvantage of many who are already socially disadvantaged.

There is, however, a scarcity of evidence about the direct influence of any one of the variables discussed in this chapter. It is rarely possible to say more than that they *may* contribute to educational disadvantage. There has been a much greater volume of research on familial factors and attainment, even though it has been noted how rarely research evidence demonstrates a direct influence on educational outcome. To what extent, and how, teachers and schools make a difference to children is still seriously under-researched. Although Rutter *et al.* argue for the importance of the influence of school, their study is not able to estimate the relative importance of this influence, *vis à vis* that of the home. Unlike Jencks (1973), except in one chapter dealing with the effects of the neighbourhood, they do not attempt to apportion the variance of the outcome measures to different influences.

It is interesting that, when a similar analysis to that of Jencks was carried out using English data, the effect of schooling was much stronger than had been found by Jencks (Psacharopoulos, 1977). One possible reason for this lies in the differences between the English and American systems of education. Whereas in the United States, as Jencks notes, virtually all entrants to high school who *complete the course* are rewarded by a high-school diploma, the English public examination system ensures that secondary-school pupils leave with a great range of qualifications. These qualifications exert a strong influence on entrance to further and higher education and control access to certain occupations. The credentials obtained at the end of schooling in the two education systems thus serve different purposes. The more uniform output of the American system may be a reason why the Jencks' analysis shows a comparatively weak school effect in comparison to that of Psacharopoulos.

It should also be noted that Jencks was not able to examine differences of quality between high schools. This is in marked contrast with the Rutter study, which was able to look in detail at the quality of schooling and at what the research termed 'school process'. However, in some ways the findings of the two studies are similar in that they show that resources, although important, do not necessarily explain differences between schools and, similarly, that organisational differences have comparatively little influence.

Ideally, the question of the relative importance of home and school would be addressed by a study with the details of schooling provided by Rutter *et al*. combined with the information about homes obtained, for example, by the large cohort studies of Douglas *et al*. and Davie *et al*.

It is essential to note that not all disadvantaged pupils fail to achieve at school. Wedge and Prosser found among the disadvantaged sub-group of one of the cohort studies that one in seven pupils were above average on tests of reading and mathematics, and one in seven were mentioned by their teachers as having 'outstanding ability' of some kind. Rutter *et al*. note the 'success' of schools with a positive ethos, despite the negative effects of disadvantaged intakes and environment. The question of why some disadvantaged pupils do succeed against seemingly insuperable odds is an important area which does not appear to have been the subject of much investigation. Work currently being carried out by Wedge on the NCDS 'disadvantaged' sub-sample may provide more evidence on this issue.

Notes

1 Legislation was subsequently passed and the Block Grant system was used for the 1981/82 allocations to local authorities.
2 Most of the ILEA allocation was lost through the use of penalty clauses applied to high-spending authorities in the first year of the new system, 1980–1981.

4 Positive Discrimination in Primary and Secondary Schools

Introduction
This chapter discusses the range of policies which have been introduced with the aim of preventing social disadvantage leading to educational disadvantage. The policies vary considerably both in their scope and in their target populations but all are mediated through the agency of school or college. Many of the policies emanate directly from the recommendation in the Plowden Report that the principle of 'positive discrimination' be applied to allocate extra resources according to need. The government response to the Plowden Report, the national provision which resulted and the Urban Programmes are discussed. Local authority responses, in particular the attempts made to develop objective and systematic criteria for the allocation of additional resources are examined. Description of the action research funded by the national bodies which took place in five local authorities under the direction of A.H. Halsey follows. The chapter then looks at evaluations which have been made of smaller-scale experiments with 'nurture' groups for young children and with attempts to increase parental involvement. The final sections describe interventions in the curriculum and programmes preparing pupils at school for work.

A brief description of each kind of policy will be followed by a report of any evaluation carried out. It is paradoxical that small-scale experimental interventions tend to be evaluated, whilst the effect of large-scale changes following policy decisions may not even be monitored. It is worth noting Glennerster's (1975) discussion of the dearth of evaluative research in Britain compared with the United States. Although open to criticism from a 'purist academic point of view' the American attempts at the 'systematic pursuit of relevant applied research' are impressive. Although interest in and support for research into social policy issues in Britain has increased, it remains haphazard and disjointed. Yet, Glennerster argues, it is 'the gradual accumulation of evidence with one study pointing on to others that begins to pay dividends'. Lacking this coherence some of the British work 'loses much of its usefulness'.

Turning from research to policy, it has not always been clear whether the policies and programmes introduced were intended primarily (i) to raise the education level of the lowest achievers or (ii) to reduce social class differences in educational attainment and to redistribute educational resources. It could be argued that policy-makers are, on the whole, more concerned with (i) and researchers more concerned with (ii) but the distinction, as already noted, is rarely that clear. For example, it is possible that the raising of achievement levels for both working-class children and disadvantaged children calls for some redistribution of resources. Moreover, attempting to improve opportunities for the wider group of working-class children in general may well also help the narrower category of disadvantaged children.

Section 11 Grants
Section 11 of the Local Government Act (1966) made available for local authorities the only direct central government funding specifi-cally intended to alleviate difficulties encountered by members of ethnic minority groups. The provisions of Section 11 enabled succes-sive governments to pay to eligible authorities 50 per cent (later raised to 75 per cent, now 80 per cent) of the cost of staff employed to work with Commonwealth immigrants in attempts to overcome problems of racial disadvantage.

The details of the grant and the conditions under which it is paid are listed in the Home Office Circular 15/1967. It was agreed with the local authority associations that 'a Commonwealth immigrant will normally be considered to be a person, adult or child, born in another country of the Commonwealth, who has been ordinarily resident in the United Kingdom for less than ten years or the child of such a person.' Thus, the Government indicated that it did not intend to indefinitely categorise as immigrants those who had made their homes in Britain. Local authorities are eligible if 2 per cent or more of their school population are the children of Commonwealth immigrants. The grants are not for capital expenditure but are intended to pay for extra staff. Although it is not confined to education about 85 per cent of the expenditure is educational, predominantly for extra teachers, ancillary staff and Educational Welfare Officers. There is no limit to the amount which an authority can claim but the authority must contribute 20 per cent (formerly 25 per cent) of the total and payment is always 'after the event'. Since 1974 the EEC Social Fund has made contributions for programmes qualifying under the Social Fund Programme for migrant workers. This has enabled some local authorities to get part of their contribution reimbursed. The 1967 circular listed forty-six authorities as being eligible. By May 1978 this had increased to eighty-six. The

take-up of grants, however, falls far short of this. An NUT sur.
1978 found only about forty-five authorities had claimed or we
intending to claim grants. Moreover, according to the NUT, 'the
relationship between the amount of grant claimed and the estimated
number of 'immigrants' appears to be tenuous in some cases' (NUT,
1978).

Little (1978) provides evidence that neighbouring authorities with
similar racial compositions make different claims. But there is no
evidence that 'those authorities with higher expenditure per head of
immigrant population are also those which have developed more
intensive programmes for the education of minorities'. Differences
may reflect political and professional willingness to use the grant.

Whilst there is much to recommend the use of a percentage grant to
jointly fund provision for the needs of ethnic minorities the NUT
report highlights problems in the interpretation and the administration
of the grant. The NUT report points out that immigrants from countries outside the Commonwealth, or second or third generations of
ethnic minority groups settled in this country are also in need of special
provision. The most important criticism is that Section 11 staff are
allocated to schools with no specified task so that the 'special provision' which the authority has to make under the terms of the grant
becomes absorbed into the ordinary provision for all children. The
NUT report suggests that the criteria for eligibility be broadened by
abolishing the rules relating to ten-year residence and Commonwealth
origin; by substituting the term 'people from ethnic minority groups'
for 'immigrants'; and by reviewing the 2 per cent formula. It also
suggests that the administration should be transferred to the DES who
could advise local authorities and supervise provision made under the
grant.

The Plowden Report

In 1967 the Plowden Committee argued that 'the principle that special
need calls for special help should be given a new cutting edge'. The
'special help' was to be in the form of 'positive discrimination' which
would give priority to schools in disadvantaged areas. The Report
stated, 'The first step must be to raise the schools with low standards to
the national average; the second, quite deliberately to make them
better. The justification is that the homes and neighbourhoods from
which many of their children come provide little support and stimulus
for learning – the schools must provide a compensating environment.'
The Report suggested ways in which extra resources could be chanel-
led to children in need. It was believed that such children were concentrated in certain schools or groups of schools in deprived areas, and by

identifying those schools or areas and by giving them extra resources those children would be helped.

The Plowden Committee, in fluctuating between the terms priority *schools* and priority *areas* created an ambivalence never satisfactorily resolved. It suggested a wide variety of criteria be used initially and experience would show which were the most useful. The Report suggested eight criteria[1] which, on the basis of information supplied by the local authority, could be used to identify schools in need of special help. Glennerster and Hatch (1974) describe this as 'the first systematic attempt to identify objective grounds for giving extra resources to areas in special need'. The Committee also made suggestions about the form which the special help might take. These included the recruitment of more experienced and better qualified teachers to such areas, who would be paid a special allowance; the provision of teachers' aides; the improvement of dilapidated buildings; the expansion of nursery education to allow for the part-time attendance of all four and five year olds and the full-time attendance of 50 per cent of them; and the development of social work associated with the school and of community schools. The Committee envisaged its proposals being implemented in two stages. In the first experimental stage up until 1972, compensatory measures were to be introduced in schools and areas with 10 per cent of the most disadvantaged children, starting with 2 per cent in the first year and rising to 10 per cent by 1972. Research would be mounted to evaluate the programmes. The programme was estimated to cost an extra £11 million. The second stage was to be longer-term but would depend to some extent on the evaluation of the first stage. The committee considered that additional resources should be made available for 10 per cent, possibly more, of the population and that the resources should be in addition to, not redistributed from, existing allocations. The Plowden Report recommended that 'research should be started to discover which of the developments in Educational Priority Areas have the more constructive effects, so as to assist in planning the longer-term programme to follow'.

The Response of Central and Local Government

The recommendations of the Plowden Committee that Educational Priority Areas be established was welcomed although the DES did not commit the government to the increased expenditure called for in the Report. The Government would not commit itself to definite proposals until it had received reactions to the Plowden Report from the various professional bodies. The views of these groups are set out in Halsey (1972). On the whole the teachers' associations were positive, as were the local authority associations. The reactions of the Associations of Education Committees were 'notably restrained'. But in general the concept of EPAs was acceptable on grounds of both social justice and efficiency.

In 1967 the sum of £16 million was allocated by the Government for a two-year building programme in urban priority areas. The programme was to include replacement of, or renovation of, unsatisfactory schools, and additions which could facilitate community life. The EPAs were not at this stage identified or designated. Local authorities were invited to submit claims on the £16 million and ninety-two did so. Halsey (1972) considers that 'the government was rather hesitant about pressing the general EPA notion on local authorities' and that there was an 'unwillingness to try to influence or impinge upon the responsibilities of local education authorities to implement the Plowden proposals'. By 1968 the Government would not commit itself to expanding nursery education on the grounds not only of increased costs but that any expansion would take teachers from primary schools. However, in their bids for grants from the £16 million, local authorities could submit plans for extra nursery classes and by the summer of 1968 twenty-three such proposals were approved.

In 1967 the Burnham Committee had awarded an extra £75 per year (Plowden had suggested £120) for teachers in schools with special difficulties, on condition that local education authorities applied to the Secretary of State for recognition of such schools, according to certain criteria. These criteria, closely resembling those suggested by Plowden, included the social and economic status of parents, the lack of amenities in the home, the proportion of children receiving free meals or whose families were receiving supplementary benefits and the proportion of children with language difficulties. Initially the Secretary of State argued that it was not possible to select the schools without creating 'serious anomalies' but he later agreed to do so and the money was paid from April 1968. Nearly 150,000 children were in 572 schools where their teachers received the extra allowance. With a primary-school population of three-and-a-half million there was a long way to go before provision was made for the 10 per cent which Plowden had suggested by 1972. By April 1968 fifty-one authorities in England and six in Wales had shared the £16 million allocated in a total of 150 school building programmes, not the 10 per cent or 3000 schools which Plowden had considered would merit the EPA rating. The identification of schools needing priority treatment was, as the Minister of State admitted, a somewhat arbitrary procedure based on selections made from local authority bids.

In July 1968 the Government announced the Urban Programme under which £25 million was to be allocated over four years to education, housing, health and welfare programmes, payable retrospectively on expenditure on approved schemes. A number of local authorities considered to be in urgent need of such help would be selected and projects agreed with them. The Government indicated their expectation that, initially, most projects would be concerned with nursery education and child care. Thirty-four authorities were selected and invited to submit proposals. In February 1969 the second phase of the Urban Programme, up until the end of 1970, was announced. A further £2 million was allocated. *All* local authorities could submit proposals for grants of 75 per cent on approved projects. The schemes were no longer limited to provision for younger children, but could include plans for teachers' centres, in-service courses, language classes for immigrants, family advice centres, aid to voluntary societies and for expenditure on materials, equipment and transport.

By the end of 1969 eighty-six local authorities had benefited from the £16 million building allocation, the teachers' allowance and the educational element in the Urban Programmes and 10,000 nursery places had been created. In 1970 the third phase of the Urban Programme was extended until 1976 with proposed expenditure between 1972 and 1976 of between £35 and £40 million. By 1971 18,000 new nursery places had been provided under the Urban Programme. The Plowden committee had recommended an increase of over 500,000 placed by 1975.

In accordance with the suggestion by the Plowden Committee that research be initiated in Educational Priority Areas £175,000 was allocated by the Department of Education and Science (DES) and the Social Science Research Council (SSRC) for action research in five EPA areas – Birmingham, Liverpool, London, Dundee and the West Riding of Yorkshire. The action researchers had four aims: to raise educational standards; to raise teacher morale; to improve links between home and school by increasing parental involvement; and to assist in giving the communities a sense of responsibility.

Under the direction of A.H. Halsey the action research teams carried out a variety of activities with the emphasis on pre-schooling and the community school, which have been described at length in the various reports published by the teams (Halsey, 1972, Midwinter, 1972, Payne, 1974, Barnes, 1975, and Smith, 1975). The attempts to increase pre-school provision, to monitor the effects of a structured language programme with pre-school children and research into the development of community school curricula are discussed later in the chapter.

The administrative bodies concerned with education produced varied but on the whole positive reactions to the Plowden proposals. The

Association of Education Committees (AEC) thought any implementation would have to be over the long term and that priorities would need to be established, since the proposals needed far more money than was likely to be available. The AEC considered it impracticable to define EPAs and so opposed extra payments to teachers working in them, but thought extra money should be available for building. It expressed doubts about trained aides creating a new grade of teacher and about increased nursery expansion placing heavy demands on existing teaching numbers. The County Council's Association (CCA) and the Association of Municipal Corporations (AMC) were more positive, whilst stressing the problem of identifying areas of need and the limitations imposed by existing resources. The AMC queried the length of time for which any designation should last and the possibility of help for deprived but not designated schools. The response to government invitations to submit bids under the Urban Programme was widespread and over 100 authorities finally had schemes approved.

Most LEAs claimed to be able to pick out EPA schools without any objective criteria and Halsey himself admits 'there is some element of truth in this claim'. However, although 'local diagnosis and flexible formulae are essential . . . the desirability of seeking more precise and widely acceptable criteria is also obvious'. The Plowden Report was somewhat muddled over the identification of areas and schools and in the DES Circular 11/67 which dealt with supplementary building programmes for educational priority areas the Secretary of State stated that he did not 'intend to designate or define educational priority areas . . . (and) that the authorities themselves are well placed to judge to what extent their areas contain districts which suffer from the social and physical deficiencies which the Plowden Council had in mind'.

The claims for building grants were much the same as previous building submissions although, unlike the post-war 'roofs over heads' policy, the claims had to be based on an assessment of need.

The second aspect of implementing Plowden necessitated the identification of schools with special needs in order to allocate the extra teachers' allowance. The Remuneration of Teachers (Primary and Secondary Schools) Act 1968 was amended to give statutory authority to the payments and Section R of the Burnham Report 1969 listed the four criteria already mentioned for identifying schools. Local authorities tended to name all the schools which met the criteria, plus a few borderline ones. 'Certain criteria were applied to all the schools and points awarded' (Halsey, 1972), although DES recognition for the purposes of the teachers' allowances was limited by the amount of money available for them which was £400,000 per annum. As a result, many schools considered by authorities to meet the criteria were not recognised by the DES as schools of exceptional difficulty. Halsey has described how the limited resources and the administration of the multiple criteria led to local anomalies and considerable difference between the numbers of LEA-proposed and DES-designated schools. The DES recognised the difficulties involved in attempting to identify objectively schools with special difficulties and Halsey states that, although the attempts by five LEAs which he and his action research teams studied were similar, there were quite substantial differences in the weightings given to various indices in order to arrive at a 'points total capable of being set in an order of priority'.

A number of local authorities (for example Cleveland, Coventry, Newcastle-on-Tyne and Walsall) developed measures for identifying social priority schools. The schemes of one large urban authority (the ILEA) and one rural authority (Northamptonshire) will be described.

The ILEA scheme is more sophisticated than any other. Under it, extra money is available to schools according to their position on an Index of Need, which takes account of factors associated with stress and disadvantage. Information on a range of measures of social and educational disadvantage is collected for each ILEA primary and secondary school. The statistics are combined to provide an overall index score for the school, and the schools are then ranked in order. A detailed account of the background to the construction of the index can be found in Little and Mabey (1972). The primary-school index was first used in 1967 and the secondary-school index in 1973. Each index is calculated biennially and the factors, measures and weightings reviewed so as to reflect changing circumstances in the schools. In 1978/79, the primary index was constructed from seven items; three related to the children as pupils (measures of behaviour in schools, attainment and transfer in and out of schools); the remaining four (poverty, parental occupation and incidence of one-parent families and of large families) related to home background. The secondary index used in 1978/9 was constructed from twelve items, including the seven used for the primary index plus five factors related to the size and age of the school building.

'Notional' allocations to schools are calculated by a formula combining the pupil roll and the school's score on the index. The notional allocations are not mandatory although in practice the room for manoeuvre is not great. Between 1977 and 1978 the total amount of money allocated in this way was increased to allow for the effects of falling rolls and inflation. The gap in the allocation between the 'top ten' index schools and the 'bottom ten' schools increased between

1977 and 1978. The average notional allowance per child in the 'top ten' schools was, in 1977, 2.84 times that per child in the 'bottom ten' schools. In 1978 this ratio increased to 3.68. Although, at present, there is no systematic monitoring or evaluation of how the additional resources are used or to what effect, plans to do this are in hand.

The index is also used in the distribution of other benefits such as the Social Priority Allowance which is paid to teachers who work in schools on the Educational Priority Area list. In 1974 the list was incorporated into a scheme controlled by the Burnham Committee. The schools in which staff were to receive the extra allowance were chosen on the basis of their position on the 1974 priority index. The position of a school on the index is also taken into consideration when building programmes are drawn up.

Boulter and Crispin (1978) devised an index of need, based on that developed by the ILEA, but concerned with pupils and schools in a rural area, in Northamptonshire. Concern was expressed by the local authority over the possibly disadvantageous effects on small rural schools of their geographic isolation, a limited curriculum and lack of certain equipment (due to the capitation system). The local education authority agreed to allocate an extra £50,000 during 1974/5 to a trial project aimed at improving the resources of small primary schools in three areas of the county. In Boulter and Crispin's study, which developed from the project, the authors address the question of whether it is possible 'to arrive at a quantifiable and explicit means of deciding where – or to whom – to allocate additional resources'. In devising their index of need Boulter and Crispin drew upon the ILEA criteria, where relevant, and added criteria relating to rural schools. In contrast to the ILEA index, five of the nine final criteria adopted were school or premises based (for example, teacher isolation, restricted curricula activities, per capita resources, quality of premises). The authors suggest that the use of such an index is a viable means of approaching disadvantage using criteria which are not only social or home-based. Moreover, local authorities have more control over school-based criteria and are able to implement what Smith (1977) calls an 'area policy' towards disadvantage which does not require identification of individual children considered to be 'at risk'.

Criticisms of EPA Policies and Programmes
Several criticisms have been levelled at the post-Plowden policies and the programmes to which they led. Some of the criticisms relate to the Government's lack of enthusiasm and to the relatively small amounts of money and time allocated to policies of positive discrimination.

Halsey (1972) considered that government interest in educational priority areas was 'uncertain' with 'a history of only half-hearted support by either political party' for the Plowden proposals. Progress on reducing class size, providing teachers' aides, forming links with colleges of education, developing community schools and increasing nursery education had been, at best, slow and still fell far short of Plowden's targets. Halsey declared 'the question now is whether the British Government is prepared to launch a full-scale national policy'. He hoped that the projects developed in his action research would go some way towards persuading the Government of the need for a policy of positive discrimination. In fact the amount of money allocated was miniscule in comparison with the educational budget as a whole (Meacher, 1974, Halsey, 1977) and the interventions 'employed only marginal resources' (Shipman, 1980). Moreover Shipman considers that the policies may become redundant and result in injustice. 'Payments once given are rarely redistributed as the conditions faced by the teachers concerned change . . . every new payment of this kind aggravates the injustice between teachers.'

The Plowden Committee had asked that schools with low standards be raised to the national average and then above it, but, as Shipman (1980) points out, 'it was never clear whether this meant standards of provision or standards of attainment'. Meacher considers that workable criteria for success have never been agreed and that the confusion of aims has resulted in there being no standardised monitoring of EPAs. Gray (1975), however, points out that if schools have contributed to social inequality then it is 'fairly improbable' that the process could be reversed in only a couple of years.

Other criticisms are concerned that the policies of positive discrimination were aimed at the wrong age group or the wrong issues. Thus, Van der Eyken (1974), whilst admitting that aid was not aimed exclusively at the youngest children (as were many American Head Start Programmes) states that '40 per cent of the money made available during the first seven years of the urban programme was spent on pre-school and day nursery provision at a time when the age-group was declining. Nothing at all was spent on fifteen to nineteen year olds, whose numbers and difficulties were increasing.' Meacher argues that there was too much emphasis on primary-school buildings, with no evidence that 'new school buildings improve educational attainment'. Since parental motivation was considered more important than such physical factors Meacher asks why, given the limited resources available, there was not a concentrated effort directed towards parental involvement.

Some critics consider that the policies have not benefited the children for whom they were intended. Both Acland (1971) in his re-analysis of Plowden data, and Barnes and Lucas (1975) in the course of the London EPA Project, argue that the majority of disadvantaged children are not in disadvantaged areas and most of the children in disadvantaged areas are not disadvantaged, and that policies effected through schools were likely to be of most benefit to 'the children of non-manual workers who were born in the United Kingdom'. Plowden was, from the outset, somewhat ambiguous about whether resources should be directed towards schools or areas and this confusion is reflected in some of the implementations which resulted. Halsey (1977) writes that the principle of positive discrimination has led to confusion between two kinds of policy; one aimed at social and the other at individual aggregates. But, 'the social approach is vulnerable to the ecological fallacy and the individual approach to the fallacy of composition.' The ecological fallacy is to predict, from average conditions, individual circumstances and performance. The fallacy of composition is to assume that the low performance of a particular community is the sum of individual low performances, whilst overlooking the social and structural forces which limit opportunities and ambition. Halsey suggests social and individual policies have to be separated and each pursued as 'complementary elements of a wider strategy'.

The former leader of the West Riding EPA team, Smith (1977) argues that the idea of positive discrimination by area, which in his opinion has never really been developed, deserves to be reconsidered. Smith admits that the original EPA policy confused two separate issues, 'reaching individual children "at risk" by designating areas where they might be concentrated, and a true area policy intended for all children in an area defined as disadvantaged, whether they are individually "at risk" or not'. If the second interpretation were to be adopted it would mean 'a series of related educational developments designed for the particular needs and conditions of specific areas' rather than a uniform policy. Smith cites the example of Saltley in Birmingham where, contrary to the rest of the city, the population, which includes many Asian immigrant families, has increased but, in accordance with the 'blanket' policy applied to the city as a whole, extra pre-school provision is not being provided. Smith considers that as a consequence 'many children in the Saltley area will be doubly disadvantaged. Faced initially with problems of adjustment to a new language medium, they are likely to have a declining chance of nursery education, to experience late entry to primary school and then to join large reception classes, containing many non-English-speaking children.' By operating at a small area level, use could be made of 'informal' educational resources and development could be related to complementary programmes.

Halsey (1977) argues that the local education system needs to be seen as only one of an area's educational resources. Education alone is unable to solve an area's problems. Development, Halsey maintains, 'has to be planned in relation to other educative and anti-educative forces, including the characteristically low level of private and public investment, and the absence of social capital in transition areas with rapidly changing populations, poor housing and poor knowledge of the political and administrative skills required in securing a fair share of resources for the district.'

If, as Barnes and Lucas and Acland suggest, more disadvantaged children are outside EPA schools than are inside them, do extra resources need to be channelled to individual *children* in a wide range of schools rather than to supposedly disadvantaged *schools*? This would obviously take more administrative time and money. It might mean funding of special programmes for which only designated disadvantaged children would be eligible (as has been the case with some of the federally funded programmes in the United States). This has implications for the autonomy of head teachers to allocate resources within schools and it has the disadvantage of labelling children who are singled out for special treatment. A recent OECD conference paper suggested further drawbacks to this approach in that it creates new bureaucracies which can lead to conflict and jealousy between existing and newly-created bodies (Blackstone, 1979a). The OECD Conference agreed that to be successful in positive discrimination more funds were necessary. It was suggested that children in need should have about 20 per cent more spent on them than children in general and there should be a variety of methods of allocating the funds. The methods would depend on the aims of the policy. Thus, additional funds might be allocated on an institutional basis, for example, to a school with multiple problems to help raise morale; or to a particular service, such as the careers service which helps school leavers; or to promote new ideas among those working with the disadvantaged; or to a particular programme for groups of children needing specific help. The programme should then be evaluated.

The financial implementation of the Plowden proposals, criticised though they are for their paucity, nevertheless resulted in a proliferation of small-scale, locally initiated intervention programmes, of which only a few are mentioned in this chapter. There is now such a host of project workers, teacher/social workers, curriculum support teams, home–school relations officers, on and off-site unit teams, that, as Shipman points out, 'it is difficult even to map where the various agencies are in the inner cities, and impossible to account for their activities'. Shipman considers that disappointment over the power of education to equalise opportunities has also reduced the incentive to define objectives and resources tend to be allocated without any clear idea about what it is hoped to achieve. This is unfortunate since the impact of extra resources can be minimised if there is insufficient control over how they are used. The different criteria used in evaluating intervention programmes leads to claims and counter claims for their effectiveness, which leads to further confusion.

Many of the projects are not part of the mainstream of education, and are not necessarily co-ordinated with it. Thus they are not able to contribute to the continuity of education; this may be considered unfortunate for the majority but disastrous for the educationally disadvantaged.

EPA Action Research
Jointly funded by central government (DES) and a national research body (SSRC) the action research took place in five areas and received some help from the local authorities concerned.

Pre-school projects
The Plowden Report suggested that pre-school provision should be extended to cater for 15 per cent of three year olds full-time and 30 per cent part-time and for 15 per cent of four year olds full-time and 75 per cent part-time. At the start of Halsey's action research none of the five EPA research areas approached this provision. The limited resources of the EPA project teams restricted the extent to which they could increase pre-school provision in any area, but they enlisted the co-operation of statutory and voluntary bodies (for example, community organisations and playgroups), parents, secondary-school pupils and college students. Halsey (1972) writes of an increased awareness of the need 'for types of provision which would maximise the effectiveness of positive discrimination and lay the foundations for radical improvement of the partnership between the educational system and the community.'

Increased pre-school provision was considered a priority by the West Riding team and with the help of the LEA and the urban programme 'they created universal provision of one kind or another in one of the two towns' (Halsey). In the ILEA overall pre-school provision was quite extensive (30 per cent in the Deptford area) but the project financed a new playgroup as part of a research project with a college of education to study pre-school language development. In the Sparkbrook area of Birmingham, even after two urban aid programmes and voluntary initiatives, the provision in 1971 was still only about 27 per cent. In Liverpool the team concentrated on support rather than provision and they attempted to draw local playgroups together 'into a loose federation for mutual benefit', although the team also provided a double-decker 'playmobile' which visited blocks of flats for a weekly play session. As well as increasing provision the EPA researchers were interested in whether the content of the pre-school curriculum could be modified to promote language development. This led to the National Pre-School Experiment.

Early results from the experimental programmes in the United States had indicated that structured 'task oriented' programmes such as that of Bereiter and Engelman (1966) achieved the greatest IQ gains. In contrast the early Head Start programmes, which were not necessarily primarily educational and often deliberately non-structured, produced disappointing results with respect to IQ gains. The EPA team considered that a structured element in the pre-school curriculum might lessen the handicap of many EPA five year olds and contribute to their later progress at school. Accordingly the American Peabody Language Development Kit (PLDK) was introduced for an experimental one-year basis into seven nursery classes and playgroups in three of the project areas. Each group had a corresponding control group which had no special programme. Teachers' reactions to the PLDK were mixed. Some felt it was too structured, others considered that the scheme was 'an efficient way of coping with a very large problem in the short time available'. Two tests of language ability were chosen to assess the children's progress.

Details of the test results can be found in Halsey (1972). The scores of the children in the PDLK groups were higher at the end of the year than at the beginning, whereas the scores of the control group were varied, some were higher but some were lower. Halsey considers that the teachers' views confirm, though with reservations, the test score evidence that children could benefit from the programme. The teachers using the PLDK claimed that the motivation and behaviour of the children had improved and that they had enjoyed learning. Although the research team did not measure these aspects Halsey expresses the hope that the gains would carry on into infant school. He also points out the importance of the teachers' attitudes to the success of the programme, 'to attempt to evaluate a programme which conflicts with the principles of the teacher using it is to give it an unfair trial.'

At the end of the first year the West Riding project found that in the infant school there was no evidence that pre-school gains from the special programmes were lost. Furthermore, Smith (1975) states that although the gains showed a decline in the second year 'children who had taken part in pre-school work had higher scores than their predecessors who had not attended pre-school even after a further year'. This was heartening in view of some evidence from American programmes, in particular the Westinghouse evaluation of Headstart, that pre-school gains 'washed out'.

A follow-up intervention programme was carried out with two randomly allocated groups of children from one of the schools during their reception year in infant school. During the first year the experimental group made significant gains. However, one year later the differences were less and after two years the groups had almost identical scores. Although the additional year of intervention had some effect at the time, Smith admits that it 'seems in no way to guarantee a long term gain in performance'. However, only those aspects of the intervention which could be measured on the standardised tests were formally evaluated and there may well have been other benefits to the children and parents involved.

The EPA action research projects involved small numbers of children and the measures of output used were somewhat limited. The results overall have not been optimistic, although it is probably unreasonable to expect to produce significant change with such a small investment which makes little impact on the total environment of the disadvantaged.

Some short-term gains which were not retained over time also emerged from a similar study carried out by the National Foundation for Educational Research (NFER) (Woodhead, 1976). The objectives of the NFER study were to implement a compensatory programme in nursery schools which included a special language programme; to examine the relationship between any changes in cognitive performance and social and personal development; and to see if the special programme in the nursery had any longer-term effect on promoting basic skills or adjustment to school. The study also set out to explore ways of involving parents in their children's pre-school education.

The results of the experiment indicated that the special programme was more effective in improving language skills than perceptual abilities. Woodhead suggests that the normal nursery experiences may provide sufficient stimulus for the development of perceptual skills but that specific training can improve verbal skills more than normal nursery education is able to do. This is not surprising given that many of the toys and much of the equipment commonly used in nurseries are aimed at promoting discrimination by colour, shape or size. However, specific language work, such as increasing vocabulary, calls for individual or small group work with adults, but various studies have indicated that individual staff–child interactions may be infrequent or concerned with children's routine physical needs rather than extending language (Tizard and Rees, 1974, Sylva, Roy and Painter, 1980, Wood, McMahon and Cranstoun, 1980). In the NFER study the special programme was successful in improving the performance of disadvantaged children relative to their peers. However, when children from different social backgrounds followed the programme they all made gains and so the gap between advantaged and disadvantaged remained. When the children started infant school the comparison group was found to be better adjusted to school than the programme group although, Woodhead suggests, this may reflect the more favourable home circumstances of the comparison group. The later follow-up, in the children's sixth term in infant school, showed that initial gains were not maintained; if anything the comparison group were at an advantage.

These initially positive but later disappointing effects were similar to much of the American experience. However, in 1977 Lewin reported the results of studies 'all showing some degree of long-term positive effect of early intervention' (Lewin, 1977). These assertions challenged the view that gains from short-term intervention 'washed out' within a year or two of schooling. Some of the researchers mentioned by Lewin believed that 'sleeper effects' had operated, with benefits to children who had earlier followed Head Start programmes becoming apparent later. (For a detailed critique of the concept of 'sleeper effect' see Clarke and Clarke, in press.) Some of the investigations referred to by Lewin were later published by Lazar, Hubbell et al. (1977), although they do not use the term 'sleeper effect'. The authors pooled early data from twelve research groups looking at the long-term effects of the intervention programmes of the 1960s, and collected uniform follow-up data in 1976/77. Evidence of the long-term effects of pre-schooling was demonstrated in four ways. The children were less likely to be in remedial classes at a later date; less likely to have to repeat a grade or drop out of school; more likely to have higher achievement in mathematics at age ten; and more likely to score more highly on an IQ test for up to three years after pre-school in some projects. This gain was maintained for longer but not above the age of thirteen. The children were also likely to be more achievement-oriented. Lazar et al. do not indicate what characteristics of the pre-school seemed to be responsible for later success.

Clarke and Clarke (1981) argue that many of the studies noted by Lazar et al. were not planned with long-term evaluation in mind and either 'lacked a data base for later comparable study or such a base was inappropriate'. A further problem following on from this is that nothing is known of what happened to the families in the intervening years between the end of the programme and the later follow-up.

Clarke and Clarke suggest alternative explanations which do not assume early changes 'lying dormant for years before becoming effective'. These explanations they term

(i)   the intervening variable model in which 'something happened to the parents, correlated with early intervention or personal circumstances, which had an ongoing or later effect upon the children';

(ii)   the random fluctuation model which suggests that in developmental studies over long periods it is common to obtain correlation coefficients of 0.35;

(iii)   the insensitive measurement model which suggests that the wrong type of measurement was used at one time but not at another. What is then interpreted as a sleeper effect might be a measurement artefact.

Clarke and Clarke (1979) also point out the need to separate sample characteristics from programme effects. They describe a parent education programme carried out by Guinagh and Gordon (1976) which showed significant differences between control and experimental groups both three years and five-and-a-half years after the programme had been completed but with considerable 'sample attrition'. At age eight-and-a-half nearly half the original sample had been lost. There is no indication of what happened to the families between the end of the programme and the follow-up testing, nor any evaluation of the drop outs except that initially they were of similar IQ to the others in the sample. As Clarke and Clarke and Bronfenbrenner (1974) point out, it is usually the most disadvantaged who drop out.

Certain specific criticisms have been levelled at the EPA projects. Whilst acknowledging that the researchers were aware of the influence of social situations, motivation and 'support in the family and community' Van der Eyken (1974) considers that the projects were, nevertheless, largely 'school oriented and school-based'.

Tizard *et al*. (1981) argue that the EPA teams did not work out the implications of some of their ideas, in particular those relating to community schools. Thus Halsey and Midwinter talk of coming to terms with the values of the community but if the community did not value educational achievement 'how could the school come to terms with this value difference *and* raise children's educational achievement?' Moreover, they point out that there are communities in Britain where a sizeable proportion of the parents hold views which the staff consider racist or sexist. 'What does coming to terms with the community values mean in this situation?'

A different sort of criticism is made by Van der Eyken and Midwinter (1972) (who himself directed the Liverpool project). They consider that the time scale, three years, to carry out and evaluate the project, was too short for an enterprise of such scope.

In the first volume of the Reports on the EPA Projects, Halsey was positive about the results of the action research and cautiously optimistic about EPAs, whilst making it plain that schools 'cannot accomplish important social reforms such as the democratisation of opportunity unless social reforms accompany the educational effort'. 'Education' could not be separated from housing, jobs, income and other social contexts. His principal conclusions were that the EPA was a 'socially and administratively viable unit' through which to apply positive discrimination, that pre-schooling was the 'outstandingly effective and economical device' by which educational standards in EPAs could be raised; the role of the community school for community regeneration had been demonstrated, as had practical ways of involving parents and of improving the quality of teaching in EPA schools. Halsey claimed that action research was an effective means of trying out policy innovations and, finally, 'the EPA can be no more than a part, though an important one, of a comprehensive social movement towards community development and community redevelopment in a modern urban industrial society' (Halsey, 1972).

The report called for an extension of the EPA concept to 'a wider variety of deprived districts' including redevelopment housing estates; 'a hybrid form of nursery centre' combining the strengths of good nursery schools and good parent-run playgroups; better pay, conditions and courses for EPA teachers and the closer involvement of 'the most under-used potential resource for positive discrimination', the colleges of education.

The Curriculum
Curriculum reform is a vast area and it will only be possible to pick out a few examples here. This section examines the curriculum developments which arose out of the EPA action research projects, some of which attempted to create a curriculum relevant to the community for primary age children; and curriculum development for less-able secondary pupils.

EPA action research projects on the curriculum
Midwinter (1972) takes the view that a community-orientated curriculum can help children to 'react imaginatively, briskly and articulately to the problems of social disadvantage' on the assumption that a more assertive community consciousness would be developed. Since Midwinter considers it likely that most children in EPA areas would spend their lives in their localities it is important that they come to

terms with their locality, not passively but critically. This is Midwinter's rationale for a community curriculum which is flexible and locality-based and in which skills take precedence over information, but in which relevance takes precedence over skills.

In the EPA projects curriculum development was related to one of the four aims of the action research – to raise educational standards – and in some cases also to the aim of arousing a sense of community responsibility. The EPA teams differed in their emphasis and activities; some concentrated on improving skills by presenting traditional subjects in new ways, others concentrated on developing a more 'relevant' education directly related to the child's environment. The Birmingham team, and, to a lesser extent, the West Riding team, concentrated on improving reading, Liverpool concentrated on a 'socially relevant curriculum' and the Deptford team worked in the three areas of environmental studies, language enrichment and mathematics.

In Birmingham attempts were made to raise the reading standards in two schools by introducing a comprehensive programme. Halsey writes that 'of course the (reading) material worked best with the best teachers who had the organisation and control necessary for using complex material and breaking the class down into smaller units.' When retested the eight and nine-year-old children had gained, which, to Halsey, suggests that 'literacy could be increased by remedial work at junior level'. One group in each school made no progress at all, which Halsey attributes to 'the performance of the teacher'.

The West Riding Project set up an audio-visual reading scheme for children who were still unable to read at the end of their time in primary school. A control group was drawn from similar schools. At the end of the year both groups were tested. The experimental group made more progress on the non-phonic test and made greater gains on the phonic test. The control group did better on the vocabulary test and had more positive attitudes to school both before and after the course. On the test of short-term memory there were 'no apparent changes related to the reading scheme'. The teachers who were enthusiastic about the scheme felt that the children had made good progress and, in some cases, has increased their confidence.

Curriculum development in Deptford centred on an environmental studies programme which attempted to improve skills and to devise an enjoyable and relevant curriculum. The project involved 400 fourth-year junior children from seven schools, fifteen teachers and numbers of students and parents who spent one day a week during the school year at an environmental studies centre in Kent. Each group was free to develop their own interests, relating the usual primary-school subjects to the area around the study centre and comparing it with Deptford. Teaching material was produced. The results, as measured by tests of academic progress, attitudes to school and motivation, were disappointing. There were no differences between the pupils following the environmental studies and the control group in performance in English and mathematics, nor in changes in attitude to school. The control group showed better study skills than the experimental group at the end of the year. Most of the teachers thought the scheme had improved the pupils' motivation and work and that their relationship with the pupils had improved. In fact, it was found that the pupils had become more hostile to the teachers.

The Deptford Project Director suggests that the optimistic views of the teachers are the self-fulfilling results of their 'persistent belief that the scheme was basically good,' but that alone was not sufficient for success. 'If children in educational priority areas are to be given an effective education, their teachers must teach them.' Moreover, the programme was superimposed on the rest of the curriculum whereas what was needed was 'a more systematic, perhaps a more radical, appraisal of what happens in our schools' (Barnes, 1975).

The Liverpool team focussed on developing a community syllabus for their 'ultimate goal' of the community school. A number of small projects were introduced with the principal aim of developing an enjoyable curriculum, relevant to the community in which the children lived and 'designed to promote a sense of community spirit and responsibility'. The improvement of skills was considered to be a subordinate aim to that of developing a relevant and enjoyable curriculum. Projects included developing social and creative studies – for example around a mock supermarket, bank or surgery to equip children to meet everyday situations comfortably and critically; and the study of local institutions (church, school, street and home). There was a strong emphasis on creative, social and dramatic work and attempts were made to involve parents, the local theatre and large stores. With student help, by the third year of the project curricular work was being undertaken in thirty schools. The Liverpool team concluded that the balance of the curriculum should change from 'academic' to 'social' and should be related to the children's experience; that schools should devote more time to creative activities involving parents and community; social environmental studies should concentrate on skills rather than on information and that both teachers and children 'should develop a critical but tolerant attitude to a range of social institutions, ideas and aspirations' (Midwinter, 1972).

Halsey (1972) wrote that the results of such projects 'cannot easily be measured by the conventional methods of educational research' but that there was a consensus among teachers that 'children had made some educational gains, particularly in terms of social relationships, language and communication.' Halsey does not indicate how these gains were measured. The net result of the EPA curriculum projects seems to be that, where one of the aims was to improve skills, only limited gains were made. There may possibly have been gains in social relationships or communication that were not easily measurable. One reason for the limited gains may have been the separation of the intervention from the mainstream of the school so that the projects lacked the integration considered by Shipman (1980) to be so vital in the education of the disadvantaged. The separation from mainstream education and the development of two differentially valued curricula, with the opportunities for transfer being too little or too late, do little to promote the educationally disadvantaged.

An interesting point to emerge from the projects is the part played by the teachers. Where they have been considered to be uncommitted or even hostile, interventions have failed. Yet, even where the teachers have been enthusiastically in favour of the interventions, measurable gains have not always been achieved and attitudes have sometimes worsened. If teachers are in favour of certain innovations then they are probably more likely to want to see improvement and, in order to avoid cognitive dissonance, to perceive gains where none exist. It is also possible that they enjoyed participating in the programme and, in the case of the Deptford environmental studies scheme, found it a stimulating change to the conventional work with the pupils in school. However, the somewhat disappointing results do suggest that curricula developments, which are 'tagged on' to an existing curriculum to which they bear little or no relation, or developments which are implemented by teachers who are not convinced of their value, are unlikely to have the desired impact.

Schools Council Curriculum Projects

The EPA strategy, exemplified in the Liverpool community school project, of making the curriculum more relevant to the everyday experience of the pupils, is similar to the rationale behind the Schools Council Curriculum Projects aimed at interesting and motivating 'less-able' secondary-school pupils.

The Schools Council was set up in 1964 soon after the publication of the Newsom Report (Central Advisory Council for Education, 1963) which had expressed concern over the large numbers of 'early leavers' and called for separate curricula for non-academic pupils. Of the many curriculum projects it has developed, the Humanities Project is relevant here, intended for secondary pupils who were of average or below average ability. It was started in 1967 as part of the Schools Council programme for the young school leaver, to offer teachers materials and support for enquiry-based courses which crossed traditional subject boundaries. It is intended that learning takes place as a result of the discussion of controversial issues with the teacher acting as a neutral chairperson. The aim is 'to forward understanding, discrimination and judgement in the human field' (Schools Council, 1965).

After pilot trials the project was launched in 1970 and was widely adopted in secondary schools to fill the curriculum gap created by the raising of the school-leaving age (ROSLA) in 1973. Rudduck (1976) says it became a 'crisis curricula' measure to meet a specific and immediate educational need. The 'ROSLA image' meant that the projects were used in divisive ways, often assigned to the fourth- and fifth-year groups considered to have no academic future. Yet Rudduck maintains that the project team 'did not like the Newsom Report's acceptance of a special curriculum for the non-academic'. She quotes Young (1971) who has argued that new courses in low-status areas of knowledge and with Newsom associations come to be seen as courses for those who have already failed so that even success with the courses can still be defined as failure. The Project Team considered that the course offered 'an intellectual challenge' to young people and a 'coherent alternative pedagogy'. Yet if it is assigned in the main to the less able its value will not be fully appreciated until it 'sheds its last Newsom veil'. The Project has been strongly criticised by White (1971) Young (1971) and Shipman (1980). White argues that an obsession with *means* (curricula development groups, reducing barriers between school and community, action research in the classroom, team teaching and audio-visual development) obscure the desired *end*. In White's view the end should be 'a "good society" where both bank manager and boiler worker are seen as contributing equally to the common good. If, as Tawney said, we think the highest culture fit for solicitors, why should we not think it fit for coalminers?'

The Schools Council is accused of perpetuating a 'dualist' framework of separate curricula for different groups of pupils or different types of school. White challenges the fact that the emphasis given by both the Newsom Report and the Schools Council on vocational education is restricted to the manual and service industries. He is particularly critical of the suggested topics in *Society and the Young School Leaver*. He suggests that some of them encourage pupils to accept their dull environment as an acceptable place in which to live. Whilst it can be argued that it is justifiable to encourage pupils to learn more about their locality, although many of them would be familiar enough with it, what is not acceptable is the limiting of environmental work to one group of pupils, whilst it is not considered good enough for others.

There is now a considerable literature on the social definition of what counts as valued knowledge and how it is differentially distributed in schools. These issues are discussed at length in Young (1971). Young criticises the Schools Council in their curricula reform for 'accepting the existing stratification of knowledge' and producing reforms only in the 'low status knowledge areas' which, since they are for the less able and disadvantaged, do not threaten the interests of power groups in the social structure. Since the courses are aimed at those already considered failures, the lack of success is attributed to an individual shortcoming in ability or motivation rather than a reflection of the education system. Separate courses for this group deny pupils 'access to the kinds of knowledge which are associated with rewards, prestige and power in our society' (Young, 1971).

Shipman (1980) maintains that the plight of the disadvantaged child and the differentiated curriculum is exacerbated in the inner city. His argument is that curricula developments were innovated most rapidly in the inner cities, where attainment has consistently been shown to be below the national average. Past investment in buildings and support services, falling rolls and more favourable pupil–teacher ratios all provided scope for innovation. But also there was in most inner areas a shortage of articulate middle-class parents who might have objected to some of the innovations. Shipman is critical of the value of much of the curriculum innovation both because of its form and content and because of the limitations it places on those disadvantaged pupils it was primarily intended to help. He considers that there has been a tendency to drop a subject if problems of motivation or discipline make it difficult to teach. This view gains some support in the HMI Secondary Survey (DES, 1979a). In their sample of 109 schools, the Inspectorate found that of twenty-five which had a concentration of problems of discipline and violence nineteen were inner-city schools. In some of these schools teachers were 'teaching for containment rather than learning' with the result that pupils experienced a more restricted curriculum. Shipman asserts that textbooks considered too demanding are replaced by worksheets; specific subjects such as history or geography are considered too difficult and replaced by integrated studies; option choices for 'O' level or CSE are delayed and assessment is minimised to avoid 'labelling'. All this contrasts with many schools elsewhere which remain subject oriented and gear their work to public examinations. The result is 'the children who need least help are given a few yards start and told to run straight. Their disadvantaged peers start later and run a zig-zag course'.

The damaging effects on teacher expectations of the 'watering down' of the curriculum, even in well-intentioned attempts at positive discrimination; in conjunction with the emphasis on the poor performance and the problems of children from ethnic minority backgrounds, may have nullified any positive effects of the additional resources made available to certain schools. This has important implications for both initial and in-service teacher-training.

In the last three sections in this chapter various small-scale initiatives that researchers have evaluated are described.

Nurture Groups
In the ILEA, nurture groups have been established in some primary schools or child guidance clinics to help nursery or infant-age children who are considered to be unable to meet the expectations or demands of school because of their disadvantaged home backgrounds. The nurture groups are intended for children 'who have not had the normal relationships and experiences of very early childhood and are emotionally and socially younger than their actual age' (Briault, 1976). In describing them Boxall (1976) states that the work of the nurture groups is 'based on the attachment of the child to the teacher and helper at an early level of dependency'. Because the children are assumed to lack supportive care and positive interaction with, in particular, their mothers, the nurture group aims to 'relive' early developmental experiences but in a more positive way than is presumed to have occurred before. The theory is that teacher and helper share early basic needs, feelings and experiences with the children, help them to explore the immediate world 'intuitively "letting go" a little at a time' as would a mother with her own child, helping the child to control infantile aggression and to develop their powers of waiting, sharing and toleration. The nurture group setting is deliberately domestic and the teachers and helpers take as their model the ('ideal') mother–child relationship. Children who are unresponsive, aggressive, anti-social or in other ways appear unable to participate in normal classroom life are selected by the school for attendance in the nurture group. Many of the children live under 'conditions of hardship and stress, in overburdened and fragmented families'.

Most groups take about twelve children at a time. Some contact with the mainstream of the school is retained to enable the child to re-enter the ordinary class, at a later date, and to establish rapport between nurture group staff and staff in the rest of the school.

Boxall emphasises the importance of physical contact. Children are given individual attention and their activities aided by a running commentary. Priority is given to controlling behaviour problems, desirable behaviour is praised, undesirable behaviour is as far as possible ignored. Food, which Boxall considers is 'fundamental in the mother–child relationship' and has 'special symbolic value' also plays a part in establishing teacher–child relationships in the nurture group and is used as a means of social training and, where necessary, as a form of social control.

An ordered routine, early intervention in potential disputes, distractions and talking about feelings of anger and aggression are among the strategies used by the staff. Boxall claims that the children become very dependent on the staff (the use of transitional objects is described) and there is obviously a danger that they may become overdependent. The children are sometimes taken to the teacher's or helper's home. Importance is attached to the constructive interactions between teacher and helper which are seen as a positive model for the child and, where possible, 'a peripheral man' (head teacher or caretaker) is introduced to the group. Schools vary in their policy of involving the parents. Some schools carry out home visits. Others have social evenings at school for parents and children.

Boxall claims that the staff know when the children are making progress because it is reflected in their more mature relationships with each other and the staff, they are more eager to please and 'not surprisingly, with this developing maturity, is a trend to a marked improvement in their academic work'.

As soon as they are deemed ready, children are placed in the normal class in the school for short, planned periods, although many still need the kind of help 'a supportive mother intuitively provides' when her child first starts school. Boxall claims that those involved in the project consider that 'growth can be initiated and maintained, and wellbeing fostered, in children whose life situation is difficult and, in many cases, appalling beyond belief.' A full-scale evaluation is planned.

This form of provision is expensive and is only likely to be available for a small percentage of children in relatively generous local authorities. Such costly provision is arguably justified, if in the long term it prevents children, who might otherwise grow up to be disturbed or delinquent, from doing so. However, such evidence is not likely to be forthcoming.

In addition to the high costs of nurture groups any provision which draws children out of the mainstream of schooling risks the children being labelled. There is a danger that difficult children will be shunted into the nurture group which will become a 'sin-bin' where the highly individual treatment and the extra attention which they receive will make it even harder for them to transfer back into the mainstream. They may become accustomed to the more attractive environment of the nurture group. They may fall behind their peers in terms of what they have learned. An alternative approach could be to employ teachers' aides in the classroom to provide support and help for children (and staff) as well as staff training in behaviour modification strategies along the lines developed by Berger, Yule and Wigley (1980) which might enable teacher and aide to cope with children needing extra help, but in the context of the classroom.

Parental Involvement
In the past fifteen years the belief has grown that children cannot be satisfactorily educated unless teachers enlist the co-operation of parents. There are several reasons for the developing emphasis on the importance of the parents' role in the education of their children. For example, the Playgroup Movement has demonstrated that a sizeable proportion of parents want to be involved in their children's education and have the initiative and skills to establish pre-school provision for under-fives. Indeed Holdsworth (1970), in a study of Devon playgroups, found that almost half the parents said they would not prefer a state nursery school to the playgroup, 'because parents are included in the playgroup'. As far as educational disadvantage is concerned, the widespread disillusionment with the effectiveness of schooling as a force for social change was undoubtedly an important factor in the growing emphasis on parental involvement.

The development of interest in parental involvement has been traced by Tizard *et al*. (1981) who suggest that the rise of environmental theories of intelligence and changing political and social beliefs were important influences. For example, various explanations were offered for the continuing under-achievement of children from the lower socio-economic groups despite post-war educational reform. Explanations such as working-class ignorance about education, lack of interest and inadequate mother–child communication emphasised the need for parental involvement in school. Thus, parental involvement was considered to be one way in which more equal educational opportunity might be achieved, by increasing parents' interest in, and knowledge of, education; by influencing mother–child interactions; by intervening in the early years of life; or by altering the relationship between schools and community. The expression of these beliefs coincided with the growth of the consumer-type pressure groups and movements, with increasing demand for accountability in other public spheres and, as already noted, the burgeoning parent-run playgroup movement. Several of these factors are noted by Blackstone (1979b) who presents three cases which have been used to justify parental involvement: citizenship, instrumentality and utility. The three justifications, not mutually exclusive, are that first, in a participatory democracy all members of the community have the right to some control over their social institutions; second, that parents themselves must be changed in order to meet their children's needs and, by implication, facilitate their children's achievement; and third, that parental involvement would make life 'easier and better' and create 'healthier social relationships' between parents and teachers.

The Plowden Committee considered that 'one of the essentials for educational advance is a closer partnership between the two parties to every child's education'. It suggested a programme for home–school contacts which included meetings with parents before children start school, individual consultations between teacher and parent, open days, written reports and special efforts to contact parents who do not visit the school. A further recommendation was that community schools should be tried out in educational priority areas since 'the gains that could be made in mutual understanding between teachers and parents through the work of a well-run community school in a priority area makes the scheme well worth trying'. In the years since the Committee's recommendations attempts to involve parents have been numerous and varied.

The EPA projects experimented with different ways of involving parents in their children's education described in detail in Halsey (1972) and in the individual Project Reports. The most ambitious undertaking in parental and community involvement in the EPA action research, the 'Red House' in the West Riding, has not been repeated elsewhere. The activities of the Red House included a pre-school group, discussion groups and classes for mothers, outings, children's and parent's parties, holiday play schemes, residential 'breaks' for children under stress and advice on welfare matters for families. However, several other ideas developed in the EPA projects have contributed to later attempts at parental involvement, for example the work at Belfield Community School (Garvey, 1975). Although most efforts to involve parents have probably been made by nursery teachers, Taylor, Exon and Holly (1972) found that they encouraged contact with parents mainly to keep informed about the child's background. In their study of 'good practice', Parry and Archer (1974) found that contacts with parents were used to seek assistance with fund-raising and to help parents understand the purpose of nursery education. In other words, as a form of parent education. Other reports of work carried out in parental involvement programmes emphasise the opportunities increased contacts give parents to discuss their 'problems' and the advisory role which staff can adopt. For example Halsey (1972), writing about the Red House, states 'sometimes the main need was the time and sympathy of another adult to listen to family or individual troubles' and Woodhead (1976) quotes a teacher who said 'parents need to be able to walk into the school and discuss any problem'. Both these approaches, however well-intentioned, present the parent as in some way inadequate, and make the Plowden 'partnership' harder to achieve. However, in their study Tizard *et al.* (1981) attempted to draw on parents' strengths and encourage their active contribution to their children's education. The researchers were interested in seeing what kinds of parental involvement were practicable, in monitoring the success of a programme and in studying any problems encountered. Extra resources were put into seven nursery schools and classes in order to increase parental involvement. In two of the schools the parents were predominantly indigenous working class; two schools were in largely immigrant areas, one Asian the other multi-racial.

In one school a group of parents were loaned a different commercially-produced activity pack each week for a term. The activities were carried out at home and the mothers met with the nursery teacher every fortnight to discuss the child's progress with the activities. In the multi-racial nursery it proved difficult to get mothers to come to the nursery to take part in a programme of activities. Yet it was considered that the mothers, from many different countries, had much to offer the school curriculum in a multi-racial, inner-city area. Several mothers were persuaded to write and illustrate a story, often about their own childhood. Most of the mothers preferred to do this in their own home with the encouragement of one of the research team. A photocopy of the completed 'book' was presented to the nursery class and formed part of the library (Sutton and Tizard, 1979). These two examples, of parents discussing their child's progress in joint activities with their child's teacher, or of contributing to the curriculum, were among the more successful interventions in the project. However, the study also highlighted gaps in communication between even the best intentioned staff and parents. In the course of the project the parents' take-up of the activities, and the teachers' and parents' attitudes to each other and to the activities provided, were investigated and an attempt made to analyse the resistance encountered. Whilst all the teachers considered that home was a much more important influence on the child than school, half of them thought that the parents made little contribution to their child's intellectual development because they did not spend enough time talking to, reading to or playing with them. The staff were keen to increase parental involvement, mainly so that parents would understand the aims of nursery education and because some of the teachers thought they would be able to influence the parents' child-rearing practices. However, the great majority of the parents did not see the nursery school as educational. Many Asian mothers were baffled by the purpose of the equipment, except for books, and few West Indian mothers appeared to know that the children were intended to learn from play materials. Indeed, a number raised strong objections to the use of sand, water and paint. The majority of parents saw their role, not in talking to and reading to their child, but in instilling good manners and discipline and helping with the 'three Rs'. Most parents were appreciative of the programme but the teachers' aims, to get parents to understand nursery education and to change what they did with the children at home, had only limited success. Although parents became well informed about *what* their children did, few understood *why* the activities were provided and how they were supposed to help the child. 'What the mothers saw were children filling bottles with water, not children acquiring the foundations of maths and science' (Tizard, 1978).

Other aspects of the project, such as developing the kind of two-way communication between parents and teachers which would enable parents to contribute to the school curriculum or to have a say in decision-making proved much harder to implement. One year after the intervention about half of the parents whose children were in infant school by then would have liked more involvement there. The authors of the study conclude that if parent involvement means frequent, friendly home–school contact and making school more open to parents, it is not difficult to achieve. If it means giving parents a real understanding of the education offered by the school, helping parents to contribute to it and exchanging information and opinions, then there are obstacles. These derive from lack of resources and time, and the lack of appropriate training and role definition for the teacher, the difficulties of communicating with parents from different cultures or different educational backgrounds whose values and attitudes may differ, teachers' and parents' belief in professionalism and parents' fear of offending teachers, who hold a 'hostage to fortune' in the form of their child.

It was noted in Chapter 2 that the research undertaken for the Plowden Committee found that a high proportion of parents of all socio-economic groups would have liked the school to have sent home work for the child to do at home but this was less likely to happen in the case of children from families in the lower socio-economic groups. One project has tried to reduce the possibility of future educational disadvantage by involving parents with teachers in assisting children's reading. The project by Tizard, Schofield and Hewison (1980) arose out of earlier work which found that, in working-class families, children whose mothers said they heard them read at home had markedly higher reading attainments at age seven and eight than children who were not heard read by their parents. This survey finding was not explicable on grounds of IQ, maternal language behaviour or any of the other aspects of upbringing style which were investigated. The possibility was therefore raised that parental involvement in the teaching of reading might have a beneficial effect on the reading attainment of seven- and eight-year-old children. The project was designed to explore this possibility and to develop parent–teacher collaboration. A cohort of children was studied in the final year of infant schooling and in the first year of junior schooling. The project was carried out in six multi-racial schools in the poorest part of a London Borough. The experiment involved teachers sending home reading material three or four times a week and the parents hearing the child read and recording this on a card sent from school.

Preliminary analysis suggests that in two multi-racial inner-city schools, which formed half of the experimental group in the project, parental involvement in the teaching of reading has led to a significant improvement in the children's reading attainments and that small group teaching by the reading specialist appeared to make little or no difference to the children's reading test success as compared to those of the two control schools.

At the conclusion of the organised parental involvement, there were no non-readers in the experimental class at either school, except for one child who was at the borderline. This was not the case for the parallel control classes in the same school; nor was it the case for classes at the other schools where the children had been given extra reading tuition in school. The authors draw six main conclusions from their study: first, in inner-city schools, it is feasible to involve nearly all parents in formal educational activities with infant and first-year junior children, even if some of the parents are non-literate, or even non-English-speaking. Secondly, the reading attainments of children who receive parental help are markedly better than those of comparable children who do not. Thirdly, most parents express great satisfaction at being involved in this way by schools, and the teachers report that the children show an increased keenness in learning in school. Fourthly, the teachers involved also report that they have found the experience worthwhile, and are continuing to involve parents in the teaching of reading, even though the project has ended. Fifthly, small-group instruction in reading given by a highly competent specialist teacher did not result in improvement in attainment comparable to that obtained from the help with reading at home. Sixthly, parental assistance was found to be particularly effective at raising the performance level of the weakest readers.

The success of this project may be related to the three components which Shipman considers to be of crucial importance in education for the inner-city child: specificity, continuity and accountability. The task that the parents undertook with the child was not removed from the usual school tasks but was an extension of one of them. It had clear, specific objectives and it was part of a continuous sequence of their child's learning. There was mutual accountability in that the teacher had to ensure that appropriate material was sent home and the parent had to record progress on a card which was returned to the school.

The majority of parents are interested in their child's education and the two studies discussed here suggest that many parents can be involved in educational activities with their children. There are, however, difficulties involved in promoting parent involvement, such as those already noted above by Tizard *et al.* (1981). Some of these problems might be overcome if teacher education included specific training for working with parents. Teachers' and parents' views of professionalism tend to prevent teachers from seeing what a valuable educational (as distinct from fund-raising) resource parents can be, and to inhibit parents from asserting their views. Newson and Newson (1977) and Blackstone (1979b) note, for example, what little use schools make of parents' work experience either as a contribution to a class topic at primary level, or as a form of career information at secondary level.

There is also a need for extra resources (including extra staff) which would, for example, enable teachers to make home visits or to work with parents in the community. A further possibility is the provision of home–school counsellors who would be relatively independent of the school. They would be in a position to ask for information about the child which would help the teacher, or they could show parents how to help the child with whatever skills he is being taught at school. Yet another alternative is the establishment of local educational 'shops' where curriculum materials could be demonstrated and information and advice given.

However, the key to successful and effective parent involvement remains the teachers. Both Smith (1975) and Halsey (1972) have noted how teacher support and commitment to the aims of an innovation is vital for it to be effective and, by implication, how the reverse can sabotage interventions. Many teachers find parents potentially threatening, both to their authority in what is often a relatively isolated situation and to their professional presige (see Sharp and Green, 1975). Better preparation in their training may be insufficient to overcome the resistance felt by some teachers. Goodacre (1970) found that the negative stereotypes held by some teachers towards parents were not carried over in their attitudes to the children. Goodacre attributed this to the greater knowledge and contact. If this is so then, as Blackstone suggests, increased contact with parents 'might break down stereotypes and enable more positive attitudes to develop'. At present the degree and kind of parental involvement undertaken is a matter of personal choice by the head and staff concerned. If a vigorous national policy of parental involvement were to be pursued it might be necessary to adopt the American strategy of earmarking funds specifically for parent involvement programmes. Although the element of coercion might prove counter-productive the increased contact and knowledge might convert more teachers to parent involvement.

Preparation in School for Employment

The relationship between education and employment and, in particular, the problem of unemployed school leavers is currently being studied in the EEC Transition to Work Project. The target population of the project is the group who, at the end of their full-time compulsory education 'have achieved minimal success as measured either by their preparedness for work or by the level of the school qualifications award' and who are likely to join the long-term unemployed, thus becoming not only educationally but socially disadvantaged (Little and Varlaam, 1980).

Projects in Sheffield, London and Bradford have three aims:
(i)   to improve the quality, style and relevance of provision for pupils nearing the end of secondary schooling
(ii)   to meet the needs of specific groups of pupils who are at risk of being unemployed.
(iii)   to establish closer links between the various agencies seeking to help young people make the transition from school to work.

The number of unemployed school leavers is rising rapidly. The unqualified, along with girls, ethnic minorities and the handicapped are the hardest hit.

The Projects try to offer a new approach to young people who will otherwise be 'at the bottom of the heap'. In many cases this means concentrating on basic skills. All the projects are also concerned with the development of social and life skills ('reasonable personal behaviour and adaptability') along the lines suggested by the Manpower Services Commission. There is also more emphasis on the 'world of work' than in most secondary curricula. The different forms this takes in the three project areas includes visits from outside agencies to the classroom, 'skill tasters' at further education colleges, visits to work sites and techniques of job application and interviews. 'Raising the horizons of both staff and pupils, through better knowledge of the local community and economy' is considered important in all the projects and to this end pupils have been taken on visits and 'encouraged to learn to use public transport to get around their city with ease'. Little's comment that 'Familiarity with only one or two bus routes can be a big hindrance to employability' is similar to views expressed by Bazalgette (1979) and Millham *et al*. (1978a) who make the point that in both London and Sunderland many of the young unemployed are unwilling to travel any distance to work in unfamiliar areas. The curriculum developments in the EEC Project are often accompanied by attempts to increase pupil motivation to learn by modifying the teaching process towards a less authoritarian, workshop approach. It is recognised that such changes do little to solve lack of certification so attempts are being made to alleviate this problem. Three basic strategies are employed. The first one is to raise the pupils' level of basic skills and motivation so that they have the chance to follow public examination courses or some form of vocational training later, although Little considers that because of their Project experience 'the *employability* of the Project leavers . . . will be enhanced even without certification'. The second strategy is to develop a Pupil Profile System 'to record initial aptitudes, attitudes, interests and difficulties and noting progress and change'. The third is to develop alternative means of assessment and certification. This may involve introducing options designed for slightly older pupils and more usually found in courses in further education rather than in schools (for example, some of the components of the City and Guilds courses in numeracy and communication skills). The project has negotiated validation by the City and Guilds Institute of a course comprising the level 1 course of the City and Guilds in conjunction with other units designed by the Project. The problems of the external credibility of both profile systems and new credentials, particularly with potential employers, are recognised. But since the young people would probably have otherwise left school with no credentials 'it is arguably better to leave with something meaningful to the pupil and his project Institution, however unfamiliar it may be to outsiders.'

Evaluation of the many local initiatives which have arisen from the EEC Project takes the form of a free flow of information between all project teams and small-scale evaluations of specific local projects. For example, in Sheffield pupils recently involved in the project are being interviewed about their post-school experience. In Bradford, in addition to project participants, a group who were not able to be included in the project are being treated as a control group and are being interviewed about their post-school work and educational experiences. In addition, 'contextual studies' of local labour markets are being undertaken in all three project areas. The follow-up studies and the labour-market studies are seen by Little as 'the crucial link between the two sides of the transition to work equation'.

Another curriculum development relevant to the educationally disadvantaged is the Ashridge/ILEA Project, which is funded partly by the ILEA and partly by the Manpower Services Commission (MSC). Its aim is to establish a model for developing curricula which are relevant to the needs of local labour markets and young people aged sixteen to eighteen who are poorly qualified and have low motivation, unrealistic job expectation, learning and other problems and are prone to long-term unemployment.

Results of previous MSC research into generic and transferable skills are used as a framework for obtaining job profiles which are relevant to three different local labour markets in London. The areas are Lewisham, Paddington and Putney. Job profiles are obtained by selecting a random sample of job vacancies registered at the Careers Service in these areas and analysing them in terms of generic and transferable skills. The job profiles are then translated into curricula for use by the teachers of the thirteen-week Youth Opportunities Programme entitled 'Introduction to Work'. These Programmes are available in a college in each of the three areas. The outcomes of the Project will be monitored by the MSC.

'Access' courses have been developed by some further education colleges to enable potential students without the conventional qualifications to reach an acceptable standard for the course they wish to pursue. In London two colleges have developed a course to help West Indian school leavers. The City and East London College and the Polytechnic of North London have combined to pilot an Access Course, which creates an alternative academic route for West Indian students who wish to become teachers. The students spend a year at the further education college on the preparatory BEd. course and then move on to the standard degree course at the Polytechnic. The preparatory year's study is accepted by the Polytechnic as an entry qualification instead of the conventional number of 'O' and 'A' level Certificates of Education. The pilot scheme will operate for three years and it is intended to extend the opportunity to other ethnic groups and possibly to indigenous groups. The scheme is similar to another access course offered by the same two colleges leading to a diploma in social work. It is claimed that over three years the results for the diploma indicate that students who came from the alternative access route did as well as those with conventional qualifications.

The scheme is seen by the colleges as one way of contributing to equal opportunity for disadvantaged groups by providing an alternative route for intending black teachers. There is also the hope that the provision of more black teachers will provide valuable models for school pupils in a multi-racial society.

Conclusion

This chapter has discussed a number of disparate initiatives. Some of these have yet to be evaluated, others have achieved only limited success. What they represent, however, are attempts by practitioners and researchers to overcome the usual barriers that exist to high attainment by the disadvantaged. In most cases the co-operation and support of teachers has been gained by the enthusiasm and commitment of the instigators. The possibility of the sabotaging of new initiatives, noted by Halsey, by teachers who do not understand or sympathise with the aims of the intervention, has not always been realised. Caution is needed however in evaluating the contribution of these interventions. There seems little doubt that many of the curriculum developments considered to be of potential benefit for disadvantaged pupils have resulted in 'two nations' within one school. But the problem of how to interest and motivate some groups of pupils taxes many teachers and is not solved by offering the traditional academic curriculum to all. It is argued by Smith (1979) that the basis of the present curriculum in the majority of secondary schools is historical rather than rational and that decisions affecting ways in which knowledge is classified into discrete subjects or in which certain knowledge is considered 'acceptable' are quite arbitrary. Smith supports Bernstein's (1971) contention that only rarely is the 'ultimate mystery of the subject' attained. This means that many are doomed to frustration, disappointment or to divisive dual curricula which contribute to the alienation of many, in particular the less able pupils. Smith also accepts Bruner's (1966) claim that most things can be taught to most pupils in a 'philosophically and conceptually coherent manner' and he argues that unless schools offer a broad common experience 'equality of opportunity is a meaningless phrase'. The *aims* of education should be the same for all pupils even if the *content* could not be the same for varied groups of pupils for 'unless we accept the fact that all children are entitled to the same broad types of experience and unless we try to develop in them all the same broad types of understanding, we are perpetuating a recipe for individual dissatisfaction and social unrest' (Smith).

Shipman's view, and that expressed in the HMI Primary Survey (DES, 1978d) is that there is a lack of sequence and continuity at all stages of learning (between subjects, between one school and the next and between schooling and education outside school). Further, Shipman argues, there is resistance to organising for continuity, exemplified in the reactions of some nursery teachers in the EPA projects to the use of the Peabody Language Development Kit. Citing from Tizard (1974) that there was no evidence of the long-term impact of pre-schooling, Shipman suggests that this is not surprising since there was no 'apparent commitment to using nursery schooling for systematically building a base for later attainment' (Shipman, 1980).

The initial success of some of the structured learning programmes such as the Follow Through Planned Variations Programme (Kennedy 1978), suggests the value of structure and organisation in both intervention programmes and mainsteam schooling rather than the inefficient 'ad hoc' approaches described by Hilsum and Cane (1971) and Taylor (1973).

A systematic approach to education is crucial for disadvantaged pupils who may find it harder to cope with 'discovery methods' that depend on the child 'being able to find the necessary human and material resources ... middle-class parents support child-centred schooling because they teach the basic skills at home' (Shipman). This is a view supported by Bernstein (1977) in his discussion of the 'invisible pedagogy' in infant schools, by Tizard (1976) in her plea for the development of a nursery curriculum, and by Sharp and Green (1975) in their study of an East End primary school.

To conclude, complex educational problems, many of which have their roots in social and economic problems, are unlikely to be solved by single solutions in the form of one-off small investment programmes. Sustained reinforcement is necessary. Specially designed programmes may be able to attain specific objectives but no programme is likely to have a deep and lasting impact if it is not a planned part of the mainstream of education.

Note

1 The eight criteria were: occupation; size of families; supplements in cash or kind from the State; overcrowding and sharing of homes; poor attendance and truancy; proportions of retarded, disturbed or handicapped pupils; incomplete families; and children unable to speak English.

5 Other Policies Designed to Alleviate Educational Disadvantage

This chapter is concerned with policies to alleviate educational disadvantage which have been implemented outside statutory school provision. The chapter is divided into three sections. In the first section one kind of family support for disadvantaged mothers and their pre-school children, including home-visiting, is discussed. Quite different kinds of family support in the form of financial benefits are dealt with in section two. The third section is concerned with policies for disadvantaged school leavers.

Home-Visiting Projects

Some researchers have suggested that much more could be done to help disadvantaged pre-school children if they, and their mothers, were taken out of their home environment and given an intensive parent education/child-stimulation programme. A small-scale British study and a more ambitious American project are described.

Evidence on the importance of the early years, including language and play, for children's subsequent development has already been noted. Once a child starts school he or she has to adapt to a school environment which assumes certain linguistic and cognitive skills. The child who has not acquired these skills, or who is unable to use them in the required way in school, is at a disadvantage. The most frequently used method for combating this disadvantage is to provide some form of pre-schooling. This gives the child the opportunity to be with other children and with trained adults who will guide their learning experience to a greater or lesser degree depending on the philosophy of the particular nursery.

Yet, as already stated, the results of nursery education have been mixed (see Tizard, 1974). Cognitive gains have not always been sustained and it has not always been easy or possible to involve parents in their child's nursery education. Parents of 'disadvantaged' children do not always see their role as educative and they may be hostile towards school. In an attempt to overcome some of these problems, to reach children at an early age and to build on learning at home, home-visiting projects have been developed. Studies in the USA by Gray and Klaus (1970), Gordon (1973) and Levenstein (1972) suggested that the strategy of developing the potential of the parent to educate their own pre-school child was a viable one. All three studies used professionals or para-professionals with the mother, exposing the child to cogni- tively or verbally stimulating play. Poulton and James (1975), in a review of fifteen educational home-visiting schemes, state that parents always welcomed the visitors and noticeable improvements in adult–child communication had taken place during the programme. They conclude that 'it has been possible for the visitors to demonstrate and articulate to parents that learning can take place in the home and involve those not able or willing to participate in a group.' Bronfen- brenner (1974), who has studied the findings of the major pre-school intervention studies, also concludes that home-visiting programmes 'are clearly impressive in terms of productiveness, permanence and practicability'. The Bullock Report (DES, 1975) recommended that 'authorities should introduce home visiting schemes to help the par- ents of pre-school children play an active part in the children's lan- guage growth'.

Two home-visiting projects are described here, the first arose out of the West Riding Educational Priority Area action research (Smith, 1975) and the second has been developed as part of community work in Deptford, in south-east London.

The West Riding Home–Visiting Project
The project had five basic assumptions:
1. It is possible in a non-school setting to change attitudinal factors in such a way that they foster school success.
2. The 'educational environment' which influences achievement includes the home, the school and the community.
3. The potential for change is greatest during the child's early years.
4. At this early stage mothers feel they play an important role in their children's lives and early intervention could help them sustain this role.
5. In a small, close-knit community, the influence of community norms or mothers' attitudes to education had to be accepted and built on rather than be rejected in favour of new, possibly conflict- ing, ideas.

The home-visiting project had four aims: to study the educational environment of the young child and the mother–child relationship; to study the child's stages of development in play and learning; to dis- cover with the mother any problems in the child's progress; to work out with the family and the community an acceptable programme to over- come the difficulties.

To avoid any families feeling neglected, the home-visiting programme was offered to every family in the catchment area of one school with children who met the age criterion. The programme ran for eleven months and dealt with twenty children aged between one-and-a-half and two-and-a-half years at the start of the project. Mothers were interviewed about their child's development and ability. Since attempts were to be made to assess the impact of the programme on the child's development, the home conditions and the mother–child relationships, an independent assessment was made by a psychologist and background information on parental occupation and on the age and number of siblings was collected. A control group of children matched for age, sex and father's occupation was drawn from a similar mining community. The children in the experimental group were visited every week and were presented with toys or games or puzzles to develop concepts and motor skills. They were also given books and sometimes a painting activity. The mothers were always encouraged to involve themselves in what their child did.

The results of the home-visiting programme were assessed in two ways. The first was to compare the pre- and post-test scores of the experimental and control group children on standardised tests. The second method was to compare the scores of both the groups on a 'home environment' rating scale which attempted to identify those aspects of the home which might relate to the child's development and which might be influenced by the programme. At the pre-test stage the two groups of children all had similar test scores but by the post-test stage the experimental group had higher scores equivalent to about four months in mental age. The gains in test scores were supported by informal observations that the experimental children were more constructive and logical in their play and more advanced in their speech. The 'home environment' measure included an assessment of the 'objective environment' (for example, the number of toys and books) and the relationship between mother and child (such as the forms of positive or negative reinforcement used). On most items on the 'objective environment' scale there were no differences between the two groups at the start of the project or at the end. By the post-test the differences in mother–child relationships favoured the experimental group with these mothers being less likely to use negative verbal or physical reinforcements. Both groups, however, used more such reinforcements at the post- than at the pre-test stage due, Smith suggests, to their children's increasing independence as they grew older which led to conflict with the mother.

This project appears to have been moderately successful in terms of test score gains. Moreover, it is likely that the families gained in other, less measurable, ways. One surprising finding was the little difference between the groups on the measure of books and toys, given that the experimental group had spent so much time using those items during the year and that, as part of the West Riding Project, a stall selling educational toys had been set up in the local market. Possibly some parents from the experimental group could not afford to buy them and Smith does not discuss the local library facilities. It is also possible that the mothers had become used to a passive role; while books and toys were delivered, like bottles of milk, to the house, they did not take the initiative to purchase them. It may be that the project's aspirations were too high: the effect of a weekly visit on deeply embedded community norms of child-rearing attitudes and practices could only at best be marginal.

The Deptford Educational Home–Visiting Project
The Deptford Educational Home–Visiting Project arose out of the Urban Aid programme which provided money for community projects and the ILEA's 'Education Service to the Whole Community', an attempt to extend the traditional role of education. Its aim was 'to develop what Halsey calls the 'teaching triangle' of parent, child and teacher' in the early learning years before the child started school (Jayne, 1976). It was hoped to develop the educational skills of parents who traditionally consider that education begins at school, to bring parents together in groups in the nursery school and, perhaps, to enable parents to become home visitors themselves.

It was decided to offer the visiting service to all the families within a small geographical area rather than to those described as 'disadvantaged'. This was to avoid the stigma of the label of 'bad parenting'. The area in fact had a high level of unemployment and social service needs, and was considered disadvantaged. The five Educational Health Visitors (EHVs) tried to establish a good relationship with both parent and child. They took books, toys, musical instruments and craft materials on their weekly visits and attempted to involve the mother in planning the session and in discussing how activities introduced during the play session could be developed in the following week. Jayne sees the project as offering a model of two-way adult–child communication since mothers, she claims, frequently 'underestimate their children's awareness and knowledge'. The local adult education institute provided courses and classes for the mothers' groups which formed during the course of the project and coffee mornings enabled the more socially isolated mothers to get out and meet others and provided opportunities for the children to mix.

When the EHV scheme was evaluated by the ILEA (Jayne, 1976

and 1977) the number of families being visited had dropped to fourteen, mainly due, it is claimed, to high mobility in an area of rehousing. The children were tested on the Pre-School English Picture Vocabulary Test (EPVT), parents were interviewed, informal assessments were made by the EHV of their 'degree of impact' on the mother–child interaction and teachers were asked to comment on the 'ease of adjustment' to school of the experimental group. Despite the very small numbers involved (fourteen EHV families and five control families) Jayne claims that the results of the parent interview show that visited mothers were more likely to prefer 'educational' play materials and were more likely to attach greater importance to the role they played in their child's education than the control group mothers. Similarly, more of the visited mothers thought that the home, or the home and the school together, played the major part in helping the child with certain learning activities. The home visitors' subjective assessments of the project impact were very favourable and all the visited children were considered by their teachers to have settled in easily and quickly at school. Once they reached the age of three all the visited children attended some form of pre-school provision and the author claims that the project increased parental awareness of what was available in the locality. A spin-off from the project was the links formed between the schools, their mothers' groups, local health centres and social security departments, and the adult education institute. In the later Research Report Jayne (1977) describes how the home-visiting project expanded to include more widespread group activities, to develop training schemes for volunteer visitors (some of them mothers who had formerly been visited themselves) and to deploy the expertise of the EHV more widely in neighbouring areas. Group activities which developed included mother and toddler clubs, coffee mornings, a toy library, classes, talks, a Christmas party and summer outings. Seven volunteer visitors started visiting families with the support of the professional EHVs and the heads of nursery schools involved in the project.

Both these home-visiting projects showed modest benefits to the children. There may well have been social benefits to the mothers, particularly those isolated in tower blocks, not only in the weekly visit but in the ensuing community activities which developed. However, home-visiting schemes are extremely costly in both financial and manpower terms and it hardly seems feasible to consider introducing such schemes on a national scale even for those families considered to be 'disadvantaged'. Furthermore they might then be stigmatised as 'bad parents'. Smith states how the parents in the West Riding Project were certainly interested in their child's education but tended to consider that education was the school's job and that if the child 'had it in him' he would succeed. They did not consider they had a role as educator. Perhaps this is where effort should be concentrated.

The importance of teacher commitment to changes in their relationship with parents and the implications for the role of teachers and for their perception of professional status have been noted in the preceding chapter. Another approach would be to teach child development to *all* pupils in secondary schools as a matter of course. The developmental landmarks and the accompanying needs of young children are rarely taught in a school 'child development' course. If it *is* part of the curriculum, it will usually be offered to pupils considered to be 'less able', and probably to girls rather than to pupils of both sexes. However it could be argued that for the majority of pupils child-rearing will still be so remote that such courses would make little impression. An additional problem is that of finding the time for it. As well as the traditional subjects there are now pressures for so many areas to be covered in the syllabus. For example, with courses on employment, leisure, health and citizenship there is a danger of 'curriculum-overload'. Yet another approach which avoids expensive, individual home-visiting might be 'drop-in centres' or one-o'clock clubs attached to baby clinics. Advice on physical child care in the clinics could be supplemented by advice and discussion on developmental needs in the drop-in centre. The two Open University Courses 'The First Years of Life' and 'The Pre-School Child' could possibly be used in such settings.

None of these measures would have the intensive, one-to-one attention that individual home-visiting schemes offer and it is likely that some mothers who are willing to be visited at home would be unwilling or unable to go with their child to a centre. However, more prospective parents and more disadvantaged mothers and children might be reached in this way.

In some inner-city areas the smaller numbers of children resulting from out-migration and the declining birth rate have enabled schools to admit children before they are five years old. Some of these areas have also benefited from increased nursery provision under various urban or inner-city programmes. This has sometimes resulted in fewer children using the local voluntary pre-school playgroups. In such cases some playgroups have extended their functions to provide drop-in centres for mothers with younger children, and mother and toddler clubs. This might be encouraged further.

The Milwaukee Project
The modest short-term gains achieved in many pre-school projects

raises the question of whether programmes started earlier, for a longer period of time, and attempting direct explicit teaching of mothers and manipulation of the whole environment of the child would be more effective. One such 'ecological' experiment is the Milwaukee Project (Heber and Garber, 1975), The longitudinal study was designed to see whether cultural, familial or socio-cultural mental retardation could be prevented by a programme of family intervention from early infancy. The project worked with two groups of twenty children of black, low IQ mothers, who lived in Milwaukee. The children were divided into an experimental and a control group. The experimental group received a two-part programme from the time the child was three or four months old until they started school. The children were collected five days a week and taken to an Education Centre where they received an individual intensive language and sensory-motor stimulation programme designed 'so that the children were exposed to the widest range of experiences' (Heber, et al. 1972). The centre had a sufficiently high teacher–child ratio to enable each child to be assigned the same teacher until they were twelve to fifteen months old, when they were gradually paired with other teachers and children. Each teacher was responsible for the total care of the infant and followed the individually adapted programme of activities. The teacher also established rapport with the child's mother.

The mother's programme was designed to prepare them for employment and to increase their home-making and child-rearing skills. They took part in vocational and home economics classes and were taught basic reading, writing and arithmetic. Job training was carried out in two large nursing homes which provided a suitably rehabilitative environment and job opportunities. Group counselling sessions took place daily. The job training programme was considered a success but some major problems in the care and treatment of children and in the home-making skills remained with a few families so the emphasis moved to more training in these areas.

Repeated measures were taken of the progress of both the control and the experimental children. Up until the children were aged two these were mainly developmental scales, after that learning and performance were measured. When the children were six years old the mean difference points between the two groups on two measures of IQ was over 30 IQ points. The majority of the controls scored below 90. Similar differences were found on tests of language usage. The gains of the experimental group were not only in performance on IQ tests, but were evident in their language ability, in social behaviour and in adjustment to school.

Heber and Garber explain the differences between the two groups in terms of their different learning environments. They maintain that children's desire to learn may be 'dampened or shut down by negative learning experiences' in the 'restricted learning environment created for him in early life by a mother who is incapable of providing otherwise' and that this will hinder the chance of success at school. The authors contend that 'the mitigation of the environmental influences for which cultural–familial retardation is a consequence can be accomplished if help is given to that large population of mothers who are unaware of the critical nature of early childhood.'

Heber does raise the question of whether the IQ gains of the experimental group may have resulted from training relevant to the tests and the possibility that the group may have reached certain developmental stages earlier than usual. But what *is* significant is the differential performance between the two groups. Clarke and Clarke (1974) point out that whether or not the gains are maintained will depend on the child's experience of primary schooling. They consider that the differences in life style of the two groups would need to be maintained and that if the experimental group 'were to revert to control conditions, remaining in these until early adulthood, it would be our assumption that there would be little or no difference between these groups at the age of, say, 20.' In fact, those children for whom the programme ceased when they reached school age did show a relative decline in their IQ scores although they were still above average and the gap between them and the control group remained about the same. Clarke and Clarke suggest that 'far larger intervention, perhaps twelve to fifteen years, is necessary to establish any permanent development change.'

Garber and Heber (1978, cited in Clarke 1981) have followed the two groups of children for four years since the end of the intervention. Although the gap between the two groups had narrowed, the experimental group still had on average a 20 IQ point advantage and remained above the national average. However, on scholastic achievement tests the performance of the experimental group, whilst remaining above the control group, declined first to the level of the city of Milwaukee and then to the level of Milwaukee inner-city schools. Clarke also points out that Craig Ramey (1979) achieved much smaller IQ differences in his similar long-term intervention programme.

It would appear that one reason for the success of the Milwaukee Project was the amount of time children spent in the Education Centre away from their own home (seven hours a day, for five days a week), yet in such a 'total' situation that it must have been, as Tizard, Moss and Perry (1976) point out, a 'second home' to them. The Milwaukee approach is obviously an expensive policy to pursue. Moreover, gains may decline without similar improvements in school and the general environment. However, Smith and James (1975) suggest that the social and economic changes required to alter the ecology of poor areas may, in the long term, 'prove an easier and less costly alternative to the increasingly elaborate attempts to compensate the child for, or even remove him altogether from, his environment.'

Bronfenbrenner (1974) concludes that programmes which involve parents have a more positive outcome. He calls for ecological intervention which would attempt to improve all aspects of the living conditions of disadvantaged families to enable them to care for their children, which would involve adequate health care, housing and employment.

In a much smaller project, carried out by Athey at the Froebel Educational Institute, twenty pre-school children and their mothers were brought to the Institute's nursery for three hours a day for 340 days over a period of two years. The project aimed at 'describing, documenting, summarising, finding commonalities and continuities' (Athey, 1980). Eight of the twenty families were non-indigenous. There was a comparison group of twenty families whose children attended the fee-paying Froebel Kindergarten. The two groups 'came from opposite ends of the socio-economic scale'. Both groups were given language and intelligence tests at home before the programme started.

The project families, usually the mothers, participated in the children's play and activities and went on frequent outings. They were, Athey says, 'drawn into an ongoing dialectic of what their children were doing and the possible significance of the behaviour'. Athey does not give the results of the pre-test but writes that 'during the project the children from the low socio-economic group made outstanding gains' on standardised tests and the gains were maintained over two years in primary school. Older siblings were also tested and at the end of the project. The project group were 20 IQ points ahead of older siblings, six months ahead of their chronological age in reading accuracy and three months ahead in comprehension tests. The comparison group made no significant gains except on the English Picture Vocabulary Test.

Unfortunately, as Athey admits, there is no way of knowing which aspects of the programme brought about the gains but the fact that 'the parents were involved in the process of observing and supporting' their children's patterns of behaviour is considered central to its success. Athey considers that the nursery curriculum needs to move from what she terms 'arbitrary content-centred provision' as for example when the teacher decides what 'topic' will be covered next without reference to the children's spontaneous interests, to provision based on children's concerns which could be discussed with, and then extended by, the parents.

Financial Measures

Financial measures in the education sector which aim to help disadvantaged families include uniform grants, the provision of free milk and meals, and education maintenance allowances. This section will describe the various forms of financial support and attempt to assess to what extent they have been successful in alleviating educational disadvantage.

Uniform grants

Although local authorities have the power, under the 1944 Education Act, to pay school uniform grants for children in their secondary schools, there is no information on the overall numbers of children in the country who receive such grants. Townsend (1979) obtained some information from his poverty survey and the Child Poverty Action Group (CPAG) collected data from thirty-five areas (Tunnard, 1977). Townsend found that about a third of children in poor households and about two-thirds of children in relatively prosperous households attended primary or secondary schools which had a uniform. Among families whose secondary-school children were expected to wear uniform only 1 per cent had received a uniform grant in the previous year, half of them were given the grant by the local authority and half by the Supplementary Benefits Commission. Among parents with incomes below the poverty line 76 per cent of those with children at secondary schools which required pupils to wear uniform had never heard of uniform grants. Townsend concludes that 'there is no evidence then that local authorities have even begun to provide the service envisaged in the Education Act, 1944'.

The CPAG Survey of uniform grants found considerable variation between local authorities in the amount given. Many families on the official poverty line, on supplementary benefits, or low income families with several children, did not qualify for grants. No authority in their survey used direct cash payments. Instead vouchers stating the amount of the grant and the items for which they could be exchanged, were issued and were accepted by specific, named shops. The parent selected the clothes and the local authority paid the shops. Tunnard points out one advantage of the voucher system is that, where it is earmarked for a specific item rather than a specific amount, it adjusts automatically to increased prices. However, not surprisingly, 'this public branding of the poor' (Tunnard) created feelings of humiliation and frustration on the part of parents who complained that because only named shops could be used, delays occurred (when the needed item was out of stock in the shops) and the money was sometimes wasted in stores not offering the best value. Uniform grants rarely covered more than half the cost of specified uniforms, and often far less. When the CPAG carried out their survey in 1977 eight out of the thirty-five local authorities were already reducing uniform grants, or cutting them out altogether. Further cuts in expenditure are likely to lead to more authorities abandoning them.

CPAG have proposed that a national scheme of cash grants of £60 (1977 value) for uniform and sports kit be introduced and that those who qualify for free school meals should automatically qualify for a uniform grant. Tunnard links the provision of uniform grants to other discretionary awards, such as educational maintenance allowances (see below) and recommends that the provision of such grants be made legally binding upon the local authorities.

Some parents in the CPAG survey said their children refused to wear second-hand or jumble sale clothes and that this caused friction between parents and teenagers. Some schools do organise uniform sales where outgrown articles of uniform are offered for sale; if this was more widespread and frequent it might reduce the stigma felt by some pupils and parents at having to resort to second-hand clothes. Alternatively, school uniforms could be abolished altogether in the two-thirds or so of schools which still demand them.

Those in favour of uniform argue that it contributes to the corporate identity of the school, it is practical, avoids 'unsuitable' clothes being worn to school and helps to reduce disparities between children whose families are financially well-off and those who are less fortunate. Those who oppose the wearing of uniform point to the financial hardship it can create (since only the poorest of the poor qualify for grant aid), to the inessential items which may be included and to the inflated prices charged by retailers who have a monopoly for supplying specific schools. A great deal of wasted energy is also spent by teachers enforcing the rules about uniform. If the battle for abolition is lost it should be possible to limit both the number of items and their style and colour and for these to be sold in chain-stores. Many of these stores do sell standard school clothing but children whose school demands more subtle shades or more unusual colours or designs have to pay the often higher prices of a named supplier.

School milk and meals
The 1944 Education Act imposed upon local authorities the duty of providing milk and meals for pupils attending state schools. The Milk and Meals Regulations under Section 49 stated that the authorities should provide 'a meal suitable in all respects as the main meal of the day' and specific nutritional standards were recommended. The Education (Milk) Act 1971 reduced the provision by stating that the law

did not 'require an LEA to provide milk after the summer term after a child was 7, unless in special schools or requested on medical grounds'. Unlike milk, school meals have been paid for by parents although often at a highly subsidised price and always with the possibility of completely free provision according to need. In May 1978, of the 4,870,000 children taking school meals (62.3 per cent of all school children in England) 23 per cent (1,151,000) claimed free meals. To meet the criteria for claiming free meals their parents had to be claiming supplementary benefits, family income supplement or earning below a certain level.

The provision of free school meals to children whose family income falls below a minimum level is intended to ensure that such children receive a nutritionally balanced hot daily meal. The non-take-up of means-tested benefits is well documented by the CPAG (1974) and the Supplementary Benefits Commission (1975). Townsend estimated that 400,000 children were eligible for, but not receiving, free school meals in 1976, either through lack of take-up, or lack of provision. Calculations for 1978 raised the figure to 460,000 (Walker, 1980). Expenditure cuts by some local authorities have reduced the eligibility criteria which will exclude many of those previously able to claim. Townsend found that overall about 70 per cent of school children had meals at school. Among the poorest households in his survey the proportion rose to 85 per cent, of whom two-thirds did not pay for them. He estimated that 15 per cent of children in the poorest households and 24 per cent of all children in or on the margin of poverty did not have meals at school, although many of them would have qualified for free meals. Townsend admits that some of the families lived in areas where the schools lacked the necessary facilities and some parents preferred the children to go home, if for example, a meal was cooked anyway for younger siblings, but 'there is no doubt some would get meals at school if it were an automatic right'. When parents of the 30 per cent of children not having school meals were asked the reason why, just over one-third of them replied that their children did not like the food and 7 per cent said the children did not get enough to eat in a school meal. However, the data were dependent on information gathered from the parents not the children, and the numbers in this group in the sample were small.

The Education Act of 1980 changed the law so that Authorities are now given discretion as to what is to be provided, although free meals still have to be provided for children whose families are in receipt of supplementary benefits or Family Income Supplement. Regulations making it the duty of local authorities to provide meals suitable as 'the main meal of the day' and milk for certain categories of pupils are discontinued.

In attempts to reduce costs and wastage at a time of government expenditure cuts many local authorities are abandoning the mid-day hot meal in favour of a cafeteria system. This may or may not be a good thing. Pupils will have more choice than formerly but they may not have such a balanced diet. More important, the rising cost to parents of the school meals (from £1.25 per week to £2.50 in many local authorities) means that fewer children are taking them. Local education authorities can provide meals of whatever nutritional standards they think fit and charge whatever price they like for them.

Walker (1980) cites evidence from two studies which suggest that 'free school meals may be a much more important benefit to the poor than one might suppose in a society where undernutrition is no longer a very obvious problem'. In the first study Rona, Chinn and Smith (1979) analysed the height of 10,000 primary-school children from twenty-eight areas in England and Scotland in 1973. The found that children receiving free school meals were significantly shorter than children who had subsidised school meals or packed lunches. These findings were supported by the second study cited by Walker in which Baker et al. (1979) presented evidence from a study of 900 eight year olds in South Wales which indicated that free meals were provided most often to shorter children. Both studies were set up and funded by the DHSS sub-committee on Nutritional Surveillance to monitor the effects of the withdrawal of school milk for seven to eleven year olds after the 1971 Act. What this evidence confirms is that poor children are still of smaller stature than their peers. If this difference is to be eliminated in the long term, then diets must be improved among the poor. The more stringent criteria of eligibility for free school meals reduces the likelihood of this happening, since there is evidence that, for many poorer children, the school meal represents the main meal of the day. But, as Walker points out, 'the low paid also more often have children with an additional problem – obesity'. Where local authorities choose to provide meals either at prohibitive cost or with reduced nutritional, but increased carbohydrate value, this problem will be exacerbated. Walker suggests that as the DHSS agreed to evaluate the withdrawal of one-third of a pint of milk, approximately 120 calories, 'they should certainly evaluate the potential withdrawal of 880 calories worth of dinner'.

Educational Maintenance Allowances (EMAs)

Regulations under Section 81 of the 1944 Education Act give local authorities the power to pay allowances to low-income parents to ease the financial burden of their children staying on beyond the statutory school-leaving age. Payments are at the discretion of the local authority and vary considerably both in number of grants made and their financial worth. According to a survey in 1976, quoted by Shirley Williams (1980a) the average annual EMA was about £130. No local authority makes generous provision and, as Townsend points out, anomalies and inconsistencies exist. For example, in some areas parents with a seventeen-year-old son or daughter who do not qualify for an EMA may find that in the following year, with the same income, they qualify for a maximum grant (£1,245 in 1979/80) for students in higher education living away from home other than in London. Yet, EMAs were designed with the specific aim of helping poor parents to keep their children at school, so that, presumably, some of them would have the opportunity to qualify for entry to higher education, with its relatively generous mandatory awards. A further anomaly is that whilst parents in receipt of supplementary benefit may, in some local authorities, automatically qualify for EMAs, employed parents with the same net income do not.

More than twenty years ago education maintenance grants were the subject of a government enquiry, the Weaver Report (Ministry of Education, 1957). The Report examined the costs borne by parents and recommended that EMAs be high enough to cover the cost of the pupil's food, clothing, holidays and spending money and for heating and lighting a study bedroom. It was suggested that the grant be divided between pupil and parents, that it be paid in advance and that EMAs should be advertised during the pupil's fourth year at school and by local press and radio before the beginning of each new school year. The Report also suggested that the grant be one-and-a-half times the supplementary benefit for an adult. Tunnard calculated that, in 1977, that would give a weekly grant of about £18 and by today's level it would be about £27 per week. The recommendations of the Weaver Report were not implemented. But in 1974 the Parliamentary Expenditure Committee took up the issue again. Its report stated 'the years from 16 to 18 are the bridge between compulsory school and preparation for a career. It is an excellent national investment to ensure that all with the will to cross that bridge should be able to do so.' The Report supported the Weaver Report which saw the purpose of EMAs 'to enable pupils to take advantage, without hardship to themselves or their parents, of any educational facilities open to them' (DES, 1976d).

However, some of the groups who gave evidence to the Expenditure Committee did not accept the Weaver philosophy. The National Union of Teachers (NUT) and the National Union of School Students (NUSS) argued (the former with reservations) that the relationship between sixteen to eighteen year olds and their parents had changed between the late 1950s and the early 1970s, that young people were more ready to handle their own affairs and that EMAs should be considered as a means of the young people maintaining themselves. In a memorandum to the Report the NUT argued that parents should no longer have to make sacrifices for their children's education and, whatever their financial circumstances, should be reimbursed for maintaining their children at school after the statutory age. In addition to a mandatory EMA 'without consideration of parental means' the NUT suggested a further discretionary element 'so that an additional award may be made by the authority in cases of severe financial hardship' and that this would be facilitated by adjustments to the Rate Support Grant in areas where the demand was high.

If this suggestion by the NUT were to be implemented it would entail a direct redistribution away from the disadvantaged. The financial costs would be enormous and would benefit the advantaged groups whose children, in any case, stay on at school.

The 1974 Expenditure Committee Report cited figures from 1971, the latest date for which they were available. In that year 28,080 pupils in England and Wales were receiving EMAs at a cost of £1.5 million a year. The grants were worth on average £72 per year, an amount so negligible as to be hardly worth applying for. It recommended that all existing educational allowances should be incorporated into one educational maintenance allowance which should be mandatory and paid by local authorities to families in need who fulfilled the criteria for free school meals. The grant should be graduated according to income, re-calculated each year and paid in a lump sum, part to the parents and part to the pupil. It was considered that pupils and parents should be told about EMAs during the pupils' fourth year in secondary school, that applications should be treated in confidence, that the award of an EMA should not depend on the level of achievement but that every school should have 'the right to exclude a voluntary pupil on the grounds of lack of effort'. Finally EMAs should not be considered as a substitute wage and 'nothing we recommend should undermine the responsibility of parents for bringing up their children'.

The Secretary of State, Fred Mulley, responded to the Report in 1976 saying that no immediate action was contemplated (DES, 1976e). He stated that the Government was still studying the problem and that a prime consideration was that the maintenance of boys or girls under nineteen in full-time education and living with their family 'is part of the maintenance of the family as a whole, for which public support, if it is needed, is given through the social security system'. In other words, the responsibility should lie with the DHSS, not the DES. However, Tunnard maintains that in the Annual Report of the Supplementary Benefits Commission for 1975, the Commission 'was making clear declarations that it did not intend to remedy the defects of other government departments, including the one responsible for education'.

In November 1978 the subsequent Secretary of State, Shirley Williams, announced a £10 million pilot scheme of nationally financed EMAs. It was intended to cover 15 per cent of the relevant age groups in fifteen to twenty authorities which had high unemployment rates, low staying-on rates and a large proportion of disadvantaged families. The maximum grant was likely to have been £7.50 a week which, with the £4 child benefit allowance, would have provided £11.50. This was comparable to the £11 paid to sixteen and seventeen year olds on Supplementary Benefit. Similar schemes had been introduced in September 1978 by Wakefield, Sheffield, Newcastle-on-Tyne, Sunderland and the ILEA. These five local authorities offered a means-tested benefit of £7–£7.50 to sixteen to eighteen year olds. Maclure (1979) states that the cost of implementing the means-tested EMA pilot scheme nationally would be in the region of £110 million a year for England and Wales. At a NUT Conference in June 1978 Shirley Williams said the proposal for the pilot scheme had met with 'an enthusiastic welcome', from the Council of Local Education Authorities (DES, 1978b). But with the change of government in 1979 the plan was abandoned, so that 'we will not, therefore, know how many boys or girls capable of more advanced education have been precluded by financial considerations, but the figure almost certainly runs into tens of thousands' (Williams, 1980a).

A number of studies have demonstrated the inadequacy of the present system. Townsend, drawing on the same survey as the Expenditure Committee, showed the wide variation in the size of the grants, and in the proportion of pupils receiving them. The amount ranged from £123 p.a. in East Sussex to £18 in Burton-on-Trent. Grants were received by 16.6 per cent of all pupils over school-leaving age in West Suffolk and by 0.4 per cent in Reading. In some authorities (for example Harrow) several pupils received a small amount. In 1975 the ILEA paid a maximum of £192 a year to a family with one child whose net income was £15.50 a week, or less (Stone and Taylor, 1976).

The Child Poverty Action Group carried out a survey in eighteen areas during 1976/77. They found that 'provision was as varied as it was meagre, and light years short of the suggestions put forward 20 years ago' by Weaver (Tunnard, 1977). The grants were poorly advertised to pupils. One authority gave out leaflets five years too early when children left primary school. Another gave out leaflets '(a) if they remembered and (b) if they could get copies'. No authority used local press or radio to advertise EMAs. Some authorities did not have a joint claim form for EMAs and other education welfare benefits, but used separate forms which, in some areas, had to be completed anew each term. The experimental use of a multi-purpose claim form for benefits in an area of Liverpool resulted in a 25 per cent increase in the take-up of EMAs.

It is hardly surprising then that Townsend found extensive lack of knowledge of the existence of EMAs. Only 15 per cent of parents of fourteen year olds and only 30 per cent of parents of sixteen to eighteen year olds had heard of them. Only 2 per cent of the latter group had applied successfully for a grant and almost 2 per cent had applied but had not been successful. Townsend states that 'as many as 80 per cent of parents of children of this age in the sample who were living in households in poverty or on the margins of poverty had not heard of educational maintenance allowances and another 18 per cent had not applied. This compared with 6 per cent and 32 per cent respectively in households with higher incomes.' The CPAG also found that the stringent financial qualifications meant that only the 'poorest of the poor' qualified; that no local authorities normally paid the allowance before term started when it was needed to buy clothes and materials and some did not pay out until towards the end of term; and that only three out of the eighteen authorities made any payment direct to the pupil. In short there is 'a haphazard and discriminatory system of financial support for 16 to 19 year olds' (NUT, 1979).

Some of those advocating reform have stressed the need to increase incentives to stay on at school. At present there is little financial incentive, other than the long-term one of higher earnings later, to stay on and work for the qualifications to enter higher education. The financial independence that a job offers is attractive to many young people. Moreover, the fact that the unemployed sixteen year old can obtain supplementary benefit or financial support from the Manpower Services Commissions (MSC) Special Programmes is thought to be a further disincentive to stay at school (NUT, 1979, Tunnard, 1977, Maclure, 1979). Maclure argues that EMAs are needed because it is socially and economically desirable to encourage young people to stay on in full-time education to improve their skills and qualifications. If financial support is provided for school leavers, then financial support most also be provided for those who stay on in full-time education, for 'it must be against public policy to create a powerful disincentive to continued education'.

However many of those benefiting from the MSC Youth Opportunities Programme or Supplementary Benefits are just those young people who are least likely to stay in full-time education. Even with a widespread and more generous system of EMAs there would probably still be a high proportion of poorly qualified school leavers who did not want any more education and for whom the EMA would not provide an incentive to stay on at school. Some research has been done which throws a little light on how far EMAs would provide an adequate incentive.

Gordon (1980) carried out a postal survey of 1500 young people after one year of post-compulsory education or one year of work experience, as a follow-up to an earlier survey carried out on 3000 fifth-formers which had touched on the potential impact of EMAs (Fulton and Gordon, 1979). Information was collected on examination results and destinations of pupils at sixteen, as well as information from parents on income and family size. Young people who had left school at the end of the fifth form were asked whether they would have stayed on if grant aid had been available for them personally, or for their parents, for each week they remained in full-time education and what amount would have been considered a sufficient incentive to stay on. Gordon found that a year after leaving school 56 per cent of the school leavers said they might or probably would have stayed on with an EMA paid to themselves and 50 per cent if it were paid to their parents. The amount of money seemed to be more important than who received it. One-quarter of the boys and almost one-third of the girls said they regretted leaving school at the end of the fifth year and showed great interest in continuing their education with the aid of a grant. There was not a close relationship between current earnings, attitude towards staying on and the amount of financial incentive needed. However, those who would have considered staying on with the help of an EMA were much more likely to have some GCE or CSE passes and, Gordon considers, would probably have added to these or pursued 'A' level courses.

Too much weight cannot be attached to Gordon's evidence since it is hypothetical data based on young people's retrospective view about what might have been and there were also various biases in the sample. The responses are likely to be considerably affected by the young people's experience of work and their level of job satisfaction.

In 1980 the Government introduced new regulations governing eligibility for supplementary benefit for sixteen-year-old school leavers. Whereas previously young people leaving school at the end of the summer term, who were unemployed, were entitled to draw benefit straight away, they now have to wait until the end of the school summer holidays. If, on the other hand, they are old enough to leave school early, and choose to do so, at the end of the Easter term, they are then entitled to supplementary benefit approximately five months sooner than their peers who stay on for the examination term. This change in policy, which has been strongly criticised by teachers, particularly in areas of high unemployment, is likely to encourage children from poorer families to leave school without taking external examinations.

In summary, to what extent can these financial measures be said to have helped the disadvantaged? There is no up-to-date national picture of the provision and take-up of uniform grants, but from the evidence available their contribution is negligible. Only the very poor are eligible and many of those who are do not know about the grants or do not apply for them. There is wide variation between local authorities both in the amounts given and the proportion of the population receiving them. In some areas it is hardly worth the bother of claiming the grants. Scant as the provision is, it is being eroded even further by cuts in local authority expenditure. The suggestion by CPAG that cash grants (£60 in 1977) of a reasonable amount be made mandatory and that application and eligibility be linked to the benefits would go some way to improving the situation. But, ironically, poor pupils attending the one-third of secondary schools which do not have, or do not enforce, the wearing of uniform would be further disadvantaged since they would not be eligible for uniform grants. This problem would be avoided if the extra payment were called a clothing grant, which would automatically be paid to those who, for example, qualified for free school meals.

The supply of free milk to school children of all ages, and the provision of a nutritious hot mid-day meal, available free to those children whose families met the relatively generous criteria of need, undoubtedly benefited many of the disadvantaged. Unfortunately since 1971 this benefit has been systematically eroded. Now, fewer authorities are providing free milk even for infant age children, and in many authorities the criteria for free meals are more stringent. Under the new Education Act no local authority has any legal compulsion to provide free school milk. The DES estimates that under half the local authorities in England still provide milk for the under-sevens *and* those with medical and special education needs, whilst about half make provision for medical and special education cases only. The relatively generous income-related scales (1971) for free meals have been abolished. In many local authorities the introduction of cafeterias may reduce the nutritional value whilst increasing the carbohydrate content of what children choose to eat, thus enhancing the likelihood of obesity and tooth decay.

Many of the criticisms of uniform grants also apply to EMAs. The amounts vary and are usually so small as to be almost negligible. They are not well publicised and their provision is hedged about with inconsistencies and anomalies. Of those knowledgeable and persistent enough to apply only the poorest qualify for the grant. Educational maintenance allowances can hardly be said to have contributed greatly to the reduction of inequality or disadvantage for an age group where peer pressures and commercial exploitation of peer group tastes are strong. Moreover, those young people who do stay on at school into the sixth form have approximately three times more spent on them than the average pupil below sixteen. The scale of the aid EMAs offers to the disadvantaged becomes derisory when viewed in relation to the scheme of the present Conservative Government to spend £3 million increasing to £12 million on the assisted places scheme for which parents earning less than £11,000 p.a. will be eligible. In addition to financial assistance towards the school fees, grants will be available for uniform, travel and meals. The uniform grant of up to £80 in the first year for pupils taking up assisted places is considerably more than that paid by many local authorities.

Lister (1980) has estimated that under the revised income scale a family with two children and an income of £9,600 a year (approximately £192 per week) in 1980/81 could, in 1981/2, send the children to an independent school charging £1,500 per pupil and receive a government subsidy of £1,740 towards the total cost of £3,000 p.a. In effect this would mean that the family received a subsidy of around £35 a week towards the total cost of fees of around £60 a week. This 'generous definition of need' contrasts starkly with the change in the definition of need in order to qualify for, for example, free school meals, since the actual right to free school meals is now confined to those on Family Income Supplement or Supplementary Benefit. Thus, a two-child family earning £3,835 a year or more (approximately £76 a week) does not qualify for free meals.

Policies Designed to Help Disadvantaged School Leavers
This section examines educational policies designed to help those who are disadvantaged because they have experienced, or are likely to experience difficulty in obtaining employment when they complete their statutory schooling. In many but by no means all cases the young people will be poorly qualified. The different policy initiatives are described along with any evaluations which have been carried out.

By June 1981 unemployment in Britain totalled almost 2.7 million. This is the highest level since the war and if the present trend continues the figure may reach 3 million or even more by the end of the year. The impact of unemployment has been uneven. There are differences between regions and between age groups. Unemployment has increased on a national scale from 2.1 per cent in 1973 to 10.4 per cent at the present time. The rate of increase has accelerated over the past year. From October 1979 to October 1980 the figure rose from 5.3 per cent to 7.8 per cent. The worst hit regions have been the North West, the Midlands, Wales and Northern Ireland. For every 1 per cent increase in adult unemployment there is a 1.7 per cent increase in unemployment among young people. During the 1970s unemployment among the under-twenties went up more than for any other age group.

In January 1971 there were 33,000 young people aged sixteen to nineteen on the unemployment register who had been out of work for six weeks or more. In January 1977 the figure had risen to 177,000. By January 1980 the figure was 216,000 although only 160,000 were registered as unemployed. The rest were on MSC special programmes (see pp. 164–70). By January 1981 the figure had risen to 262,000. Ball (1980) estimates that the numbers of sixteen to nineteen year olds who will be unemployed for six weeks or more may rise to 490,000 by January 1982 and to 570,000 by January 1983. Again national figures mask regional differences and differences between social groups. Long-term unemployment is a more acute problem on Merseyside, where 10 per cent of unemployed young people have been out of work for more than a year, and in the West Midlands where unemployment is disproportionately higher amongst ethnic minority groups.

It is not possible to go into the causes of youth unemployment in any depth here. It is worth recording, however, that many commentators consider that they are largely structural. Technological changes and the growth of capital-intensive industry are leading to a higher proportion of sixteen to eighteen year olds being surplus to labour market requirements. There is now less need of unskilled labour and what vacancies there are call for specific skills which school leavers do not possess. There is also a geographical mismatch between the demand for labour in some regions and the supply of labour in others and there are still shortages in some areas. However, evidence from American studies cited by Cohen and Nixon (1981), suggest that, on completing their vocational education, many young people enter unskilled or semi-skilled work for which they need little or no training and that many employers would prefer the schools to concentrate on the basic skills of literacy and numeracy rather than job-related skills. Government anxiety about the employability of young people is now manifest in attempts to improve the work habits, maturity and motivation of the young employed and to ease the transition from school to work.

There are three goals which policy-makers must have in attempting to deal with the educational aspects of youth unemployment: first, the provision of appropriate vocational courses for those young people who stay on either at school or in further education but who do not want or are not able to follow academic courses; second, the provision of more part-time courses for those who leave school and enter employment; third, the provision of education and training and jobs for the young unemployed. It should, however, be noted that the three groups of young people are not totally separate. There is movement from courses to employment and back and in and out of employment.

There are now numerous agencies involved, at both central government and local government level, in the education and training of all three groups. These include colleges of further education (FE) which provide courses validated by the City and Guilds of the London Institute, the Technical Education Council and the Business Education Council; the Manpower Services Commission (MSC); the Careers Service and the Youth Service; and secondary schools, sixth-form colleges and tertiary colleges. The plethora of agencies creates certain problems. The provision is criticised on the grounds of financial complexity and the difficulties involved in planning and monitoring programmes. It is argued that the provision is unco-ordinated and lacks a coherent national framework. Cohen and Nixon maintain that college staff often feel that preference is given to schools and sixth-form colleges and that they fare badly in the competition for funds. Where courses are funded by the MSC, FE staff may have to 'reconcile conflicting objectives within NAFE (Non-Advanced Further Education) courses of education and training, in terms of both content and standards'. Maureen O'Connor (1980) discusses the variety of student financial support for education and training in further education and Cohen and Nixon suggest that the 'courses have to be designed to meet the different rules of income support systems rather than the academic needs of the students.' An additional problem relating to vocational education is the low status it is accorded in the education system. This, O'Connor suggests, creates tension between the further education sector and the training services such as the MSC. Furthermore, the academic hierarchical structure of colleges rewards higher-level work more than non-advanced courses, which further militates against great interest being taken in the school leaver with few or no qualifications. Full-time vocational education and careers advice may have importance for attempts to reduce the mismatch between labour supply and demand and to improve career prospects once young people are in employment. However, this area of provision is not discussed here since those young people who stay on in full-time vocational education are not the most disadvantaged. The emphasis in this chapter is therefore on part-time post-school education for sixteen to nineteen year olds who are employed, and on education and training for the young unemployed.

Part-time education and training for the employed
Concern has been expressed over the paucity of provision for the
education and training of young people who are in unskilled employment. Estimates suggest that only around 27 per cent of males and 7
per cent of females aged between sixteen and eighteen who are in
employment participate in non-advanced further education on a day or
block release (*Report*, December 1978). Since the Industrial Training
Act of 1964 the Industrial Training Boards (ITBs) have operated a
system whereby employers either had to provide sufficient training for
their own needs or pay a levy to the ITB which provided grants for
others to undertake the responsibility for training. The emphasis was
on apprenticeships or other long-term training in transferable skills.
However this system has done little to aid the more disadvantaged who
were not able or not qualified to enter long apprenticeships.

A more concerted attempt to bring together schools, further educa-
tion colleges, employers, the training services and young people is the
Unified Vocational Preparation (UVP) pilot programme launched by
the Labour Government in 1976. The programme developed from an
Inter-Departmental Group Study in 1974 entitled 'Getting Ready for
Work', a discussion paper from the Training Services Division of the
MSC (1975) and the HMI Working Party Report (The Sudale Report,
DES, 1976a), on provision for sixteen to nineteen year olds who were
not participating in organised post-school education or training. One
of the guidelines laid down for the programme was that schemes
should be designed 'to overcome any kind of past or present disadvantage whether social, economic, physical or educational' (DES, 1976b).
Initially planned for three years, the pilot scheme was later extended
until 1981. Its aim is to expand the learning opportunities for young
people aged between sixteen and eighteen by offering those who enter
jobs with little or no education or training a programme of experimental vocational preparation schemes. It was considered that 'properly
conceived vocational preparation at this crucial stage would not only
raise the economic contribution of these young people, but would
enhance their chances for development in a personal as well as a
vocational sense' (Government Statement, DES 1976c).

The education and training services were to be jointly responsible
and elements of both were to be combined in a unified approach.
Provision was to be focussed on the place of work and was to be seen as
relevant by both the employers and the young people. Employers are
reimbursed for each day the young workers are involved in UVP. The
potential target population for UVP was estimated by the Government
to be about 300,000 in 1976, but the MSC reduced this estimate to
200,000. The group consists of the more disadvantaged of the 600,000

school leavers who enter the job market. That is, those young people who are less well qualified, who move between jobs and in and out of employment and who enter industries which traditionally provide no systematic education or training below craft level. Not only do they lack the opportunities provided for those who stay on in part-time education beyond sixteen but they do not have the support of a programme of continued education.

Between Autumn 1976 and 1979 approximately 200 pilot schemes were launched, catering for around 2200 young people. It was anticipated that the pilot programme would eventually cater for up to 6000 young people per year. Most schemes were under the aegis of the Distributive Industry Training Boards, but some were launched by other Industry Training Boards, by the Training Services Division of the MSC or by colleges of further education. Schemes last from three to twelve months. Participants are tutored both off-the-job and on-the-job. Off-the-job tutoring usually takes place outside the company premises in a college of further education. The work includes literacy, numeracy and the development of personal and communication skills. In addition, aspects of work such as health, safety and industrial organisation, which are not specific to their employing company are covered. On-the-job tutoring is mainly concerned with job training and task rotation. The Further Education Curriculum Review and Development Unit (FEU) of the DES and the Sudale Report (1976a) both suggested that UVP Schemes include a short residential course. These usually take place in YMCA hostels or Outward Bound Centres.

The UVP pilot programme was launched without any accompanying curriculum development. But during the second year of the experiment members of the Further Education Unit of the DES (the FEU) prepared curricula guidelines for organisers of schemes. The FEU suggested a framework which can be developed according to local needs. It is intended to help organisers identify trainees' learning needs and decide how best to care for them. The guidelines stress the importance of 'experience . . . reflection . . . and learning' (DES/FEU, 1978).

The FEU guidelines also suggested ways in which organisers and participants could assess their scheme. In addition the first phase (until September 1979) has been evaluated by the NFER (Wray, Moor and Hill, 1980) and evaluation of the second phase is under way. The scope of the NFER brief was wide since it included an evaluation of all the different types of UVP schemes launched between 1977 and 1979. The Government offered no blueprint for schemes but defined a list of objectives. Schemes which demonstrated different patterns of organisation and which catered for young people from different occupations were used as case studies. Information was gathered from interviews, observations and questionnaires.

Overall the UVP organisers and participants were positive about the pilot programme. About half of the 308 employers involved returned the NFER questionnaire. The majority (77 per cent) thought the scheme in which they had participated had been successful for both the company (in terms of more committed skilled and interested workers) and the young trainees (in terms of improved confidence and social skills); and that a joint approach was feasible and enabled them to disseminate the needs of industry (60 per cent). Eighty-four per cent expressed their willingness to participate in future schemes. Reservations were concerned with problems of staff coverage and resentment by other employees of UVP trainees 'getting time off work to attend college' (30 per cent), constraints of time and money (19 per cent) and dissatisfaction over the content or organisation of schemes (8 per cent). Wray et al. suggest that these problems will remain while UVP is seen as an 'extra' and is not 'an automatic and accepted part of every young person's introduction to work'.

Three-quarters of the organisers (mostly Industrial Training Boards and colleges of further education) considered that the 'real synthesis' of education and training aimed for in the Government Statement had been achieved in their schemes and 85 per cent thought that UVP should be made a national programme. Two-thirds of tutors had found the UVP a rewarding experience and half considered trainees had increased in self-confidence and knowledge of work. Reservations tended to be concerned with the need for greater employer commitment and closer liaison between the parties involved both on and off the job to ensure the unified approach.

In an attempt to find out if the actual participants on UVP matched the target population, questionnaires were sent to trainees. The response rate was low (36 per cent), which means that this self-selected group may not be representative of the UVP participants as a whole. Whilst a fifth of the respondents had no qualifications, almost a half had CSE qualifications and a third had 'O' levels. Thus they were somewhat better qualified than expected. The group consisted of almost equal numbers of boys and girls, whereas it has been noted that in 1976/77, 60 per cent of boys and 85 per cent of girls aged sixteen, who were in work, received no further education (DES, 1979b). The majority of trainees considered they had benefited, mostly by gaining self-confidence, a better knowledge of their work and an increased ability to communicate. Wray et al. admit that the greater confidence may have occurred in any case with maturation but that participation in the scheme may have helped to overcome the disaffection engendered by school failure and that, for the recipients, it was a case of participating in UVP or nothing.

Wray *et al.* consider that there was not always the flexibility and liaison necessary for a truly unified vocational approach. The integration of the education and the training components of schemes depends on the extent of shared responsibility between employers and the education and training services. Sometimes schemes had to be designed around who or what was available rather than around the needs of trainees. In addition, it did not always prove easy to attract employers. Many of those who did participate were already 'training-conscious' and prepared to accept the disadvantages of lost production and staff cover which results from releasing young people for schemes. This suggests that, unless they are very committed to the need for continuing education, small firms in particular are less likely to be interested in UVP.

It is disappointing that the UVP pilot scheme reached only a fraction of its target population, 3000 out of a hoped-for group of 18,000. The organisers were possibly over-optimistic about the number of employers who would be willing to bear the cost of releasing young workers on a regular basis. It will take time to persuade many of them of the value of participating in the UVP or, in the long term, to initiate their own training scheme without incentive payments. Wray *et al.* also note discrepancies in the system of financial reimbursements which need to be resolved.

Whilst there is still much to be done in the area of curriculum and staff development Wray *et al.* conclude that without the UVP or something similar approximately 200,000 school leavers per annum will probably receive no further education and little, if any, systematic training.

Courses for the young unemployed

Most of the projects and policies aimed at helping the young unemployed to obtain education and training emanate from the Manpower Services Commission (MSC), which was established in 1974 with two principal aims:

(i)   to assist in the development of manpower resources and contribute to the nation's economic well-being;

(ii)   to help secure for each worker the opportunities he or she needs in order to lead a satisfying working life.

Its functions include the overseeing of the Industrial Training Boards and the implementation at local levels of national policies concerned with the training and employment of young people.

In September 1976 the MSC launched the Work Experience Programme (WEP) which in 1978, as a result of the recommendations of
the Holland Report (MSC, 1977), became part of a wider overall
strategy, the Youth Opportunities Programme (YOP). The Programme aims to offer unemployed young people, under nineteen years
of age, constructive alternatives to unemployment and the opportunities of training and work experience that will improve their prospects of obtaining satisfactory permanent employment at the earliest
possible moment. When YOP was initiated it was considered that the
size of the programme should be related to the number of young
people unemployed for six weeks or more over the months when the
annual cycle of youth unemployment reached its lowest level. This led
to a target being set for the period September 1978 to August 1979 of
187,000 entrants to the programme, with 80,000 young people in the
programme at the end of March 1979. Another objective (the 'Easter
undertaking') was meant to ensure that no Easter or Summer school
leaver of 1978, who remained unemployed by Easter 1979 should be
without the offer of a suitable place on the programme.

From the start the programme has offered three different types of
work preparation courses and four different types of work experience.
The intention is that they should be flexible enough to meet individual
and local needs. Work experience can be on an employer's premises,
project based, in community service or in training workshops. Work
Experience on Employer's Premises (WEEP), which caters for the
majority of entrants to YOP, is particularly relevant to the needs of the
educationally disadvantaged. In addition to providing young people
with a variety of different types of work, under supervision, the scheme
includes a specific education component. In fact the Holland Report
recommended that work experience opportunities should, wherever
possible, include an integrated element of further education. The
importance of off-the-job learning to the development of young people was reiterated at the time YOP was set up. A recent survey of
young people on Work Experience schemes showed that about a
quarter of respondents were receiving off-the-job training, over half of
these in a college of further education. The percentage receiving
off-the-job training varied from 40 per cent of those doing Community
Service to 13 per cent of those working on employer's premises (MSC,
1979).

Whilst it is acknowledged that work experience schemes are an
attempt to create more employment opportunities for young people,
criticisms are levelled at them. It is argued that they do not provide
'real' jobs but concentrate on small-scale, short-term 'fringe' activities
or that many of the projects, in particular the environmental projects,

provide opportunity for little more than unskilled labour at a time when the demand for this kind of employment is falling and will continue to fall. Others argue that the financial incentives in the form of employer subsidies to encourage employers to take on the young unemployed, result in job displacement of older or married women workers. A further criticism is that the educational and training elements are of limited value in altering the imbalance between demand for and supply of particular skills. However, it can also be argued that any scheme which enables young people to perform tasks of value to the community, which provides some training, however limited, and which may prevent them from becoming unemployable, has value. A final criticism is that, although YOP caters for the least qualified school leavers, the programmes have not attracted the most disadvantaged, such as young blacks in inner-city areas, who may need an 'out-reach' service such as that introduced by the careers service (Cohen and Nixon, 1981).

A programme of research and surveys into YOP is being undertaken by both MSC and external institutions. The programme includes longitudinal studies in which school leavers are followed through YOP in particular areas and similar studies concentrating on certain groups such as ex-offenders and ethnic minorities. These studies hope to provide insight into the contribution of YOP and of particular elements in the programme, such as life and social skills training, towards the young people's employability on leaving the programme. The studies will cover such aspects as improvement in job seeking and other skills, willingness to travel, increase in confidence and interest in further training. Other projects focus on the organisational and delivery aspects of the programme, seeking to identify areas for change and development. They include studies of trades union involvement, the use of the media and ways of involving voluntary organisations.

One study which has been completed is a follow-up of WEP participants (Smith and Lasko, 1978). This indicated that 72 per cent of respondents were in full-time employment when they were interviewed almost a year after taking a WEP course; 61 per cent had gone straight from WEP into full-time employment; 38 per cent had transferred to the permanent work force of the WEP employer on completing the course. Smith and Lasko point out that the experience of the first group of trainees may not be typical, for instance it is doubtful that such a high proportion joining the permanent work force of the WEP employer would be repeated for each 'generation' of trainees. The first follow-up of YOP trainees indicated that 72 per cent had gone straight into employment and 84 per cent were employed at the time of the survey some seven months later (MSC, 1979).

A review team of the MSC recommended that YOP be expanded, with more formal educational opportunities. This would mean that YOP would change from a scheme primarily intended to get young people off the unemployment register and onto a programme, to one which set out to train them. It would entail greater expenditure since education and training would have to be provided for those on WEEP courses which cost relatively little (Jackson, 1980). Youthaid also recommended that YOP should become a comprehensive scheme for vocational preparation open to all the young unemployed (Jackson).

In the areas most affected by unemployment some young people complete YOP courses and then find themselves back on the dole. It is argued by Ball (1980) that expansion of YOP is not enough, and may even be counter-productive. The positive aspects of YOP, such as the skills and experiences it provides and the 'learning/earning' curriculum which is being developed, may be overshadowed by negative aspects, such as loss of credibility and accusation of 'buying time', if increasing numbers of YOP trainees join the dole queue. Ball considers that there is a need to diversify the aims of YOP and to expand the context in which it operates. He makes three proposals which are concerned with the role of the school, the community and the administration of YOP. He is concerned about the disaffection of many young people with school (or 'academic learning centres'). Certain types of provision, for example 'sanctuary units', have been developed in response to this disaffection. Ball likens the attributes of such provision ('adult styles, experiential content') to YOP courses. This leads to the suggestion that the 'earning/learning' curriculum could be developed before pupils are sixteen in what are termed 'experimental learning centres' which would co-exist with traditional schools. Pupils would be able to divide their time between both centres. The 'experiential learning centre' would offer work experience, community service, leisure pursuits, apprentice-type tuition and opportunities for part-time work. It would be course-based rather than subject-based and pupils could participate on a monthly rather than a yearly basis.

With regard to the community, Ball suggests there is scope for developing lay participation along the lines of the 'industrial coach' project developed by the Grubb Institute. This involves skilled workers outside the usual FE structure acting as tutors to YOP participants (Bazalgette and Reed, 1977).

The third recommendation is that the existing administrative arrangements of YOP are replaced by a network of Work Education Councils. These would consist of representatives from local industry, unions, teachers/administrators, community groups, parents, young people and the careers/employment services. These Councils would be concerned with the school and community contexts detailed above, but also with the diversification of YOP. One such diversification suggested is 'entitlements', such as wage and education vouchers which could be traded in for full or part-time work/education/leisure opportunities or the 'wage' vouchers could be 'cashed' to provide capital for self-employment enterprises.

Whilst these suggestions are interesting and thought-provoking they raise problems of organisation and accountability. For example, it may not be practical for young people to transfer between monthly participation in experiential learning centres and schools where courses tend to be organised on a termly or yearly basis. Ball does not say whether he envisages the under-sixteens receiving payment for their part-time work. With rising numbers of school leavers unable to find paid employment this suggestion is likely to encounter opposition. Furthermore many employers consider that schools should be concentrating on basic literacy and numeracy.

Whilst in some respects the Work Education Councils would resemble the Area Boards of the MSC, Ball sees them as being more representative of local interests (including parents and young people), less remote and fragmented and more collaborative than the MSC provision. It is not clear, however, to whom the Work Education Councils would be accountable. Nor is it clear what measures of control would be exercised over those who "cashed" their vouchers for their own enterprises.

In summary the policies described go only a small way towards alleviating the problem of youth employment and improving the post-school educational opportunities of the most disadvantaged group who leave school at the first opportunity. So far the various agencies involved in the transition from school to work have not managed to eradicate problems of mismatch between labour supply and demand. An increased awareness of the need to provide for those who are staying on in education, but who would not benefit from academic courses, has led to the Further Education Unit to argue for a "comprehensive pattern of tertiary provision".

The provision of further education and training for employed young people has ostensibly been a high priority of both Labour and Conservative Governments over the past decade but in practice our provision for this disadvantaged group still compares badly with many other countries. The Unified Vocational Preparation Scheme represents an important new initiative but so far it has only been introduced on a pilot basis. The results for participants who took part in the evaluation were on the whole positive. Decisions have to be made about the future of UVP soon: priority should now be given to devising a programme of expansion that will eventually lead to universal provision for all sixteen-year-old school leavers. However, it is likely to take time to persuade some employers of the benefit of participation. As regards provision for the most disadvantaged group, who have few qualifications, no jobs and little money, there seems little doubt the YOP schemes have considerably benefited the young people, many of whom leave school having gained little from the education system. It is probable (although we cannot be certain) that many of them benefit from the remedial education and the training in work habits, and a high proportion do go on to permanent employment. Although the present government has reduced its financial support for the MSC it has pledged its continuing commitment to YOP. With increasing numbers of unemployed young people, the programme seems likely to be under great strain and further new initiatives will be necessary.

In May 1981 a consultative document, *A New Training Initiative*, was produced by the MSC (MSC, 1981). The document proposes three aims for the Government:

(i)   to provide skill-training to an agreed standard for young people entering at different ages and with varying levels of attainment;

(ii)   to eventually provide all under-eighteens with an opportunity to stay in full-time education, to enter training or to have work experience combined with work-related training and education, and

(iii)   to increase opportunities for adults to acquire, increase or update skills.

The document states that 'there is a compelling need for a training system which enables all workers to acquire a basic range of skills and to develop and adapt them through their working lives'. Under the provision of the Initiative the YOP will be expanded and developed with an expanded UVP Programme. It is planned to provide 444,000 young people with opportunities on YOP courses in 1981/82 and to increase UVP sixfold to cater for 20,000 young people in employment. It is suggested that young employees/trainees be paid at a lower rate than other employees, as are apprentices. The question of who should pay for the scheme is left open but it is likely to be funded jointly by employees and the state.

The document does not, as many had hoped it would, present a one-year programme for *all* school leavers who wanted it. Nor does it resolve the need for agreements to be worked out between employers and the unions, but it is a welcome first step towards a unified system of post-school provision.

YOP schemes have been criticised for not providing 'real' jobs and for displacing older and/or women employees for the benefit of the young worker. In a period of shrinking employment it is, however, inevitable that training programmes of this kind will have this effect, squeezing out other groups. A conscious change was made to concentrate efforts and resources, though not exclusively, on young people. There may be an element of social control in this decision for large numbers of unemployed and unoccupied young people are likely to be more of a 'problem' than similar numbers of women or older workers. However, it is not just a question of employment, but also of training. The Government has given a higher priority to training sixteen to eighteen year olds than the other groups mentioned above. This may partly be motivated by an altruistic desire to demonstrate that society is concerned on their behalf. It may also reflect a wish to give unemployed young people first-hand experience of work at a crucial age. Whatever the social justice of such decisions current projections indicating that unemployment will increase must lead to speculation over whether there will be enough resources to cope in the future.

Conclusion

This chapter has reviewed a variety of initiatives designed to help disadvantaged children and young people. In many cases policies have not been systematically evaluated or if they have, their *educational* impact has not been assessed. In the first section various studies which sought to enhance the link between pre-school experience at home and subsequent experience in the education system were discussed. Whilst some of these experimental projects appear successful, it is important to note that they are expensive. Reviewing the statutory provision of free milk and meals, it was suggested that changes in legislation and provision may reverse trends towards healthier childhood amongst some disadvantaged children. This section also dealt with the present limitation of school uniform grants and EMAs.

The second half of the chapter covered aspects of provision for post-school education and training, in particular the Unified Vocational Preparation pilot programme and the Youth Opportunities Programme. Because of the effects of an economic recession and a diminishing need for unskilled labour, the employment opportunities for those pupils achieving least in secondary school have declined. As a consequence the Government has introduced job creation and compensatory training schemes. These schemes may prove successful if the recession is short. If there is a longer period of youth unemployment the provision will appear inadequate. One of the highest priorities should be to combine UVP and YOP into a universal and permanent programme for all school leavers who are not going on to further education or training.

During this period of growing youth unemployment successful school students have continued to take up the opportunities in higher education leading to enhanced employment prospects. In 1980, when there were over 200,000 unemployed young people between sixteen and nineteen, the opportunities for graduates or equivalent were still good. Thus, even more than in previous years, secondary education became a selective process in which the gap between successful and unsuccessful students widened.

6 Conclusions

This report has sought to examine the relationship between social disadvantage, educational attainment and educational policy. It has concentrated on primary and secondary schooling but has also considered aspects of pre-school and post-school provision. The persistence of a negative relationship between social disadvantage and educational attainment has been well documented in the research literature. In order to understand why this has remained so powerful a force following the introduction of free, compulsory schooling, various aspects of home and school life have been investigated, by reviewing available research evidence. There has been little research *directly* concerned with the inter-generational nature of educational disadvantage. Insofar as it examines the association between parents' education and socio-economic status and their children's education it does however reveal, at a general level, the significance of inter-generational factors.

There have been a number of attempts to overcome the effects of disadvantage by initiatives of both a directly interventionary nature and of a solely financial type. Some of these initiatives have had very limited success. In none, however, has success been so noteworthy that it has been seen as a solution. The negative relationship has proved to be exceedingly robust. In this concluding chapter we briefly discuss the limited nature of these policies and their consequent lack of effectiveness. This will be followed by a consideration of three areas where changes might provide some educational help to the disadvantaged.

This report began by reviewing the literature which illustrated the continuing association between socio-economic status and educational attainment. It concluded that, despite the optimism engendered by the 1944 Act and the subsequent expansion of provision, educational disadvantage, defined in terms of poor performance and limited access to educational opportunities after the statutory school-leaving age, remains closely associated with social disadvantage. Chapter 2 examined possible social and environmental reasons which might contribute to this association. The literature reviewed in Chapter 3 suggested several ways in which certain cultural or attitudinal school factors may also transmit educational disadvantage. Chapters 4 and 5 described educational policies which have been put into effect in order to reduce the strength of the relationship between social disadvantage and educational disadvantage.

Why have the policies and programmes enjoyed such limited success? Several reasons have been considered. It has been argued that we have not really practised positive discrimination – that the resources allocated were far too few and the innovations too piecemeal to be able to achieve any lasting impact. For example, the EPA policy was not clear in its objectives, there was confusion over whether it was aimed at groups or individuals and there was little systematic monitoring of programmes. But most important of all, the resources involved were miniscule.

The EPA action research led to some improvements in certain measurable aspects of the programmes, although quite frequently they were disappointingly small and many were not sustained. However, there may have been other gains, particularly of a social nature, which were not measurable. The research did, however, serve to draw attention to the importance of some of the unanticipated 'side effects' of such initiatives, such as the importance of teacher commitment to innovation and the potentially isolating effects of, for example, curriculum changes which are not incorporated into mainstream education.

Some of the later parent involvement projects, which have been able to draw on earlier EPA experience, have been successful in engaging parents in their children's learning. Others have indicated where some sources of difficulty lie and suggest possible strategies for overcoming them.

Policies aimed at making it easier for parents to support their children whilst they are at school, have, like those associated with the Plowden Committee's proposals for positive discrimination, also suffered from pitifully inadequate resources. For example, policies concerning the provision of uniform grants at present and Educational Maintenance Allowances give so little to so few that they can hardly be considered successful attempts at reducing disadvantage. Free meals and school milk have been available for larger numbers, though now they too are being eroded. Of considerable promise are the pilot Unified Vocational Preparation Scheme and the Youth Opportunities Programme, although these policies at present help a relatively small proportion of the age groups in need of a joint approach to education and training. Moreover they come relatively late in the educational experience of the young people concerned. Many have argued that early intervention which is followed up continuously throughout the child's educational experience is essential.

The conclusion to Chapters 4 and 5 was that at whatever stage of the educational process policies are introduced, one-off, small-scale programmes which are not part of a coherent approach to the mainstream of education, and which are not entirely supported by those responsible for their implementation, are unlikely to succeed.

In addition to general and specific criticisms of the shortcomings of policies designed to help the disadvantaged, shortcomings which, with hindsight, might have been avoided, there are other factors which have militated against their success. These are to do with the inter-generational power of advantage and two particular aspects of the education system – the expansion of the higher education sector and the maintenance of the private sector.

It has already been noted that there is little direct research into inter-generational transmission of educational disadvantage, but it seems likely that poverty, low status and concomitant poor self-image may lead to failure to utilise educational opportunities. Lack of educational opportunities in turn may lead to poor job opportunities, low status, low income and, eventually, poverty. As the evidence in Chapters 1 and 2 indicates, the children of low income, low status families are more likely to be those who have low levels of participation in the education system and low levels of achievement. However, Rutter and Madge (1976) have argued that only some of these continuities involve familial continuity, and that regional continuities and school continuities are also important. Moreover, even where there appears to be marked disadvantage, there are striking discontinuities. Further evidence on the extent of intra-generational or inter-generational continuity in educational disadvantage is likely to emerge from the NCD longtitudinal study. In addition the follow-up of the 'disadvantaged' sub-sample, initially studied by Wedge and Prosser (1973) may prove to be a valuable source of information on the likelihood of parental disadvantage being reproduced and on the mechanisms which might lead to discontinuities.

Evidence from the Oxford Mobility Study (Halsey et al., 1980) suggests however that educational advantage, at least in the recent past, has been mediated to a considerable extent via the family. In the cohorts studied by Halsey et al., three-quarters of working-class boys went to elementary, secondary modern or comprehensive schools, whereas nearly three-quarters of the sons of the middle class (or 'service class' as the authors call it) went to some kind of selective secondary school. More important was the fact, noted earlier by Klein (1975), that the middle classes were able to get more than they were entitled to by merit alone.

However, Halsey rejects the notion of a concentration of 'cultural capital' as an exclusive means of social reproduction. His figures do, in fact, demonstrate considerable upward inter-generational mobility and the presence, in state selective schools, of a substantial number of 'first generation novitiates' into the 'national cultural heritage'. Moreover, Halsey *et al.* maintain that, once in a selective secondary school, the notion of cultural capital was less important for examination results, which were similar for both working-class and service-class boys. The inequalities were in *access* to selective schools and then to the sixth form. Thus continuities in educational advantage occur to the extent that middle-class parents have the power to retain their advantage and pass it on to their children. This includes their use of private education, with its subsequent enhanced opportunities (see Boyd, 1973) and the advantage they have taken of the expanded opportunities in higher education which Glennerster (1972) has described.

As already mentioned, the policies of positive discrimination have absorbed only a small amount of resources. Education expansion over the past twenty years has been concentrated in higher education where per capita expenditure is high. Per capita expenditure is also high in sixth forms. Yet these are both areas of provision which give most aid to the already advantaged and are least used by the disadvantaged. Glennerster has argued that, as the proportion of working-class children participating in any level of education decreases, so resources devoted to it increase. And Halsey states that 'at each stage from primary to secondary to post-secondary education and at each historical stage of the expansion of secondary and higher education, merit is modified by class distinction.'

Not only do the middle class disproportionately benefit from the expanded, most expensive sector of State education, those that choose to send their children to fee-paying schools in the private sector also benefit from a variety of subsidies from central government. These include tax exemptions, for those schools with charitable status, direct grants paid in respect of pupils admitted before 1977, boarding allowances for the children of military and diplomatic personnel, tax-relief schemes through educational trusts for fee-paying and the assisted places scheme to be introduced in September 1981. Furthermore the costs of training many of the 40,000 teachers in private schools have been met by the State. Private schools are thus subsidised by the tax payer, the majority of whom send their children to state schools. These subsidies represent the most extreme example of support for the privileged within the education system.

It is exceedingly difficult, without major structural changes in the distribution of life chances, to achieve all one might wish by means of education. Some might argue, for example, that to give all children an equal opportunity we would have to do away with the family as it exists at present. For if children benefit from certain parental qualities and home life, by the same token they must suffer from parental and family shortcomings. However such an extreme policy would be in direct contradiction with deeply held values about the role of the family, and as such is quite unacceptable. There are other, less extreme, changes which could be made.

Although some of the suggestions we make in this final chapter do call for additional expenditure some need only the imaginative and flexible use of existing plant and resources and others call for attitudinal changes. We accept that the policy recommendations we make will not revolutionise the situation, but they would be relatively easy to implement and we believe they would help to reduce educational disadvantage.

It is not possible to list all the changes which might be introduced in order to reduce educational disadvantage. Suggestions made below concern three areas:

(i)   pre-school provision and home-school links;
(ii)   assessment;
(iii)   continuing education.

The need for many other changes are implicit in many of the comments we have made about resource allocation and about particular policies earlier in this report.

Pre-school Provision and Home–School Links

Despite the modest success of the initiatives described earlier, perhaps one of the potentially most fruitful areas for further work is that of the links between homes and schools. The Plowden Committee – and many others since – have stressed that parents and teachers must be partners in the education of their children. Neither party has the sole direction of the child; both contribute to the child's happiness and development, so each needs to be aware of the contribution of the other. In the past, educationists have been drawn to an explanation of educational failure based on a 'deficit model' of homes; some critics of schools are now posing a 'deficit model' of teachers. Common sense dictates, and this report assumes, that maximum benefit for the child will be where both parents and teachers are aware of each other's contributions which at times are distinct and, at other times, overlap, so that each may reinforce the work of the other. The studies by Tizard, Schofield and Hewison (1980) reviewed in Chapter 4 and by Clarke and Cheyne (1980) have indicated that parents, even those who are disadvantaged on economic or educational criteria, can contribute to their children's progress. Both Blackstone (1973 and 1979b) and Tizard, Mortimore and Burchell (1981) have discussed the need for teacher-training in parent involvement and effective, even statutory, parent involvement programmes in schools.

Part of the home–school link must be the provision of adequate pre-school facilities. The aims and objectives of pre-school education are themselves the subject of debate, as has been noted earlier, and their relationship to the current style of statutory schooling rather obscure. Clearly this is unhelpful. A common approach to day care and education, coupled with a critical consideration of the curriculum, the role of staff and 'the models of play the school establishes in the minds of children through group activity' (Bruner, 1980) might allow the learning capacities of the under-fives to be better used.

The 1978 Report of the Central Policy Review Staff (CPRS) on 'Services for Young Children of Working Mothers' discusses the inadequacies and inequalities of existing day-care provision available to the 900,000 under-fives whose mothers work. The CPRS recommended that day care and nursery education should be combined whenever possible, and that there should be greater flexibility in the use of existing provision. Both the CPRS, the Oxford Pre-school Research Team (Bruner, 1980), Blackstone and Crispin (1980), Hughes *et al.* (1980) and Tizard, Moss and Perry (1976) suggest changes in policy in order to alter the emphasis 'from expensive service for a small number to a reasonable service for a much larger number' (CPRS). But within this it is essential that special attention is paid towards the disadvantaged so that extra resources are channelled in their direction, through, for example, full-time places and home visitors schemes for them. If the service is to provide for those most in need and thus have some redistributive effect, full-time provision needs to be expanded, particularly in inner cities and other deprived areas. This could go some way towards enabling single parents (five out of six of whom are women), and the working-class wives of husbands on low incomes, who both want and need to work to secure an adequate standard of living for their families, the chance to do so. The CPRS advocated the conversion of part-time nursery class places to full-time places and the provision of an extended day after normal school hours for the minority of children whose mothers were working full-time. The inevitable costs of such a policy could be reduced by the use of the voluntary movement (some pre-school playgroups are experimenting with an extended day); by drawing on paraprofessionals or parent volunteers rather than highly-trained, expensive staff after school hours; and by converting spare classrooms (available as a result of declining school populations) at less cost than providing purpose-built accommodation. The CPRS suggested an earmarked sum be allocated for pre-school education since in the present climate few local authorities are likely to expand provision without some special financing.

Assessment

In most secondary schools assessment is by means of public examinations taken by pupils at the end of the period of compulsory schooling. Several recent publications have been highly critical of the system (Broadfoot, 1980a, Flude and Parrott, 1980, Burgess and Adams, 1980, Mortimore, 1980b). Criticisms have centred on the narrowness of the assessment (testing as it does one kind of academic ability), the lack of comparability of grading from one syllabus, subject or board to another, and the dependence on norm-based statistical techniques which take no account of absolute standards. The existence of a dual system of 'O' level and CSE poses serious difficulties to pupils, parents and teachers which need resolution. Whilst the popular view is that 'O' level currency is much stronger in the eyes of parents and employers, some of the more imaginative syllabuses and techniques of marking, including the use of continuous assessment, have been pioneered by the CSE Boards.

Some of these difficulties may be resolved by the introduction of a joint system combining CSE and 'O' level, a version of which was recommended by the Waddell Committee (1978) and another of which has been accepted, in principle, by the current Secretary of State for Education. However, even with the operation of such a joint system which will still only be intended to cater for 60 per cent of the age group, many educationally disadvantaged pupils will leave school after eleven years with no formal qualifications, no record of achievement and the possibility of a poor self-image which it may take years to improve. Some of these problems might be lessened if schools operated an assessment procedure which, whilst including examinations where possible, would also assess specified objectives, take account of ongoing work and include an element of non-academic evaluation (it is to be hoped involving the pupils themselves). A start in this direction has been made by the introduction, in some local authorities, of pupil-profile schemes such as the Swindon Record of Personal Achievement (RPA) and the Scottish Student Profile Scheme (SSPS) (Stansbury, 1980, Swales, 1980, and Broadfoot, 1980b). The limitations of such schemes are that so far they have been used principally for non-examination pupils and have not been widely received by parents and prospective employers. Burgess and Adams have suggested how this kind of assessment might be introduced in the form of a three-stage, nationally validated programme for all pupils in the third year and beyond (see Chapter 3). A system of examinations for some pupils and profile schemes for others is in danger of institutionalising educational disadvantage.

Continuing Education

The case for the development of a system of continuing education is argued both on the grounds of equity and efficiency by Schuller and Bengtsson (1977). The historical parallels between the struggle in the 1920s and 1930s for paid holidays and holiday credit schemes and the current debate over entitlement to paid educational leave are drawn by Schuller (1978).

The present system of post-secondary educational provision contributes to educational disadvantage since, as we have emphasised throughout this report, it is principally geared to, and used by, the well-qualified eighteen to twenty year old. The majority leave school at sixteen, of whom only a small proportion are able to take advantage of opportunities for further education and training (see Chapter 5). Shirley Williams has argued 'vocational education everywhere in Europe has long been the form of further education reserved for the socially inferior . . . yet the divorce between the thinkers and workers, those that study and those that do, is one of the most profound sources of social difference' (Williams, 1980b). In future, distinction between academic and vocational education should be less important. And, given the unpredictability of future employment patterns and the overwhelming need for an adaptable labour force, it will be essential for young people to be rapidly retrained in specific areas.

This pattern will not, of course, be restricted to young people. The growth in long-term unemployment amongst adults, many of whom are unskilled, poses a substantial problem of education and training. Long-term unemployment is likely to be a continuing phenomenon which means that growing numbers of men and women will probably be made redundant and require retraining. Workers of all ages will need to retrain at periods during their working lives. At other periods, it is possible there will be no work available and education will be followed for its own intrinsic sake rather than on an instrumental basis. There is thus a need for continuing education.

The present declining numbers of young people means that educational plant and personnel can be made more widely available (see Blackstone and Crispin). Rising unemployment means that the real costs of people studying rather than working are altered, both to the individual who will not be foregoing earnings in order to study, and to the state which, for relatively little more expenditure, can enable the unemployed to study.

France, Italy and Norway all operate schemes for employees to take paid educational leave (see Schuller and Bengtsson). With the European experience to draw on it should be possible to devise an educational credits system whereby everyone over eighteen is entitled to a specified amount of time either taken in one block or spread over time on an accredited course with grant or loan support. Job safeguards for those in employment would need to be built into the system.

There would be a need for an information and counselling service to advise people at home, at work and in the community of what was available and appropriate to their needs. Institutions would need to be more flexible in the range of courses offered, in the provision of part-time or cumulative modular courses and in the scope for interchange between courses and colleges. The challenge that these changes would present to universities and polytechnics and other further and higher education institutions are noted both by Blackstone and Crispin and by Ellwood (1976). It will not be sufficient merely to use existing educational plant in the traditional manner. A research project into adult education by Fordham, Poulton and Randle (1979) found that the adult education provided by local authorities often resembled an extension of school. Participants were 'taught by teachers at fixed times over well-defined periods' and for some, premises and paraphernalia evoked unwelcome memories. The authors note the importance of providing a community-oriented service with, if possible, 'outreach' tutors and support systems.

Some of these suggestions about making educational resources available for the whole community and developing special approaches towards acceptable provision for groups who have participated little in the education system are not new. They were, for example, among the recommendations of the Russell Report on adult education (DES, 1973). Whilst the Russell Report was not directly concerned with continuing education, a source of regret to Ellwood, the Report may have helped pave the way towards the implementation of one policy specifically aimed at the educationally disadvantaged, the Adult Literacy Campaign. The different groups whose efforts coincided in the campaign have been described by Jones and Charnley (1978). The outcome was that in February 1975 the Government announced that it was sponsoring the Adult Literacy Resource Agency (ALRA) which would allocate a £1 million government grant, would act as a national referral service, co-ordinate an army of volunteer 'teachers' and liaise with the BBC in a literacy series. Local authorities and voluntary organisations were able to submit bids for initial allocations, although they had to be prepared to meet continuing expenditure from their own resources. All local authorities requested an allocation which suggests that improving adult literacy was universally considered to be of some priority. Most local authorities, with the help of trained, paid personnel and volunteers, were able to offer one to one tuition. Referrals were made locally or via the BBC as a result of their series *On the Move*. By February 1976, 55,000 'students' and 40,000 volunteer 'teachers' were involved in a network of provision that covered every local authority in England and Wales. An additional £2 million was made available. By 1978 the numbers of students had risen to 125,000 and the number of volunteer teachers was 75,000.

The government 'pump priming' ended in March 1978, when local authorities took on the responsibility for maintaining provision with financial help from an adjustment to the Rate Support Grant Settlement of £1.3 million. Subsequent government support came from the establishment of an Adult Literacy Unit (ALU) as an agency of the National Institute of Adult Education. The function of the ALU is to advise and consult local authorities, to co-ordinate provision, to publish material and to commission projects. The present cuts in public expenditure must put at risk the continuation of the programme. Some local authorities will be tempted to regard it as somewhat peripheral and as such an easy target for cutting.

An early survey of 6,500 students by the NIAE found that twice as many men as women were enrolled, that about two-thirds of the students were between twenty-one and forty years and married, and that the vast majority had left school at sixteen or under. The third report on the Campaign (DES, 1978a) indicates that there was a high drop-out rate but that some later returned to the course. Jones and Charnley estimated that only about a third of participants continued for a year but that about half stayed long enough to improve their skills and confidence. The scheme also revealed considerable reserves of goodwill in the large number of volunteers who took part.

The existence of adult illiteracy highlights more dramatically than anything else the need for increasing the opportunities for post-school education for those who have gained least from the education system. The Russell Report talked about helping those who had missed their 'first chance', but Hopkins (cited in Hutchinson and Hutchinson, 1978) points out 'for many a "first chance" was never really presented'. But whilst adult illiterates are perhaps the most deserving group of all, there are many more who, whilst they can read and write, have hardly had the education which the citizens of an advanced industrial society deserve. Further research is needed to identify the numbers of the adult educationally disadvantaged, and to attempt a breakdown of their social class background, sex, ethnic origin and geographical location.

In addition to attempting to assess the numbers, characteristics and location of the educationally disadvantaged as a whole, it is important to try to find out more about how they became so. The point has been made in different chapters of this report that we know little about exactly how or to what extent social disadvantage or the education system affect educational disadvantage. It seems likely that it is mediated in some way by social circumstances and the family and that it can result from or be exacerbated by certain aspects of the education system. But the *processes* by which this occurs are still not understood and merit a good deal more research. Much of the work described in the preceding chapters has been of the input/output type. Some of it was not instigated with the aim of assessing disadvantage, which makes extrapolation difficult.

Research into processes is not easy. If it is conducted on too large a scale it is unlikely to yield rich enough data. If it is too fine-grain it is of dubious value out of its context. That being said we would suggest that research is needed into the processes by which familial factors, such as overcrowding or maternal depression or mother–child interaction, may affect educational outcomes. But we consider that there is an even greater need for the balance between familial and educational research on attainment to be righted by more research into the processes by which the structure and organisation of the education system and the attitudes and expectations of teachers may put certain groups of pupils at a disadvantage.

Appendix A

Table A   Analysis of (a) recurrent expenditure[1] by local and central government by sector, and (b) local government expenditure: England and Wales, 1970/71 to 1977/78

	1970 –71	1972 –73	1974 –75	1975 –76	1976 –77	1977 –78[2]
(a) Total recurrent expenditure						
(i) Actual £ million	1932	2661	4168	5356	6105	6559
(ii) As % by sector						
Nursery schools	0.3	0.3	0.3	0.4	0.4	0.4
Primary schools	24.2	24.1	24.7	24.6	24.1	24.0
Secondary schools	27.6	28.1	29.8	29.8	29.8	30.3
Special schools	2.3	2.8	3.0	3.2	3.3	3.4
School health, meals and milk	6.7	6.4	6.4[3]	6.5	6.8	6.1
Further and adult education	14.8	14.8	14.3	14.7	15.9	16.2
Training of teachers	3.9	3.7	3.5	2.9	1.1	0.9
Universities	13.1	12.1	10.8	10.6	11.2	11.2
Other[4]	7.1	7.7	7.2	7.3	7.4	7.5
(b) Local education current expenditure[5]						
(iii) As % of total local current	58.1	57.9	54.7	54.0	54.5	54.9

Notes

1. Includes maintenance grants and allowances to pupils and students.

2. Provisional.

3. From 1 April 1974 medical inspection and treatment functions of school health were transferred to Area Health Authorities.

4. Includes administration, transport, unspecified awards and grants, and the Youth Service.

5. Includes libraries, science and arts.

Sources: Department of Education and Science (1979), *Statistics of Education, 1977 Finance and Awards*, Vol 5; *The Government's Expenditure Plans*, 1979/80 to 1982/83, Cmd 7439, January, 1979 and earlier White Papers.

Table reproduced from Blackstone, T. and Crispin, A. (1980), 'Education', in Blake and Ormerod (eds.), *The Economics of Prosperity*, Grant McIntyre.

Appendix B

Table B   Analysis of (a) Captial expenditure by local and central government by sector, and (b) local government capital expenditure: England and Wales, 1970/71 to 1977/78

	1970 −71	1972 −73	1974 −75	1975 −76	1976 −77	1977[1] −78
(a) Total capital expenditure						
(i) Actual £ million	340.9	487.7	528.8	593.5	573.9	485.8
(ii) As % by sector						
Nursery schools	0.3	0.3	0.5	1.4	1.2	0.9
Primary schools	25.4	26.8	26.4	23.8	23.3	20.1
Secondary schools	31.3	38.1	39.8	37.6	36.8	42.9
Special schools	2.6	2.7	3.8	5.1	5.5	4.4
Further and adult education	14.2	10.8	11.2	12.3	12.9	13.6
Training teachers	2.1	1.8	1.4	0.8	0.2	0.2
Universities	18.7	14.1	12.6	14.4	15.4	13.2
Other[2]	5.4	5.4	4.3	4.6	4.7	4.7
(b) Local education capital expenditure[3]						
(iii) As % of total local capital	16.4	20.0	12.1	12.2	12.9	12.7

Notes

1. Provisional.

2. Includes school health, meals and milk, administration and Youth Service.

3. Includes libraries, science and arts, and key and locally determined sectors.

Sources: Department of Education and Science (1979), *Statistics of Education, 1977 Finance and Awards*, Vol 5; *The Government's Expenditure Plans*, 1979/80 to 1982/83, Cmd 7439, January, 1979 and earlier White Papers.

Table reproduced from Blackstone, T. and Crispin, A. (1980), 'Education', in Blake and Ormerod (eds.), *The Economics of Prosperity*, Grant McIntyre.

Bibliography

Acland, H. (1971), 'What is a "bad" school?', *New Society*, 9 September.

Acland, H. (1973), *Social Determinants of Educational Achievement: an Evaluation and Criticism of Research*, Ph.D. Thesis, University of Oxford.

Acland, H. (1980), 'Research as Stage Management: The Case of the Plowden Committee' in M.I.A. Bulmer (ed.), *Social Research and Royal Commissions*, George Allen and Unwin.

Acton, T.A. (1980), 'Educational criteria of success: some problems in the work of Rutter, Maughan, Mortimore and Ouston', *Educational Research*, **22**, 3 June.

Allnutt, D. and Gerlardi, A. (1980), 'Inner Cities in England', *Social Trends*, **10**.

Anastasi, A. (1956), 'Intelligence and family size', *Psychol Bull.*, **53**.

Apple, M.W. (1979), *Ideology and the Curriculum*, Routledge and Kegan Paul.

Ashton, D.N. and Maguire, M.J. (1980), 'The function of academic and non-academic criteria in employers' selection strategies', *British Journal of Guidance and Counselling*, July.

Assistant Master and Mistress Association (AMMA) (1979), 'Report of the Primary and Preparatory Education Committee on Nursery Education', *Report*, **2**, 4, January 1980.

Association of Metropolitan Authorities (AMA) (1980), Statement on DES *Framework for the School Curriculum*, *Times Educational Supplement*, 18 July.

Athey, C. (1980), 'Parental involvement in nursery education' submitted for publication to *Early Childhood*, 1.

Averch, H.A., Carroll, S.J., Donaldson, T.S., Kiesling, H.J. and Pincus, J. (1972), *How Effective is Schooling? A Critical View and Synthesis of Research Findings*, Rand Corporation.

Baird, D. and Illsley, R. (1953), 'Environment and childbearing', *Proc. Roy. Soc. Med.*, **46**.

Baker, I.A., Elwood, P.C. and Sweetman, P.M. (1979), *Lancet*, 29 September.

Ball, C. (1980), 'Expansion is not enough', *Times Educational Supplement*, 17 October.

Ball, S. (1981) *Beachside Comprehensive*, Cambridge University Press.

Baratz, J.C. and Baratz, J. (1969), 'A bi-dialectal task for determining language proficiency in economically disadvantaged Negro children', *Child Dev.* **40**, 3.

Baratz, J.C. and Baratz, J. (1970), 'Teaching Reading in an Urban Negro School System' in F. Williams (ed.), *Language and Poverty*, Markham, Chicago.

Barnes, J. (ed.) (1975), *Educational Priority*, Vol. 3, *Curriculum Innovation in London's EPAs*, HMSO.

Barnes, J. (1978), 'Education and the Urban Environment', *Open University Course E. 361, Unit 3*.

Barnes, J.H. and Lucas, H. (1975), 'Positive Discrimination in Education: Individuals, Groups and Institutions' in J. Barnes (ed.), *Educational Priority* Vol. 3, *Curriculum Innovation in London's EPAs*, HMSO.

Bates, A., Bell, R. and Mackenzie, J. (1974), *Decision-making in Schools*, Open University Press.

Bazalgette, J. (1979), Lecture delivered to the Association of Child Psychol. and Psychiat., September.

Bazalgette, J.L. and Reed, B.D. (1977), *The Industrial Coach*, Grubb Institute of Behavioural Studies.

Becher, T. and Maclure, S. (1978), *The Politics of Curriculum Change*, Hutchinson.

Becker, H.S. (1963), 'Education and the Lower-class Child' in A.W. Gouldner and H.P. Gouldner (eds.), *Modern Sociology*, Harcourt Brace.

Bee, H.L. (1969), 'Social class difference in maternal teaching strategies and speech patterns', *Developmental Psychology*, 1, 6.

Beez, W.V. (1970), 'Influence of Biased Psychological Reports on Teacher Behaviour and Pupil Performance' in M.B. Miles and W.W. Chartess, *Learning in Social Settings*, Allyn and Bacon.

Belsen, W.A. (1975), *Juvenile Theft: the Causal Factors*, Harper and Row.

Benjamin, H. (1939), Foreword to J.A. Peddiwell, *The Saber-tooth Curriculum* McGraw Hill. Also reproduced in R. Hooper, (ed.) *The Curriculum: Context, Design and Development*, Open University Press.

Benn, C. (1980), 'Selection still blocks growth of comprehensives', *Where*, 158, May.

Bereiter, C. and Engelmann, S. (1966), *Teaching Disadvantaged Children in the Pre-school*, Prentice Hall.

Berger, M., Yule, W. and Rutter, M. (1975), 'Attainment and adjustment in two geographical areas. II. The prevalence of specific reading retardation', *Brit. J. Psychiat*, 126.

Berger, M., Yule, W. and Wigley, V. (1980), 'Intervening in the classroom', *Contact*, ILEA, 12 September.

Bernstein, B. (1962), 'Social class, linguistic codes and grammatical elements', *Lang. and Speech*, 5.

Bernstein, B. (1971), 'On the Classification and Framing of Educational Knowledge' in M.F.D. Young (ed.), *Knowledge and Control,* Collier Macmillan.

Bernstein, B. (1977), 'Class and Pedagogies: Visible and Invisible' in J. Karabel and A.H. Halsey (eds.), *Power and Ideology in Education*, Oxford University Press. Also in *Class, Codes and Control*, Vol. III (1975), Routledge and Kegan Paul.

Bernstein, B. and Davies, B. (1969), *Perspectives on Plowden*, Penguin.

Berthoud, R. (1976), *The Disadvantages of Inequality: a Study of Social Deprivation*, Macdonald and Jane.

Billington, B. (1979), 'Patterns of attendance and truancy', *Educational Review*, **10**, 2.

Birch, H.G. and Gussow, J.D. (1970), *Disadvantaged Children: Health, Nutrition and School Failure*, Harcourt, Brace and World.

Black, D., Townsend, P., Smith, C. and Morris, J. (1980), *Inequalities in Health*, DHSS/HMSO.

Blackburn, J.N. (1945), *Psychology and the Social Pattern*, Kegan Paul.

Blackstone, T. (1973), *Education and Day Care for Children in Need: The American Experience*, Bedford Square Press.

Blackstone, T. (1979a), 'Conference on Inner City Schooling: Final Report', Unpublished, OECD.

Blackstone, T. (1979b) 'Parental involvement in education', *Education Policy Bulletin*, **7**, 1, Spring 1977.

Blackstone, T. (1980a) 'Fifteen Thousand Hours: Review Symposium' in *Brit. J. Sociol. of Ed.*, **1**, 2.

Blackstone, T. (1980b) 'The Challenge of the Inner City' in M. Marland (ed.) *Education for the Inner City*, Heinemann Educational Books.

Blackstone, T. and Crispin, A. (1980), 'Education' in D. Blake and P. Ormerod, *The Economics of Prosperity*, Grant McIntyre.

Blank, M. (1973), *Teaching and Learning in the Pre-school*, Columbus Merrill.

Bloom, B.S. (1964), *Stability and Change in Human Characteristics*, John Wiley.

Boaden, N. (1971), *Urban Policy-making*, Cambridge University Press

Boudon, R. (1973), *Education, Opportunity and Social Inequality*, John Wiley.

Boulter, H. and Crispin, A. (1978), 'Rural disadvantage: the differential allocation of resources to small rural primary schools', *Durham and Newcastle Research Review*, **8**, 41.

Boulter, P. (1979), *OECD Project on Sparsely Populated Areas*, DES/OECD.

Bourdieu, P. (1973), 'Cultural Reproduction and Social Reproduction' in R. Brown (ed.), *Knowledge, Education and Cultural Change*, Tavistock.

Bowlby, J. (1953), *Child Care and the Growth of Love*, Pelican.

Bowles, S. and Gintis, H. (1976), *Schooling in Capitalist America: Educational Reform and the Contradictions of Economic Life*, Routledge and Kegan Paul.

Boxall, M. (1976), *The Nurture Group in the Primary School*, ILEA, August.

Boyd, D. (1973), *Elites and their Education*, NFER.

Brandis, W. and Henderson, D. (1970), *Social Class, Language and Communication'*, Routledge and Kegan Paul.

Briault, E.W.H. (1976), Introduction to M. Boxall, *The Nurture Group in the Primary School*, ILEA.

Brimer, M.A., Madaus, G.F., Chapman, B., Kellaghan T, and Wood, R. (1977), *Sources of Difference in School Achievement*, Report to Carnegie Corporation, NFER.

Broadfoot, P. (1979), 'Assessment, Schools and Society' in J. Eggleton (ed.), *Contemporary Sociology of the School* Series, Methuen.

Broadfoot, P. (1980a) 'How exams cheat our children', *New Society*, 19 June.

Broadfoot, P. (1980b), The Scottish Pupil Profile System' in T. Burgess and E. Adams (eds.), *The Outcomes of Education*, Macmillan.

Bronfenbrenner, U. (1974), *Is Early Intervention Effective? A Report on the Longitudinal Evaluations of Pre-school Programmes*, Office of Child Development, US Dept. of Health, Education and Welfare.

Brooks, C. (1966), 'Some Approaches to Teaching English as a Second Language' in S.W. Webster (ed.), *The Disadvantaged Learner*, Chandler Publishing Company.

Brophy, J. and Good, T. (1974), *Teacher/Student Relationships: Causes and Consequences*, Holt, Rinehard and Winston.

Brown, G.W., Bhrolchain M.N. and Harris, T. (1975), 'Social class and psychiatric disturbance among women in an urban population', *Sociology*, **9**.

Brown, M., Madge, N., DHSS/SSRC Review (in preparation).

Bruck, M. and Tucker, C.R. (1974), Social class differences in the acquisition of school language', *Merrill Palmer Quarterly*, **20**.

Bruner, J.S. (1966), *Towards a Theory of Instruction*, Belknap Press.

Bruner, J.S. (1974), *Relevance of Education*, Penguin.

Bruner, J. (1980), *Under Five in Britain*, Vol. 1 of the Oxford Pre-school Research Project, Grant McIntyre.

Burgess, T. and Adams, E. (1980), *Outcomes of Education*, Macmillan.

Burgess, T. and Travers, T. (1980), *Ten Billion Pounds: Whitehall's Takeover of the Town Halls*, Grant McIntyre.

Burstall, C. (1979), 'Time to mend the nets: a commentary on the outcomes of class-size research', *Trends in Education*, Autumn, DES.

Burt, C. (1943), 'The education of the young adolescent: implications of the Norwood Report', *British Journal of Educational Psychology*, **13**.

Butler, N. and Alberman, E.D. (eds.) (1969), *Perinatal Mortality*, Livingstone.

Byrne, D., Williamson, B. and Fletcher, B. (1975), *The Poverty of Education: A Study in the Politics of Opportunity*, Martin Robertson.

Byrne, E. (1976), *Open University Course E.321, Unit 16*.

Central Advisory Council for Education (England) (1954), *Early Leaving*, HMSO.

Central Advisory Council for Education (England) (1959), *15 to 18* (The Crowther Report), HMSO.

Central Advisory Council for Education (England) (1963), *Half Our Future* (The Newsom Report), HMSO.

Central Advisory Council for Education (England) (1967), *Children and their Primary Schools* (The Plowden Report), HMSO.

Central Policy Review Staff (1978), *Services for Young Children of Working Mothers*, HMSO.

Central Policy Review Staff/Central Statistical Office (1980), *People and their Families*, HMSO.

Chartered Institute of Public Finance and Accountancy (CIPFA) (1980), *Education Estimates 1980/81*.

Chazan, M. (1962), 'School Phobia', *British Journal of Educational Psychology*, **28**.

Chazan, M., Laing, A., Cox, T., Jackson, S. and Lloyd, G. (1976) 'Studies of Infant School Children. I. *Deprivation and School Progress*', Blackwell.

Cherry, N. (1976), 'Persistent job changing – is it a problem?', *Journal of Occupational Psychology*, **49**.

Child Poverty Action Group (1974), 'Take-up of Means-Tested Benefits', *CPAG Poverty Pamphlet*, 18, November.

Clark, M.M. and Cheyne, W.M. (eds.) (1980), *Studies in Pre-school Education*, Scottish Council for Research in Education, Publication No. 70, Hodder and Stoughton.

Clarke, A.D.B. and Clarke, A.M. (1975), *Recent Advances in the Study of Subnormality*, National Association for Mental Health.

Clarke, A.D.B. and Clarke, A.M. (1981), *Sleeper Effects in Development: Fact or Artefact? Developmental Review*, December, vol. 1, no. 4.

Clarke, A.M. (1981), 'Developmental Discontinuities: an Approach to Assessing their Nature' in L.A. Bond and J.M. Joffee (eds.) *'Facilitating Infant and Early Childhood Development'*, University Press of New England.

Clarke, A.M. and Clarke, A.D.B. (1974), 'Genetic-environmental Interactions in Cognitive Development' in A.M. and A.D.B. Clarke (eds.), *Mental Deficiency, the Changing Outlook*, 3rd ed., Methuen.

Clarke, A.M. and Clarke, A.D.B. (1979), 'Early Experience: its Limited Effect upon Later Development' in R. Shaffer and J. Dunn, (eds.), *The First Years of Life*, Wiley.

Clarke-Stewart, K.A. (1973), 'Interaction between Mothers and their Young Children: Characteristics and Consequences', *Monograph for the Society for Research in Child Development*, Series No. 153.

Coates, K. and Silburn, R. (1973), *Poverty: the Forgotten Englishmen*, Penguin.

Cohen, G. and Nixon, J. (1981), 'Employment Policies for Youth in the UK and the USA', *Journal of Social Policy*, July vol. 10, pt. 3.

Cole, M. and Bruner, J.S. (1972), 'Preliminaries to a Theory of Cultural Differences', 71st *Nat. Soc. Educ. Yearbook*, part 2 cited in J. Bruner, (1974), *The Relevance of Education*, Penguin.

Coleman, J.S., Campbell, E.Q., Hobson, C.J., McPartland, J., Mood, A.M., Weinfeld, F.D. and York, R.L. (1966), *Equality of Educational Opportunity*, Washington DC Office of Education.

Committee on Higher Education (England) (1963), *Higher Education* (Robbins Report), HMSO.

Connolly, K. in Connolly, K. and Bruner, J. (eds.) (1974), *The Growth of Competence,* Academic Press.

Cook-Gumperz, J. (1973), *Social Control and Socialisation*, Routledge & Kegan Paul.

Cooper, M.G. (1966), 'School refusal: an enquiry into the part played by school and home', *Educational Research*, **8**.

Cope, E. and Gray, J. (1978), 'Figures and perspectives on the national problem of truancy: an opening discussion', *CES Newsletter*, June.

Corrigan, P. (1979), *Schooling the Smash Street Kids*, Macmillan.

Crosland, C.A.R. (1961), 'Some thoughts on English education', *Encounter*, **17**, 1961.

Cullen, B.D. (1979), 'Lessons from class-size research – an economist's perspective', *Trends in Education 1979/4*, DES.

Dale, R.R. and Griffiths, S. (1965), *Down Stream*, Routledge and Kegan Paul.

Davie, R., Butler, N. and Goldstein, H. (1972), *From Birth to Seven*, a report of the National Child Development Study, Longman.

Davies, Bleddyn (1967), 'Notes on Variation in LEA Provision', Appendix 14 to *Children and their Primary Schools* (The Plowden Report).

Davies, J. (1980), *Attendance at Three Secondary Schools*, ILEA RS 749/80.

Deakin, N. (1980), 'Inner City Problems in Perspective; the London Case' in M. Marland (ed.), *Education for the Inner City*, Heinemann Educational.

Denney, A.H. (1973), *Truancy and School Phobia*, Priory Press.

Department of Education and Science (DES) (1973), *Adult Education: a Plan for Development* (The Russell Report).

DES (1974a), *One Day Survey on Absence from School*, HMSO.

DES (1974b), 'Teacher Turnover', *Reports on Education*, 79, May.

DES (1975), *A Language for Life* (The Bullock Report), HMSO.

DES (1976a), *Report by H.M. Inspectors on Curricula for Non-participating 16/19s* (The Sudale Report), March.

DES (1976b), Conference Papers, *16/19 Getting Ready for Work*.

DES (1976c), *Government Statement on Unified Vocational Preparation Pilot Programme*, July.

DES (1976d), *Third Report from the Expenditure Committee Session 1974*, Educational Maintenance Allowances in the 16/18 year age group July 1974, HMSO.

DES (1976e), *Sixth Special Report from the Expenditure Committee Session 1975/76*, Educational Maintenance Allowances in the 16/18 year age group. Observations by the Secretary of State for Education and Science on the third report of the Committee Session, 1974, HMSO, May.

DES (1977), *A Study of School Buildings*, HMSO.

DES (1978a) '*Adult Literacy 1977/78: a Remarkable Educational Advance*', Report on the third and final year's operation, HMSO.

DES (1978b) *Press Notice* for Shirley Williams, 22 December.

DES (1978c), 'Mixed Ability Work in Comprehensive Schools', *HMI Series: Matters for Discussion*, HMSO.

DES (1978d), *Primary Education in England: a Survey by HM Inspectors of Schools*, HMSO.

DES/FEU (1978), *Experience, Reflection, Learning: Suggestions for Organisers of Unified Vocational Preparation*, April.

DES (1979a), '*Aspects of Secondary Education in England: a Survey by H.M. Inspectors of Schools*', HMSO.

DES (1979b), '*Education and Training for 18–18 Year-olds: a Consultative Paper*', DES/DE/Welsh Office.

DES (1979c), Statistical Bulletin 15/79, *Participation in Education by Young People in the 16–19 Age Group and its Association with the Socio-economic Structure and Population Density in an area*, December.

DES (1980a), 'The Secondary School Staffing Survey', *Statistical Bulletin*, June.

DES (1980b), *A Framework for the School Curriculum*, Proposals for consultation by the Secretaries of State for Education and Science and for Wales, HMSO.

DES (1981), *West Indian Children in our Schools*, Interim Report of the Rampton Committee, Cmnd. 8273, HMSO.

Deutsch M. (1964), 'Facilitating development in the pre-school child: social and psychological perspectives', *Merrill-Palmer Quarterly*, **10**, April.

Department of Health and Social Security (DHSS) (1975), *Report No. 10 on Health and Social Subjects*, 'A Nutrition Survey of Pre-school Children 1967–68', Report by Committee on Medical Aspects of Food Policy, HMSO.

DHSS (1976), *Fit for the Future*, Report of the Committee on Child Health Services (The Court Report), HMSO.

Department of the Environment (DOE), (1976), *Report of the Committee of Enquiry into Local Government Finance*. (The Layfield Report), Cmnd 6453, HMSO.

DOE (1977a), *Inner London: Policies for Dispersal and Balance – Final Report of the Lambeth Inner Area Study*, HMSO.

DOE (1977b), *Unequal City – Final Report of the Birmingham Inner Area Study*, HMSO.

DOE (1977c), *Change or Decay: Final Report of the Liverpool Inner Area Study*, HMSO.

DOE (1979), *Rate Support Grant for 1980/81 for England and Wales*, Report to Parliament on the RSG 1979, HMSO.

Donnison, D. and Soto, P. (1980), *The Good City: a Study of Urban Development and Policy in Britain*, Heinemann Educational Books.

Douglas, J.W.B. (1964), *The Home and the School*, MacGibbon and Kee.

Douglas, J.W.B. (Personal Communication).

Douglas, J.W.B., Ross, J.M. and Simpson, H.R. (1968), *All our Future: A Longtitudinal Survey of Secondary Education*, Peter Davies.

Drillien, C.M. (1964), *Growth and Development of the Prematurely Born Infant*, Livingstone.

Edwards, H. and Thompson, B. (1971), 'Who are the fatherless?', *New Society*, **17**.

Ellwood, C. (1976), *Adult Learning Today: a New Role for the Universities?*, Sage Publications.

Essen, J. (1978), 'Living in one-parent families: income and expenditure', *Poverty*, **40**.

Essen, J. (1979), 'Living in one-parent families: attainment at school', *Child: Care, Health and Development*, **5**.

Essen, J., Lambert, L. and Head, J. (1976), 'School attainment of children who have been in care', *Child: Care, Health and Development*, **2**.

Essen, J., Fogelman, K.R. and Head, J. (1978), 'Childhood housing experiences and school attainment', *Child: Care, Health and Development*, **4**, February.

Farrington, D. (1973), 'Self reports of deviant behaviour predictive and stable?', *J. Crim Law Criminal*, **64**.

Fenwick, I.G.K. (1976), *The Comprehensive School 1944/1970*, Methuen.

Ferri, E. (1976), *Growing Up in a One-parent Family: a Long-term Study of Child Development*, NFER.

Field, F. (ed.) (1977a), *The Conscript Army: A Study of Britain's Unemployed*, Routledge and Kegan Paul.

Field, F. (ed.), (1977b) *Education and the Urban Crisis*, Routledge and Kegan Paul.

Field, F., Meacher M. and Pond, C. (1977), *To Him Who Hath. A Study of Poverty and Taxation*, Pelican.

Fielder, W., Cohen, R. and Feeney, S. (1971), 'An attempt to replicate the teacher expectancy effect', *Psychological Reports*, **29**.

Floud, J.E. (1961), 'Social Class Factors in Educational Achievement' in A.H. Halsey (ed.), *Ability and Educational Opportunity*, OECD.

Floud, J.E., Halsey, A.H., and Martin, F.M. (1956), *Social Class and Educational Opportunity*, Heinemann.

Flude, R. and Parrott, R. (1980), 'Memorials to past problems', *Times Educational Supplement*, 28 November.

Fogelman, K. (1975), 'Developmental correlates of family size', *Brit. J. Social Work*. **5**.

Fogelman, K. (1976), *Britain's Sixteen-year-olds*, National Children's Bureau.

Fogelman, K. (1980), Smoking in pregnancy and subsequent development of the child', *Child: Care, Health and Development*, **6**, 4.

Fogelman, K. and Goldstein, H. (1976), 'Social factors associated with changes in educational attainment', *Educational Studies*, **2**.

Fogelman, K., Goldstein, H., Essen, J. and Ghodsian, M. (1978), 'Patterns of attainment', *Educational Studies*, **4**, 2.

Ford, J. (1970), *Social Class and the Comprehensive School*, Routledge and Kegan Paul.

Fordham, P., Poulton, G., and Randle, L. (1979), *Learning Networks in Adult Education: Non-formal Education on a Housing Estate*, Routledge and Kegan Paul.

Fowler, C.D., Jackman, R.A. and Perlman, M. (1980), *Local Government Finance in a Unitary State*, Allen and Unwin.

Fowler, G. (1979), 'Participation in Educational Government', Unit 9, Block 4 of Open University Course E361, *Participation and Accountability*, Open University Press.

Francis, H. (1975), *Language in Childhood*, Elek Press.

Fraser, E.D. (1959), *Home Environment and the School*, University of London Press.

Frasure, N.E. and Entwisle, D.R. (1973), 'Semantic & syntactic development in children', *Developmental Psychology*, **9**.

Friedman, N.L. (1967), 'Cultural deprivation: a commentary in the sociology of knowledge', *Journal of Educational Thought*, **1**, 2.

Fuchs, E. (1968), 'How teachers learn to help children fail', *Trans-Action*, September.

Fulton, O. and Gordon, A. (1979), 'The British pool of ability: how deep and will cash reduce it?', *Educational Studies*, **5**.

Galloway, D. (1976), 'Persistent unjustified absence from school', *Trends in Education*, **76**, 4.

Garber, H. and Heber, R. (1978), 'The efficacy of early intervention with family rehabilitation', *Paper delivered at the Conference on Prevention of Retarded Development in Psychologically Disadvantaged Children*, Madison, Wisconsin.

Garvey, A. (1975), 'Belfield Community School, Rochdale', *Where*, 102, March.

Ginsburg, H. (1972), *The Myth of the Deprived Child: Poor Children's Intellect and Education*, Prentice-Hall.

Glass, D.V. (1961), in A.H. Halsey *et al.*, *Education, Economy and Society*, Free Press of Glencoe.

Glennerster, H. (1972), 'Education and Inequality' in N. Bosanquet and P. Townsend (eds.), *Labour and Inequality*, Fabian Society.

Glennerster, H. (1975), *Social Service Budgets and Social Policy*, George Allen and Unwin.

Glennerster, H. and Hatch, S. (1974), 'Strategy against Inequality', *Fabian Research Series* **314**, *Positive Discrimination and Inequality*.

Goldstein, H. (1980), Critical Notice in *Journal of Child Psychology and Psychiatry*. **21**, 4, October.

Goodacre, E. (1967), *Teachers and their Pupils' Home Backgrounds*, NFER.

Goodacre, E. (1970), *School and Home*, NFER.

Gordon, A. (1980), 'Leaving school: a question of money', *Educational Studies*, **6**, 1, March.

Gordon, I.J. (1973), *An Early Intervention Project: a Longitudinal Look*, Gainsville: University of Florida, Institute for Development of Human Resources, College of Education.

Grace, G. (1978), *Teachers, Ideology and Control: Study of Urban Education*, Routledge and Kegan Paul.

Gray, G., Smith, A., and Rutter, M. (1980), School Attendance and the First Year of Employment' in L. Hersov and I. Berg (eds.), *Out of School: Modern Perspectives in Truancy and School Refusal*, John Wiley.

Gray, J. (1975), 'Positive discrimination in Education: a review of the British experience', *Policy and Politics*, **4**, 2.

Gray, J. (1977), 'Teacher competence in reading tuition', *Educational Research*, **19**, 2.

Gray, S.W. and Klaus, R.A. (1970), *The Early Training Project: a Seventh Year Report*, Nashville, Demonstration and Research Centre for Early Education, Peabody College.

Greaves, J.P. and Hollingworth, D.F. (1966); *World Review of Nutrition and Diebetics*, **6**.

Greenfield, P.M. (1969), 'Goal as environmental variable in the development of intelligence', Paper presented at conference on Contributions to Intelligence University of Illinois, Urbana, cited in J. Bruner (1974), *The Relevance of Education*.

Guinagh, B.J. and Gordon, I.J. (1976), *School Performance as a Function of Early Stimulation*, Final Report of office of Child Development, Gainesville, Florida, College of Education, University of Florida.

Hall, P. (1980), 'Two nations or one? The geography of deprivation', *New Society*, 14, February.

Halsey, A.H. (1972), *Educational Priority. EPA Problems and Policies*, Vol. 1, HMSO.

Halsey, A.H. (1975), 'Sociology and the equality debate', *Oxford Review of Education*, 1, 1.

Halsey, A.H. (1977), 'Whatever happened to positive discrimination', *Times Educational Supplement*, 21 January.

Halsey, A.H., Heath, A.F. and Ridge, J.M. (1980), *Origins and Destinations: Family, Class and Education in Modern Britain*, Clarendon Press.

Hargreaves, A. (1980), 'Fifteen Thousand Hours: Review Symposium', *Brit. J. Sociol. and Ed.*, 1, 2.

Hargreaves, D.H. (1967), *Social Relations in a Secondary School*, Routledge and Kegan Paul.

Hargreaves, D.H. (1972), 'Social Differentiation I: Allocation and Differentiation in Schools' in *'Sorting Them Out: Two Essays on Social Differentiation'* for the *School and Society Course Team. The Open University Educational Studies, E282, Unit 9.* Open University Press.

Harnischfeger, A. and Wiley, D.E. (1975), 'Teaching/learning processes in elementary school: a synoptic view', *Studies of Education Processes*, 9, University of Chicago.

Harrison, A.J. and Whitehead, C.M.E. (1978), 'Is there an inner city problem', *Three Banks Review*, September.

Hawkins, P. (1969), 'Social Class, the Nominal Group and Reference', *Language and Speech* 12 February, reprinted in B. Bernstein, *Class, Codes and Control*, Vol. 2, Routledge & Kegan Paul, 1973.

Heath, A. and Clifford, F. (1980), 'The Seventy Thousand Hours that Rutter left out', *Oxford Review of Education*, 6, 1.

Heber, R., Garber, H., Harrington, S., Hoffman, C. and Falender, C. (1972), *Rehabilitation of Families at Risk for Mental Retardation*, Madison: Rehabilitation Research and Training Centre in Mental Retardation. University of Winsconsin.

Heber, R. and Garber, H. (1975), Progress Report II: 'An Experiment in the Prevention of Cultural–familial Retardation', *Proceedings of the 3rd Congress of the International Association for the Scientific Study of Mental Deficiency*, Polish Medical Publishers, Warsaw.

Held, R. and Hein, A.V. (1958), 'Adaptation of disarranged hand/eye coordination contingent upon reafferent stimulation', *Percept. and Motor Skills*, 8.

Hess, R.D. and Shipman, V.C. (1965), 'Early experience and the socialisation of cognitive modes in children', *Child Dev.*, 36, 4.

Hess, R.D. and Shipman, V.C. (1967), 'Cognitive Elements in Maternal

Behaviour', in J.P. Hill (ed.), *Minnesota Symposia on Child Psychology*, Vol. 1, University of Minnesota Press, Minneapolis.

Hess, R.D. and Bear, R.M. (1968), *Early Education: Current Theory, Research and Action*, Aldine.

Hess, R.D. *et al*. (1969), *The Cognitive Environments of Urban Pre-school Children*, Graduate School of Education, University of Chicago.

Hilsum, S. and Cane, B.S. (1971), *The Teacher's Day*, NFER.

H.M. Treasury, (1980), *The Government's Expenditure Plans, 1980/81 to 1983/84*, Cmnd 7841, March, HMSO.

Holdsworth, R. (1970), *Three Thousand Children*, Devon Pre-school Playgroups Association.

Hooper, R. (ed.) (1971), *The Curriculum: Context, Design and Development*; Open University Press.

Hopkins, A. (1978), *The School Debate*, Penguin.

House of Commons Select Committee on Race Relations (1978).

Howick, C. and Hassani, H. (1979), 'Education Spending: Primary', *CES Review*, **5**, January.

Howick, C. and Hassani, H. (1980), 'Education Spending: Secondary' in *CES Review*, **8**, January.

Hughes, M., Mayall, B., Moss, P., Perry, J., Petrie, P. and Pinkerton, G. (1980), *Nurseries Now: A Fair Deal for Parents and Children*, Penguin.

Hunt, J.Mc.V. (1964), 'The psychological basis for using pre-school enrichment as an antidote for cultural deprivation', *Merrill-Palmer Quarterly*, **10**, July.

Hunt, J. McV., Kirk, G.H. and Lieberman, C. (1975), 'Social Class and Pre-School Language Skill: IV Semantic Mastery of Shapes', *Genetic Psychol. Monographs*, **91**, pp. 317–37.

Hutchinson, E. and Hutchinson, E. (1978), *Learning Later: Fresh Horizons in English Adult Education*, Routledge and Kegan Paul.

ILEA (1980), *1980 Attendance Survey*, RS 753/80.

Illsley, R. (1966), 'Early Prediction of Perinatal Risk', *Proc. Royal Soc. Med.*, **59**.

Jackson, B. (1964), *Streaming*, Routledge and Kegan Paul.

Jackson, B. and Marsden, D. (1962), *Education and the Working Class*, Routledge and Kegan Paul.

Jackson, M. (1980), 'School to work', *Times Educational Supplement*, 26 September.

Jayne, E. (1976), 'Deptford Educational Home Visiting Project', *Research Report ILEA*, RS 645/76.

Jayne, E. (1977), *Deptford Educational Home Visiting Project*, Third Report ILEA.

Jencks, C. (1979), *Who Gets Ahead: the Determinants of Economic Success in America*, Basic Books.

Jencks, C., Smith, M., Acland, M., Bane, M.J., Cohen, D., Gintis, H., Heyns, B. and Michelson, S. (1973), *Inequality: a Reassessment of the Effect of Family and Schooling in America*, Allen Lane.

Jensen, A.R. (1969), 'How much can we boost IQ and scholastic achievement?' *Harvard Ed. Rev. 39.* No. 1.

Jensen, A.R. (1980), *Bias in Mental Testing*, Methuen.

Jones, A. (1976), 'Coping in the School Situation' in C. Jones-Davis and R.G. Cave (eds.), *The Disruptive Pupil in the Secondary School*, Ward Lock Educational.

Jones, H.A. and Charnley, A.H. (1978), *Adult Literacy: a Study of its Impact*, National Institute of Adult Education.

Kay, B. (1980), 'Class-size, the wrong question', *Trends in Education, 1980/2*, DES.

Keddie, N. (1971), 'Classroom Knowledge' in M.F.D. Young (ed.), *Knowledge & Control*, Collier-Macmillan.

Kellmer-Pringle, M.L., Butler, N.R. and Davie, R. (1966), *11,000 Seven-year-olds: First Report of the National Child Development Study*, Longman.

Kennedy, M.K. (1978), *Findings from the Follow Through Planned Variation Study*, US Office of Education.

Kirk, G.F. and Hunt, J.McV. (1975), 'Social Class and Pre-school Language Skill I', *Intro. Gen. Psych. Monograph 91.*

Klein, R. (ed.) (1975), *Inflation and Priorities: Social Policy and Public Expenditure 1975*, Centre for Studies in Social Policy.

Krugman, J.L. (1956), 'Cultural deprivation and child development', *High Points*, **38**, November.

Labov, W. (1973), 'The Logic of Non-Standard English', in N. Keddie (ed.), *Tinker, Tailor . . . the Myth of Cultural Deprivation*, Penguin Education.

Lacey, C. (1970), *Hightown Grammar: the School as a Social System*, Manchester University Press.

Lacey, C. (1974), 'Destreaming in a "Pressured" Academic Environment' in J. Eggleston (ed.), *Contemporary Research in the Sociology of Education*, Methuen.

Lambert, L. (1978), 'Living in one-parent families: leaving school and plans for the future', *Concern*, **29**.

Lambert, L. and Streather, J. (1980), *Children in Changing Families*, Macmillan.

Lambert, R. (1964), 'Nutrition in Britain, 1950/60', *Occasional Papers on Social Administration*, **6**, Bell.

Lawton, D. (1968), *Social Class, Language and Education*, Routledge and Kegan Paul.

Lawton, D. (1979), *The End of the Secret Garden? A Study in the Politics of the Curriculum*. An inaugural lecture. University of London, Institute of Education also published in P. Gordon (ed.) *Inaugural Lectures in Education*, **2**, Frank Cass.

Lawton, D. (1980), 'Responsible partners', *Times Educational Supplement*, 3 March.

Lazar, I., Hubbell, V., Murray, H., Rosche, M. and Royce, J. (1977), *The Persistence of Pre-school Effects. A Long-term Follow-up of Fourteen Infant and Pre-school Experiments*, DHEW Publication No. (OHDS) 78–30129.

Le Grand, J. (1982) 'The Distribution of Public Expenditure on Education', *Economica*.

Levenstein, P. (1972), *Verbal Interaction Project*, Mineola, NY Family Service Assoc. of Nassau County.

Lewin, R. (1977), 'Head Start pays off', *New Scientist*, 3 March, pp. 508–9.

Lewis, M. and Goldberg, S. (1969), 'Perceptual-cognitive development in infancy: a generalised expectancy model as a function of mother/infant interaction', *Merrill Palmer Quarterly*, **15**.

Lewis, M. and Wilson, C.D. (1972), 'Infant development in lower-class American families', *Human Development*, **15**.

Lister, R. (1980), 'No affluence trap', *New Society*, **52**, 917, 12 June.

Little, A.N. (1977), in F. Field (ed.), *Education and the Urban Crisis*, Routledge and Kegan Paul.

Little, A.N. (1978), *Educational Policies for Multi-racial Areas*, Goldsmith's College Inaugural Lecture.

Little, A.N., Mabey, C. and Russell, J. (1971), 'Do small classes help a pupil?', *New Society*, **473**.

Little, A.N. and Mabey, C. (1972), 'An Index for the Designation of Educational Priority Areas' in Schonfield and Shaw (eds.), *Social Indicators and Social Policy*, Heinemann.

Little, A. and Varlaam, C. (1980), *EEC/DES Transition to Work Project*, Half-yearly report to IFAPLAN, Spring, Available from Goldsmith's College, London.

Low Pay Unit (1980), *Low Pay Bulletin*, 30, February.

Lunn, J.C.B. (1970), *Streaming in the Primary School*, NFER.

Maclure, S. (1979), 'Financial Support for the 16/18s', *Education Policy Bulletin* 7, 1.

Manpower Services Commission (1977), *Young People and Work* (The Holland Report).

Manpower Services Commission (1979), *A Review of the First Year of Special Programmes*.

Manpower Services Commission (1981), *A New Training Initiative*, May.

Marland, M. (1980), *Education for the Inner City*, Heinemann Educational.

Meacher, N. (1974), 'The Politics of Positive Discrimination' in H. Glennerster and S. Hatch, *Positive Discrimination and Inequality, Fabian Research Series*, 314.

Mendels, G.E. and Flanders, J.P. (1973), 'Teachers' expectations and pupil performance', *American Educational Research Journal*, **10**, 3.

Merton, R. (1948), 'The self-fulfilling prophecy', *Antioch Review*, **8**.

Merton, R.K. (1957), *Social Theory & Social Structure*, Free Press of Glencoe.

Midwinter, E. (1972), *Priority Education: an Account of the Liverpool Project*, Penguin.

Midwinter, E. (1977), *Education for Sale*, Allen and Unwin.

Miller, F.J.W. *et al.* (1960), *Growing Up in Newcastle-Upon-Tyne*, Oxford University Press.

Millham, S., Bullock, R. and Hosie, K. (1978a), *Springboard: A Study of CSVs Job Creation Project in Sunderland*, Dartington School Research Unit, 1977.

Millham, S., Bullock, R. and Hosie, K. (1978b), 'Juvenile unemployment: a concept due for recycling?', *J. Adolesc.*, **1**.

Ministry of Education (1957), *Report of the Working Party on Educational Maintenance Allowances* (The Weaver Report).

Morris, J. (1966), *Standards and Progress in Reading*, NFER.

Mortimore, P. (1980a), *Secondary Schools Staffing Sruvey*, Report No. 1. ILEA.

Mortimore, P. (1980b), 'Time to re-examine the system', *Guardian*, 24 June.

Mortimore, P. (1980c), *Non-attendance at School: Some Research Findings*, ILEA, RS 760/80.

Mortimore, P. (1980d), 'The study of secondary schools: a researcher's reply', *Perspectives*, **1**, Exeter University School of Education.

Morton-Williams, R. (1967), 'The 1964 Nat. Survey among parents of primary school children' in Central Advisory Council for Education, *Children and their Primary Schools*, 2, *Research and Surveys*, HMSO.

Morton-Williams, R. and Finch, S. (1968), *Young School Leavers: Schools Council Enquiry I*, HMSO.

Moss, H.A., Robson, K.S. and Pederson, F. (1969), 'Determinants of maternal stimulation of infants and consequences of treatment for later reactions to strangers', *Developmental Psychology*, **1**, 3.

Murchison, N. (1974), Appendix to Finer Report, see DHSS (1974), *Report of the Committee on One-parent Families*, HMSO.

Murray, R. (1974), 'Overcrowding and aggression in primary school children in C.M. Morrison (ed.), *Educational Priority*, Vol. 5, HMSO.

Nash, P. (1973), *Classrooms Observed*, Routledge and Kegan Paul.

National Union of Teachers (1978), *Section II: an NUT Report*.

National Union of Teachers (1979), *Education and Training for the 16/19 age group. A Discussion Document*.

Newson, J. and Newson, E. (1972), *Patterns of Infant Care*, Penguin.

Newson, J. and Newson, E. (1976), *Seven Years Old in the Home Environment*, Allen and Unwin.

Newson, J. and Newson, E. (1977), *Perspectives on School at Seven Years Old*, Allen and Unwin.

Nicholson, J. (1980), 'Jensen rides again' review of A. Jensen's 'Bias in Mental Testing', *New Society*, 6 March.

Nurss, J.E. and Day, D.E. (1971), 'Imitation, comprehension and production of grammatical structures', *Journal of Verbal Behaviour*, **10**.

O'Connor, M. (1980), 'Too much of a good thing?', *Guardian*, 8 July.

Office of Health Economics (1967), *Malnutrition in the 1960s?*.

Office of Population Censuses and Surveys, Social Survey Division 1976, *The General Household Survey, 1973*, HMSO.

Pack Report (1977), *Truancy and Indiscipline in Schools in Scotland*, Report of a Committee of Enquiry, Scottish Education Dept., HMSO.

Parry, M. and Archer, H. (1974), *Pre-school Education. Schools Council Research Studies*, Macmillan.

Patrick, J. (1973), *A Glasgow Gang Observed*, Eyre Methuen.

Payne, J. (1974), *Educational Priority, Vol. 2 Surveys and Statistics*, HMSO.

Peaker, G.F. (1967), 'The Regression Analyses of the National Survey',

Appendix 4, Vol. II (*Plowden Report*).

Phillips, D.L. (1968), 'Social class and psychiatric disturbance: the influence of positive and negative experiences', *Social Psychiatry*, **3**.

Piaget, J. (1955), *The Construction of Reality in the Child*, trans. M. Cook, Routledge and Kegan Paul.

Pidgeon, D.A. (1974), 'Class size as a factor of pupil performance: a policy analysis' in *New Patterns of Teacher Education and Tasks: General Analyses*, OECD.

Pilling, D. and Pringle, M.K. (1978), *Controversial Issues in Child Development*, Paul Elek.

Postlethwaite, K. and Denton, C. (1978), *Streams for the Future? The Long-term Effects of Early Streaming and Non-streaming. The Final Report of the Banbury Enquiry*, Banpubco.

Poulton, G.A. and James, T. (1975). *Preschool Learning in the Community, Strategies for Change*, Routledge and Kegan Paul.

Psacharopoulos, G. (1977), 'Family background, education and achievement: a path model of earnings determinants in the UK and some alternatives, *British Journal of Sociology*, September.

Ramey, C.T. and Campbell, F.A. (1979), 'Educational intervention for children at risk for mild retardation. A longitudinal analysis', *Paper presented at the Fifth Congress on the International Association for the Study of Mental Deficiency*, Jerusalem, August.

Raynor, J. and Harden, J. (1973), *Readings in Urban Education, Vol. 2, Equality and City Schools*, Routledge and Kegan Paul.

Report 94, (1978), Article on DES survey on non-advanced further education, December.

Reynolds, D. (1974), 'Some do, some don't', *Times Educational Supplement* 10 May.

Reynolds, D. (1980), 'Fifteen Thousand Hours Review Symposium', *British Journal of Sociology of Education*, **1**, 2.

Reynolds, D. and Murgatroyd, S. (1977), 'The Sociology of schooling and the absent pupil: the school as a factor in the generation of truancy' in H.C.M. Carroll (ed.), *Absenteeism in South Wales, Studies of Pupils, their Homes and their Secondary Schools*, University College of Swansea.

Rhodes and Moore (1976), *Appendix to the Layfield Report*, DOE Cmnd 6453, HMSO.

Riessman, F. (1962), *The Culturally Deprived Child*, Harper and Row.

Rist, R. (1970), 'Student social class and teacher expectations: the self-fulfilling prophecy in ghetto education', *Harvard Ed. Review*, **40**.

Robinson, H.B. and Robinson, N.M. (1968), 'The problem of timing in pre-school education' in R.D. Hess and R.M. Bear (eds.), *Early Education*, Aldine.

Rona, R.J., Chinn, S., Smith, A.M. (1979), *Lancet*, 8 September.

Rosenthal, R. and Jacobson, L. (1968), *Pygmalion in the Classroom: Teacher Expectations and Pupils' Intellectual Development*, Holt, Rinehart and Winston.

Routh, G., Wedderburn, D. and Wootton, B., (1980), 'The Roots of Pay

Inequalities', *Low Pay Discussion Paper 1*, Low Pay Unit.

Royal Commission on the Distribution of Income and Wealth (1977), Report No. 5, *Third Report on the Standing Conference*, HMSO.

Rubinstein, D. and Simon, B. (1969), *The Evolution of the Comprehensive School, 1920–1966*, Routledge and Kegan Paul.

Rudduck, J. (1976), *Dissemination of Innovation: the Humanities Curriculum Project*, Evans Methuen Educational.

Runciman, W.G. (1966), *Relative Deprivation and Social Justice*, Routledge and Kegan Paul.

Rutter, M.L. (1976), 'Prospective studies to investigate behavioural change' in J.S. Strauss, H.M. Batigian and M. Ross (eds.), *Methods of Longitudinal Research in Psychopathology*, Plenum.

Rutter, M. (1979), *Changing Youth in a Changing Society. Patterns of Adolescent Development and Disorder*, The Rock Carling Fellowship, Nuffield Provincial Hospitals Trust.

Rutter, M. (1980), 'Raised lead levels and impaired cognitive/behavioural functioning: a review of the evidence', Supplement No. 42 to *Developmental Medicine and Child Neurology* **22**, 1.

Rutter, M.L., Tizard, J. and Whitmore, K. (eds.) (1970), *Education, Health and Behaviour*, Longman.

Rutter, M., Yule, B., Morton, J. and Bagley, C. (1975), 'Children of West Indian immigrants III. Home circumstances and family patterns', *Journal of Child Psychology and Psychiatry*, **16**.

Rutter, M.L. and Madge, N. (1976), *Cycles of Disadvantage*, Heinemann.

Rutter, M., Maughan, B., Mortimore, P. and Ouston, J. with Smith, A. (1979), *Fifteen Thousand Hours: Secondary Schools and their Effects on Children*, Open Books.

Rutter, M.L., Maughan, B., Mortimore, P. and Ouston, J. (1980), 'School influence on pupil progress: research strategies and tactics', *Journal of Child Psychology and Psychiatry*, **21**, 4.

Schoggen, M. (1969), 'An ecological study of three year olds at home', George Peabody College for Teachers, Nashville, cited in J. Bruner (1974), *The Relevance of Education*.

Schools Council (1965), *Raising the School Leaving Age*, Working Paper No. 2, HMSO.

Schools Council (1980), 'Graded Tests Boost Interest in French', *News Release*, 80/83, 30 September.

Schuller, T. (1978), 'Leave to learn for everybody', *Times Higher Education Supplement*, 26 October.

Schuller, T. and Bengtsson, J. (1977), 'A Strategy for Equity: Recurrent Education and Industrial Democracy' in J. Karabel and A.H. Halsey (eds.), *Power and Ideology in Education*, Oxford University Press.

Seaver, W.J. (1973), 'Effects of naturally induced teacher expectancies', *J. Pers. and Soc. Psychology*, **28**.

Sharp, R. and Green, A. with Lewis, J. (1975), *'Educational and Social Control: a Study in Progressive Primary Education*, Routledge and Kegan Paul.

Shipman, M. (1980), 'The Limits of Positive Discrimination' in M. Marland (ed.), *Education for the Inner City*, Heinemann Educational Books.

Silver, H. (ed.) (1973), *Equal Opportunity in Education: A Reader in Social Class and Educational Opportunity*, Methuen.

Simon, B. (1953), *Intelligence Testing and the Comprehensive School*, Lawrence and Wishart. Extract reprinted in H. Silver (ed.), *Equal Opportunity in Education*, Methuen, 1973.

Lady Simon of Wythenshawe (1948), *Three Schools or One? Secondary Education in England, Scotland and the USA*, Frederick Muller, Extract reprinted in H. Silver (ed.), *Equal Opportunity in Education*, Methuen, 1973.

Simpson, H.R. (1964), 'The influence of home and school on test performance', Appendix II of J.W.B. Douglas,' *The Home and the School*, MacGibbon and Kee.

Sinfield, A. (1977), Memo on Unemployment to the Chancellor, Unpublished.

Smith, B.O., Stanley, W.O. and Shores, J.H. (1950), *Fundamentals of Curriculum Development*, Harcourt Brace.

Smith, G.A. (ed.) 1975, *Educational Pr.ority Vol. 4. The West Riding Project*, HMSO.

Smith, G.A. (1977), 'Positive discrimination by area in education: the EPA idea re-examined', *Oxford Review of Ed.*, **3**, 3.

Smith, G.A. and James, T. (1975), 'The effects of pre-school education: some American and British evidence', *Oxford Review of Ed.*, **1**, 3.

Smith, S. (1979), 'Slow Learners and the Secondary-school Curriculum' in D. Rubenstein (ed.), *Education and Equality*, Penguin.

Smith, S.D. and Lasko, P. (1978), 'After the Work Experience Programme', *Department of Employment Gazette*, March.

Spence, J., Walton, W.S., Miller, F.J.W. and Court, S.D.M. (1954), *A Thousand Families in Newcastle-upon-Tyne*, Oxford University Press.

Stansbury, D. (1980), 'The Record of Personal Experience' in T. Burgess and E. Adams (eds.), *The Outcomes of Education*, Macmillan.

Steedman, J. (1980), *Progress in Secondary Schools: Findings from the National Child Development Study*, National Children's Bureau.

Stone, J. and Taylor, F. (1976), *The Parents' Schoolbook*, Penguin.

Stouffer, S.A. (1949), *The American Soldier*, Princeton.

Sugarman, B. (1967), 'Involvement in youth culture, academic achievement and conformity in schools: an empirical study of London schoolboys, *British Journal of Sociology*, **18**.

Summers, A.A. and Wolfe, B.L. (1977), 'Do schools make a difference?', *American Economic Review*.

Supplementary Benefits Commission (1975), *Annual Report*.

Sutton, H. and Tizard, B. (1979), 'Parents as authors', *Times Educational Supplement*, 30 November.

Swales, T. (1980), Record of Personal Achievement: an Independent Evaluation of the Swindon RPA Scheme, Schools Council Pamphlet 16.

Sylva, K.D., Roy, C., and Painter, M. (1980), *Childwatching at Playgroup and Nursery School*, Grant McIntyre.

Tanner, J.M. (1969), 'Relation of Body Size, Intelligence Scores and Social Circumstances', in P.H. Mussen, J. Langer, and H. Covington (eds.), *Trends and Issues in Developmental Psychology*, Holt, Rinehart and Winston.

Taylor, P., Exon, G., and Holly, B. (1972), *A Study of Nursery Education, Schools Council Working Paper 41*, Evans Methuen.

Taylor, W. (1964), *The Secondary Modern School*, Faber and Faber.

Taylor, W. (1973), *Heading for Change: Management of Innovation in the Large Secondary School*, Routledge and Kegan Paul.

Terry, John P. and John, Esther V. (1979), *Project STILE (Student/Teacher Interactive Learning Environment): a Programme Designed to Improve Teacher/Student Classroom Interactions*, Mass. Institute of Technology.

Thornbury, R. (1978), *The Changing Urban School*, Methuen.

Tizard, B. (1974), *Pre-school Education in Great Britain. A Research Review*, SSRC.

Tizard, B. (1976), 'Let them turn cartwheels', *Times Educational Supplement*, 27 February.

Tizard, B. (1978), 'Carry on communicating', *Times Educational Supplement*, 3 February.

Tizard, B. and Rees, J. (1974), 'A comparison of the effects of adoption, restoration to the natural mother and continued institutionalisation on the cognitive development of four-year-old children', *Child Dev*, **45**.

Tizard, B., Burgess, T., Francis, H., Goldstein, H., Young, M.F.D., Hewison, J. and Plewis, I. (1980a), *15,000 Hours: a Discussion*, London Institute of Education.

Tizard, B., Carmichael, H., Hughes, M. and Pinkerton, G. (1980a), 'Four Year Olds Talking to Mothers and Teachers' in L.A. Hersov and M. Berger (eds.), *Language and Language Disorders in Childhood*, Pergamon Press.

Tizard, B., Mortimore, J., and Burchell, B. (1981), *Involving Parents in Nursery and Infant School: a Sourcebook for Teachers*, Grant McIntyre.

Tizard, J. (1976), 'Nutrition, growth and development', *Psychol. Med.*, **6**.

Tizard, J., Moss, P. and Perry, J. (1976), *All Our Children: Pre-school Services in a Changing Society*, Temple Smith/New Society.

Tizard, J., Schofield, W. and Hewison, J. (1980), *The Haringey Reading Project*, Unpublished report to the DES.

Tomlinson, J. (1980), Preface to T.S. Burgess and E. Adams *Outcomes of Education*, Macmillan.

Tough, J. (1970), *Language and Environment: An Interim Report on a Longitudinal Study*, University of Leeds Institute of Education (unpublished).

Tough, J. (1974), *Focus on Meaning: Talking to Some Purpose with Young Children*, Allen and Unwin.

Tough, J. (1977), *Development of Meaning*, Allen and Unwin.

Townsend, P. (1979), *Poverty in the United Kingdom: A Survey of Household Resources and Standards of Living*, Penguin.

Training Services Agency (1975), *Vocational Preparation for Young People: A Discussion Paper*, Manpower Services Commission.

Tulkin, S.R. and Kagan, J. (1972), 'Mother/child interaction in the first year of life', *Child Dev.*, **43**.

Tunley, P. Travers, T. and Pratt, J. (1979), *Depriving the Deprived: A study of Finance, Educational Provision and Deprivation in a London Borough*, Kogan Page.

Tunnard, J. (1977), ' "Battle Royal", another look at school clothing and maintenance grants', *Welfare in Action: A Child Poverty Action Group Report*, June, CPAG.

Tyerman, M. (1968), *Truancy*, University of London Press.

Tyerman, M. (1974), 'Who are the truants?' in B. Turner (ed.), *Truancy*, Ward Lock Educational.

Universities Central Council of Admissions (UCCA) (1980), *Statistical Supplement to the Seventeenth Report*.

Van der Eyken, Willem (1974), 'Compensatory education in Britain: a review of research', *London Educational Review*, **3**, 3, Autumn.

Waddell Report (1978), *School Examinations, Parts I and II*, HMSO.

Walker, C. (1980), 'How LEAs will be free to demolish school meals service', *Where*, 154, January.

Webber, R.J. (1977), 'The National Classification of residential neighbourhood. An introduction to the classification of wards and parishes', *Technical Paper No. 23*, Planning Research Application Group.

Wedderburn, D. (1970), 'Workplace Inequality', *New Society*, 9 April.

Wedge, P. and Prosser, N. (1973), *Born to Fail?*, Arrow Books.

Welton, J. (1979), 'Research report: comprehensive education and the egalitarian dream', *British Educational Administration Association Journal*, July.

Wernstein, R.S. (1976), 'Reading group membership in first grade: teacher behaviour and pupil experience over time', *Journal of Educational Psychology*, **68**, 1.

West, D.J. and Farrington, D. (1973), *Who Becomes Delinquent?*, Heinemann Educational Books.

Westergaard, J. and Resler, H. (1975), *Class in Capitalist Society: a Study of Contemporary Britain*, Heinemann Educational Books.

White, J. (1971), 'The Curriculum Mongers: Education in Reverse' in R. Hooper (ed.), *The Curriculum: Context, Design and Development*, Oliver and Boyd/Open University Press.

White, J.P. (1973), *Toward a Compulsory Curriculum*, Routledge and Kegan Paul.

White Paper (1977), *'A Policy for Inner Cities'*, Cmnd 6845, HMSO.

Williams, S. (1980a), 'Stumbling over the sixth form step', *Guardian*, 26 February.

Williams, S. (1980b), 'Broad path to the future', *Times Educational Supplement*, 9 September.

Willis, P. (1977), *Learning to Labour*, Saxon House.

Willmott, P. (1969), *Adolescent boys of East London*, Penguin.

Wood, D., McMahon, L. and Cranstoun, Y. (1980), *Working with Under Fives*, Grant McIntyre.

Woodhead, M. (1976), *Intervening in Disadvantage: A Challenge for Nursery Education*, NFER.

Woods, J. (1980), *Absenteeism in Secondary Schools*, ILEA, RS 762/80.

Woods, P. (1979), *The Divided Schook*, Routledge and Kegan Paul.

Wootton, A.J. (1974), 'Talk in the homes of young children', *Sociology,* **82**.

Wragg, E.C. (1980), *Perspectives*, 1, Exeter University School of Education.

Wray, J.M., Moor, C. and Hill, S. (1980), *Unified Vocational Preparation: An Evaluation of the Pilot Programme*, NFER.

Wrightstone, J.W. (1958), 'Discovering and stimulating culturally deprived talented youth, *Teachers College Record,* **60**.

Yarrow, L.J. (1963), 'Research in dimensions of early maternal care', *Merrill-Palmer Quarterly*, **9**.

Young, M. and McGeeney, P. (1968), *Learning begins at home: a study of a junior school and its parents*, Routledge and Kegan Paul.

Young, M.F.D. (1971), *Knowledge and Control*, Collier-Macmillan.

Zigler, E. and Butterfield, E.C. (1968), 'Motivational aspects of changes in IQ test performance of culturally deprived nursery school children', *Child Dev.*, **39**.

Index of Names

Subject Index